SWAMI VIVEKANANDA
A Great Nationalist and Spiritual Leader

Dr. Akhilesh Vasudev

Corporate Office:
EMPTY CANVAS PUBLISHERS™
2/42, Ansari Road,
Daryaganj, New Delhi-110002
Email: emptycanvaspublishers@gmail.com
www.emptycanvaspublishers.com

Edition :2025

ISBN: 978-81-949219-8-1

Swami Vivekananda:
A great nationalist & spiritual Leader
Dr. Akhilesh Vasudev

Published by:
EMPTY CANVAS PUBLISHERS™
New Delhi- (India)

Printed and Bound in India

Preface

Swami Vivekananda was one of the most influential spiritual leaders of Vedanta philosophy. He was the chief disciple of Ramakrishna Paramahansa and was the founder of Ramakrishna Math and Ramkrishna Mission. Swami Vivekananda was the living embodiment of sacrifice and dedicated his life to the country and yearned for the progress of the poor, the helpless and the downtrodden. He showed a beacon of light to a nation that had lost faith in its ability under British Rule and inspired self-confidence among Indian that they are second to none. His ringing words and masterful oratory galvanized the slumbering nation.

Swami Vivekananda was born in an aristocratic Bengali family of Calcutta on January 12, 1863. Swami's parents influenced his thinking—the father by his rational mind and the mother by her religious temperament. From his childhood, he showed inclination towards spirituality and God realization. While searching for a man who could directly demonstrate the reality of God, he came to Ramakrishna and became his disciple. As a guru, Ramakrishna taught him Advaita Vedanta (non-dualism) and that all religions are true, and service to man was the most effective worship of God. After the death of his Guru, Vivekananda became a wandering monk, touring the Indian subcontinent and getting first-hand knowledge of India's condition. He later sailed to Chicago and represented India as a delegate in the 1893 Parliament of World Religions. An eloquent speaker, Vivekananda was invited to several forums in the United States and spoke at universities and clubs. He conducted hundreds of public and private lectures and classes, disseminating Vedanta and Yoga in America, England and a few other countries in Europe. He also established the Vedanta societies in America and England. Later he sailed back to India and in 1897 founded the Ramakrishna Math and Ramakrishna Mission, a philanthropic and spiritual organization.

Vivekananda emphasizes on the fact that society will change and make progress if he identifies religion as the 'soul of humanity'- the soul that responds to the realities of life and evolution of human consciousness. He never considers humanism apart from religion and vice versa. As such, the efflorescence of religion always depends on how it best serves humans under all trying circumstances. Contrary to paying importance to rigid dogmatism, which stands in the way of dynamism of religion, he is more interested in making religion a very comprehensive and essential component of growth and development of humanity.

Swami Vivekananda was one of the most influential spiritual leaders of Vedanta philosophy. He was the chief disciple of Ramakrishna Paramahansa and was the founder of Ramakrishna Math and Ramkrishna Mission. Swami Vivekananda was the living embodiment of sacrifice and dedicated his life to the country and yearned for the progress of the poor, the helpless and the downtrodden. He showed a beacon of light to a nation that had lost faith in its ability under British Rule and inspired self-confidence among Indian that they are second to none. His ringing words and masterful oratory galvanized the slumbering nation.

This is a reference book. All the matter is just compiled and edited in nature, taken from the various sources which are in public domain.

This book has very vividly, comprehensively and yet very concisely dealt with the life and thoughts of Swami Vivekananda. His commendation of the citizens of Japan while his visit to that place and his exhortation to our countrymen to emulate their virtues is a special feature of this book.

—*Editor*

Contents

	Preface	(*v*)
1.	Biography	1
2.	Visit to America	34
3.	Swami Vivekananda on Nationalism	67
4.	Fulfilment of Hindu Religion	74
5.	Teaching and Training	102
6.	Vivekananda's Philosophy	143
7.	The Hindu View of Life	161
8.	The Science of Yoga	166
9.	Hindu Philosophic Thought	196
10.	Sacrifice as a Spiritual Discipline	226
11.	Last Days of His Life	234
	Bibliography	261
	Index	263

1

Biography

Swami Vivekananda, the great soul loved and revered in East and West alike as the rejuvenator of Hinduism in India and the preacher of its eternal truths abroad, was born at 6:33, a few minutes before sunrise, on Monday, January 12, 1863. It was the day of the great Hindu festival Makarasamkranti, when special worship is offered to the Ganga by millions of devotees. Thus the future Vivekananda first drew breath when the air above the sacred river not far from the house was reverberating with the prayers, worship, and religious music of thousands of Hindu men and women.

Before Vivekananda was born, his mother, like many other pious Hindu mothers, had observed religious vows, fasted, and prayed so that she might be blessed with a son who would do honour to the family. She requested a relative who was living in Varanasi to offer special worship to the Vireswara Siva of that holy place and seek His blessings; for Siva, the great god of renunciation, dominated her thought. One night she dreamt that this supreme Deity aroused Himself from His meditation and agreed to be born as her son. When she woke she was filled with joy.

The mother, Bhuvaneswari Devi, accepted the child as a boon from Vireswara Siva and named him Vireswara. The family, however, gave him the name of Narendranath Datta, calling him, for short, Narendra, or more endearingly, Naren.

The Datta family of Calcutta, into which Narendranath had been born, was well known for its affluence, philanthropy, scholarship, and independent spirit. The grand father, Durgacharan, after the birth of his first son, had renounced the world in search of God. The father, Viswanath, an attorney-at-law of the High Court of Calcutta, was versed in English and Persian literature and often entertained himself and his friends by reciting from the Bible and the poetry of Hafiz, both of which, he believed, contained truths unmatched by human thinking elsewhere.

He was particularly attracted to the Islamic culture, with which he was familiar because of his close contact with the educated Moslems of North-western India. Moreover, he derived a large income from his law practice and, unlike his father, thoroughly enjoyed the worldly life. An expert in cookery, he prepared rare dishes and liked to share them with his friends. Travel was another of his hobbies. Though agnostic in religion and a mocker of social conventions, he possessed a large heart and often went out of his way to support idle relatives, some of whom were given to drunkenness. Once, when Narendra protested against his lack of judgement, his father said: 'How can you understand the great misery of human life? When you realize the depths of men's suffering, you will sympathize with these unfortunate creatures who try to forget their sorrows, even though only for a short while, in the oblivion created by intoxicants.' Naren's father, however, kept a sharp eye on his children and would not tolerate the slightest deviation from good manners. Bhuvaneswari Devi, the mother, was cast in a different mould. Regal in appearance and gracious in conduct, she belonged to the old tradition of Hindu womanhood. As mistress of a large household, she devoted her spare time to sewing and singing, being particularly fond of the great Indian epics, the Ramayana and the Mahabharata, large portions of which she had memorized. She became the special refuge of the poor, and commanded universal respect because of her calm resignation to God, her inner tranquillity, and her dignified detachment in the midst of her many arduous duties. Two sons were born to her besides Narendranath, and four daughters, two of whom died at an early age.

CHILDHOOD

Swami Vivekananda, the great soul loved and revered in East and West alike as the rejuvenator of Hinduism in India and the preacher of its eternal truths abroad, was born at 6:33, a few minutes before sunrise, on Monday, January 12, 1863. It was the day of the great Hindu festival Makarasamkranti, when special worship is offered to the Ganga by millions of devotees. Thus the future Vivekananda first drew breath when the air above the sacred river not far from the house was reverberating with the prayers, worship, and religious music of thousands of Hindu men and women. Before Vivekananda was born, his mother, like many other pious Hindu mothers, had observed religious vows, fasted, and prayed so that she might be blessed with a son who would do honour to the family. She requested a relative who was living in Varanasi to offer special worship to the Vireswara Siva of that holy place and seek His blessings; for Siva, the great god of renunciation, dominated her thought. One night she dreamt that this supreme Deity aroused Himself from His meditation and agreed to be born as her son. When she woke she was filled with joy.

The mother, Bhuvaneswari Devi, accepted the child as a boon from Vireswara Siva and named him Vireswara. The family, however, gave him the name of Narendranath Datta, calling him, for short, Narendra, or more endearingly, Naren. The Datta family of Calcutta, into which Narendranath had been born, was well known for its affluence, philanthropy, scholarship, and independent spirit. The grand father, Durgacharan, after the birth of his first son, had renounced the world in search of God. The father, Viswanath, an attorney-at-law of the High Court of Calcutta, was versed in English and Persian literature and often entertained himself and his friends by reciting from the Bible and the poetry of Hafiz, both of which, he believed, contained truths unmatched by human thinking elsewhere.

He was particularly attracted to the Islamic culture, with which he was familiar because of his close contact with the educated Moslems of North-western India. Moreover, he derived a large income from his law practice and, unlike his father, thoroughly enjoyed the worldly life. An expert in cookery, he prepared rare dishes and liked to share them with his friends. Travel was another of his hobbies. Though agnostic in religion and a mocker of social conventions, he possessed a large heart and often went out of his way to support idle relatives, some of whom were given to drunkenness. Once, when Narendra protested against his lack of judgement, his father said: 'How can you understand the great misery of human life? When you realize the depths of men's suffering, you will sympathize with these unfortunate creatures who try to forget their sorrows, even though only for a short while, in the oblivion created by intoxicants.' Naren's father, however, kept a sharp eye on his children and would not tolerate the slightest deviation from good manners.

Bhuvaneswari Devi, the mother, was cast in a different mould. Regal in appearance and gracious in conduct, she belonged to the old tradition of Hindu womanhood. As mistress of a large household, she devoted her spare time to sewing and singing, being particularly fond of the great Indian epics, the Ramayana and the Mahabharata, large portions of which she had memorized. She became the special refuge of the poor, and commanded universal respect because of her calm resignation to God, her inner tranquillity, and her dignified detachment in the midst of her many arduous duties. Two sons were born to her besides Narendranath, and four daughters, two of whom died at an early age.

Narendra grew up to be a sweet, sunny-tempered, but very restless boy. Two nurses were necessary to keep his exuberant energy under control, and he was a great tease to his sisters. In order to quiet him, the mother often put his head under the cold-water tap, repeating Siva's name, which always produced the desired effect. Naren felt a child's love for birds and animals, and this characteristic reappeared during the last days of his life. Among his boyhood pets were a family cow, a monkey, a goat, a peacock, and several pigeons and guinea-pigs.

The coachman of the family, with his turban, whip, and bright-coloured livery, was his boyhood ideal of a magnificent person, and he often expressed the ambition to be like him when he grew up. Narendra bore a striking resemblance to the grand-father who had renounced the world to lead a monastic life, and many thought that the latter had been reborn in him. The youngster developed a special fancy for wandering monks, whose very sight would greatly excite him. One day when such a monk appeared at the door and asked for alms, Narendra gave him his only possession, the tiny piece of new cloth that was wrapped round his waist. Thereafter, whenever a monk was seen in the neighbourhood, Narendra would be locked in a room. But even then he would throw out of the window whatever he found near at hand as an offering to the holy man. In the meantime, he was receiving his early education from his mother, who taught him the Bengali alphabet and his first English words, as well as stories from the Ramayana and the Mahabharata.

During his childhood Narendra, like many other Hindu children of his age, developed a love for the Hindu deities, of whom he had learnt from his mother. Particularly attracted by the heroic story of Rama and his faithful consort Sita, he procured their images, bedecked them with flowers, and worshipped them in his boyish fashion. But disillusionment came when he heard someone denounce marriage vehemently as a terrible bondage. When he had thought this over he discarded Rama and Sita as unworthy of worship. In their place he installed the image of Siva, the god of renunciation, who was the ideal of the yogis. Nevertheless he retained a fondness for the Ramayana. At this time he daily experienced a strange vision when he was about to fall asleep. Closing his eyes, he would see between his eyebrows a ball of light of changing colours, which would slowly expand and at last burst, bathing his whole body in a white radiance. Watching this light he would gradually fall asleep. Since it was a daily occurrence, he regarded the phenomenon as common to all people, and was surprised when a friend denied ever having seen such a thing. Years later, however, Narendra's spiritual teacher, Sri Ramakrishna, said to him, 'Naren, my boy, do you see a light when you go to sleep?' Ramakrishna knew that such a vision indicated a great spiritual past and an inborn habit of meditation. The vision of light remained with Narendra until the end of his life, though later it lost its regularity and intensity.

While still a child Narendra practised meditation with a friend before the image of Siva. He had heard that the holy men of ancient India would become so absorbed in contemplation of God that their hair would grow and gradually enter into the earth, like the roots of the banyan tree. While meditating, therefore, he would open his eyes, now and then, to see if his own hair had entered into the earth. Even so, during meditation, he often became unconscious of the world. On one occasion he saw in a vision a luminous person of serene countenance who was carrying the staff and water-bowl of a monk. The apparition was about to say something when Naren became frightened and left the room. He thought later that perhaps this had been a vision of Buddha.

At the age of six he was sent to a primary school. One day, however, he repeated at home some of the vulgar words that he had learnt from his classmates, whereupon his disgusted parents took him out of the school and appointed a private tutor, who conducted classes for him and some other children of the neighbourhood in the worship hall of the house. Naren soon showed a precocious mind and developed a keen memory.

Very easily he learnt by heart the whole of a Sanskrit grammar and long passages from the Ramayana and the Mahabharata.

Some of the friendships he made at this age lasted his whole lifetime. At school he was the undisputed leader. When playing his favourite game of 'King and the Court,' he would assume the role of the monarch and assign to his friends the parts of the ministers, commander-in-chief, and other state officials.

He was marked from birth to be a leader of men, as his name Narendra (lord of men) signified. Even at that early age he questioned why one human being should be considered superior to another. In his father's office separate tobacco pipes were provided for clients belonging to the different castes, as orthodox Hindu custom required, and the pipe from which the Moslems smoked was set quite apart. Narendra once smoked tobacco from all the pipes, including the one marked for the Moslems, and when reprimanded, remarked, 'I cannot see what difference it makes.'

During these early years, Narendra's future personality was influenced by his gifted father and his saintly mother, both of whom kept a chastening eye upon him. The father had his own manner of discipline. For example, when, in the course of an argument with his mother, the impetuous boy once uttered a few rude words and the report came to the father, Viswanath did not directly scold his son, but wrote with charcoal on the door of his room: 'Narendra today said to his mother - ' and added the words that had been used. He wanted Narendra's friends to know how rudely he had treated his mother. Another time Narendra bluntly asked his father, 'What have you done for me?'

Instead of being annoyed, Viswanath said, 'Go and look at yourself in the mirror, and then you will know.'

Still another day, Narendra said to his father, 'How shall I conduct myself in the world?'

'Never show surprise at anything,' his father replied.

This priceless advice enabled Narendranath, in his future chequered life, to preserve his serenity of mind whether dwelling with princes in their palaces or sharing the straw huts of beggars. The mother, Bhuvaneswari, played her part in bringing out Narendranath's innate virtues. When he told her, one day, of having been unjustly treated in school, she said to him, in consolation: 'My child, what does it matter, if you are in the right? Always follow the truth without caring about the result. Very often you may have to suffer injustice or unpleasant consequences for holding to the truth; but you must not, under any circumstances, abandon it.' Many years later Narendranath proudly said to an audience, 'I am indebted to my mother for whatever knowledge I have acquired.'

One day, when he was fighting with his play-fellows, Narendra accidentally fell from the porch and struck his forehead against a stone. The wound bled profusely and left a permanent scar over his right eye. Years later, when Ramakrishna heard of this accident, he remarked: 'In a way it was a good thing. If he had not thus lost some of his blood, he would have created havoc in the world with his excessive energy.' In 1871, at the age of eight, Narendra entered high school. His exceptional intelligence was soon recognized by his teachers and classmates. Though at first reluctant to study English because of its foreign origin, he soon took it up with avidity.

But the curriculum consumed very little of his time. He used most of his inexhaustible energy in outside activities. Games of various kinds, many of which he invented or improvised kept him occupied. He made an imitation gas-works and a factory for aerating water, these two novelties having just been introduced in Calcutta. He organized an amateur theatrical company and a gymnasium, and took lessons in fencing, wrestling, rowing, and other manly sports. He also tried his hand at the art of cooking. Intensely restless, he would soon tire of one pastime and seek a new one. With his friends he visited the museum and the zoological garden. He arbitrated the disputes of his play-fellows and was a favourite with the people of the neighbourhood. Everybody admired his courage, straight-forwardness, and simplicity.

From an early age this remarkable youth had no patience with fear or superstition. One of his boyish pranks had been to climb a flowering tree belonging to a neighbour, pluck the flowers, and do other mischief. The owner of the tree, finding his remonstrances unheeded, once solemnly told Naren's friends that the tree was guarded by a white-robed ghost who would certainly wring their necks if they disturbed his peace. The boys were frightened and kept away. But Narendra persuaded them to follow him back, and he climbed the tree, enjoying his usual measure of fun, and broke some branches by way of further mischief. Turning to his friends, he then said: 'What asses you all are! See, my neck is still there.

The old man's story is simply not true. Don't believe what others say unless you your-selves know it to be true.' These simple but bold words were an indication of his future message to the world. Addressing large audiences in the later years, he would often say: 'Do not believe in a thing because you have read about it in a book. Do not believe in a thing because another man has said it was true. Do not believe in words because they are hallowed by tradition. Find out the truth for yourself. Reason it out. That is realization.'

The following incident illustrates his courage and presence of mind. He one day wished to set up a heavy trapeze in the gymnasium, and so asked the help of some people who were there. Among them was an English sailor. The trapeze fell and knocked the sailor unconscious, and the crowd, thinking him dead, ran away for fear of the police. But Naren tore a piece from his cloth, bandaged the sailor's wound, washed his face with water, and gradually revived him. Then he moved the wounded man to a neighbouring schoolhouse where he nursed him for a week. When the sailor had recovered, Naren sent him away with a little purse collected from his friends. All through this period of boyish play Narendra retained his admiration for the life of the wandering monk. Pointing to a certain line on the palm of his hand, he would say to his friends: 'I shall certainly become a sannyasin. A palmist has predicted it.'

As Narendra grew into adolescence, his temperament showed a marked change. He became keen about intellectual matters, read serious books on history and literature, devoured newspapers, and attended public meetings. Music was his favourite pastime. He insisted that it should express a lofty idea and arouse the feelings of the musician.

At the age of fifteen he experienced his first spiritual ecstasy. The family was journeying to Raipur in the Central Provinces, and part of the trip had to be made in a bullock cart. On that particular day the air was crisp and clear; the trees and creepers were covered with green leaves and many-coloured blossoms; birds of brilliant plumage warbled in the woods. The cart was moving along a narrow pass where the lofty peaks rising on the two sides almost touched each other. Narendra's eyes spied a large bee-hive in the cleft of a giant cliff, and suddenly his mind was filled with awe and reverence for the Divine Providence. He lost outer consciousness and lay thus in the cart for a long time. Even after returning to the sense-perceived world he radiated joy.

Another interesting mental phenomenon may be mentioned here; for it was one often experienced by Narendranath. From boyhood, on first beholding certain people or places, he would feel that he had known them before; but how long before he could never remember. One day he and some of his companions were in a room in a friend's house, where they were discussing various topics.

Something was mentioned, and Narendra felt at once that he had on a previous occasion talked about the same subject with the selfsame friends in that very house. He even correctly described every nook and corner of the building, which he had not seen before. He tried at first to explain this singular phenomenon by the doctrine of reincarnation, thinking that perhaps he had lived in that house in a previous life. But he dismissed the idea as improbable. Later he concluded that before his birth he must have had previsions of the people, places, and events that he was to experience in his present incarnation; that was why, he thought, he could recognize them as soon as they presented themselves to him.

At Raipur Narendra was encouraged by his father to meet notable scholars and discuss with them various intellectual topics usually considered too abstruse for boys of his age. On such occasions he exhibited great mental power. From his father, Narendra had learnt the art of grasping the essentials of things, seeing truth from the widest and most comprehensive standpoints, and holding to the real issue under discussion.

In 1879 the family returned to Calcutta, and Narendra within a short time graduated from high school in the first division. In the meantime he had read a great many standard books of English and Bengali literature.

History was his favourite subject. He also acquired at this time an unusual method of reading a book and acquiring the knowledge of its subject-matter. To quote his own words: 'I could understand an author without reading every line of his book. I would read the first and last lines of a paragraph and grasp its meaning. Later I found that I could understand the subject-matter by reading only the first and last lines of a page. Afterwards I could follow the whole trend of a writer's argument by merely reading a few lines, though the author himself tried to explain the subject in five or more pages.'

Soon the excitement of his boyhood days was over, and in 1879 Narendranath entered the Presidency College of Calcutta for higher studies. After a year he joined the General Assembly's Institution, founded by the Scottish General Missionary Board and later known as the Scottish Church College. It was from Hastie, the principal of the college and the professor of English literature, that he first heard the name Sri Ramakrishna.

In college Narendra, now a handsome youth, muscular and agile, though slightly inclined to stoutness, enjoyed serious studies. During the first two years he studied Western logic. Thereafter he specialized in Western philosophy and the ancient and modern history of the different European nations. His memory was prodigious. It took him only three days to assimilate Green's History of the English People. Often, on the eve of an examination, he would read the whole night, keeping awake by drinking strong tea or coffee.

About this time he came in contact with Sri Ramakrishna; this event, as we shall presently see, was to become the major turning-point of his life. As a result of his association with Sri Ramakrishna, his innate spiritual yearning was stirred up, and he began to feel the transitoriness of the world and the futility of academic education. The day before his B.A. examination, he suddenly felt an all-consuming love for God and, standing before the room of a college-mate, was heard to sing with great feeling:

Sing ye, O mountains, O clouds, O great winds!

Sing ye, sing ye, sing His glory!

Sing with joy, all ye suns and moons and stars!

Sing ye, sing ye, His glory!

The friends, surprised, reminded him of the next day's examination, but Narendra was unconcerned; the shadow of the approaching monastic life was fast falling on him. He appeared for the examination, however, and easily passed. About Narendra's scholarship, Professor Hastie once remarked: 'Narendra is a real genius. I have travelled far and wide, but have not yet come across a lad of his talents and possibilities even among the philosophical students in the German universities. He is bound to make his mark in life.' Narendra's many-sided genius found its expression in music, as well. He studied both instrumental and vocal music under expert teachers. He could play on many instruments, but excelled in singing. From a Moslem teacher he learnt Hindi, Urdu, and

Persian songs, most of them of devotional nature. He also became associated with the Brahmo Samaj, an important religious movement of the time, which influenced him during this formative period of his life.

The introduction of English education in India following the British conquest of the country brought Hindu society in contact with the intellectual and aggressive European culture. The Hindu youths who came under the spell of the new, dynamic way of life realized the many shortcomings of their own society. Under the Moslem rule, even before the coming of the British, the dynamic aspect of the Hindu culture had been suppressed and the caste-system stratified. The priests controlled the religious life of the people for their own selfish interest. Meaningless dogmas and lifeless ceremonies supplanted the invigorating philosophical teachings of the Upanishads and the Bhagavad Gita. The masses were exploited, moreover, by the landlords, and the lot of women was especially pitiable. Following the break-down of the Moslem rule, chaos reigned in every field of Indian life, social, political, religious, and economic. The newly introduced English education brought into sharp focus the many drawbacks of society, and various reform movements, both liberal and orthodox, were initiated to make the national life flow once more through healthy channels.

The Brahmo Samaj, one of these liberal movements, captured the imagination of the educated youths of Bengal. Raja Rammohan Roy (1774-1833), the founder of this religious organization, broke away from the rituals, image worship, and priestcraft of orthodox Hinduism and exhorted his followers to dedicate themselves to the 'worship and adoration of the Eternal, the Unsearchable, the Immutable Being, who is the Author and the Preserver of the universe.' The Raja, endowed with a gigantic intellect, studied the Hindu, Moslem, Christian, and Buddhist scriptures and was the first Indian to realize the importance of the Western rational method for solving the diverse problems of Hindu society. He took a prominent part in the introduction of English education in India, which, though it at first produced a deleterious effect on the newly awakened Hindu consciousness, ultimately revealed to a few Indians the glorious heritage of their own indigenous civilization.

Among the prominent leaders of the Brahmo Samaj who succeeded Rammohan Roy were Devendranath Tagore (1817-1905), a great devotee of the Upanishads, and Keshab Chandra Sen (1838-1884), who was inclined to the rituals and doctrines of Christianity. The Brahmo Samaj, under their leadership, discarded many of the conventions of Hinduism such as rituals and the worship of God through images. Primarily a reformist movement, it directed its main energy to the emancipation of women, the remarriage of Hindu widows, the abolition of early marriage, and the spread of mass education. Influenced by Western culture, the Brahmo Samaj upheld the supremacy of reason, preached against the uncritical acceptance of scriptural authority, and strongly supported the slogans of the French Revolution. The whole movement was intellectual and eclectic in character, born of the necessity of the times; unlike traditional Hinduism, it had no root in the spiritual experiences of saints and seers.

Narendra, like many other contemporary young men, felt the appeal of its progressive ideas and became one of its members. But, as will be presently seen, the Brahmo Samaj could not satisfy the deep spiritual yearning of his soul. About this time Narendra was urged by his father to marry, and an opportunity soon presented itself.

A wealthy man, whose daughter Narendra was asked to accept as his bride, offered to defray his expenses for higher studies in England so that he might qualify himself for the much coveted Indian Civil Service. Narendra refused. Other proposals of similar nature produced no different result. Apparently it was not his destiny to lead a householder's life.

From boyhood Narendra had shown a passion for purity. Whenever his warm and youthful nature tempted him to walk into a questionable adventure, he was held back by an unseen hand. His mother had taught him the value of chastity and had made him observe it as a matter of honour, in loyalty to herself and the family tradition. But purity to Narendra was not a negative virtue, a mere abstention from carnal pleasures. To be pure, he felt, was to conserve an intense spiritual force that would later manifest itself in all the noble aspirations of life. He regarded himself as a brahmacharin, a celibate student of the Hindu tradition, who worked hard, prized ascetic disciplines, held holy things in reverence, and enjoyed clean words, thoughts, and acts.

For according to the Hindu scriptures, a man, by means of purity, which is the greatest of all virtues, can experience the subtlest spiritual perceptions. In Naren it accounts for the great power of concentration, memory, and insight, and for his indomitable mental energy and physical stamina. In his youth Narendra used to see every night two visions, utterly dissimilar in nature, before falling asleep. One was that of a worldly man with an accomplished wife and children, enjoying wealth, luxuries, fame, and social position; the other, that of a sannyasin, a wandering monk, bereft of earthly security and devoted to the contemplation of God.

Narendra felt that he had the power to realize either of these ideals; but when his mind reflected on their respective virtues, he was inevitably drawn to the life of renunciation. The glamour of the world would fade and disappear. His deeper self instinctively chose the austere path.

For a time the congregational prayers and the devotional songs of the Brahmo Samaj exhilarated Narendra's mind, but soon he found that they did not give him any real spiritual experience. He wanted to realize God, the goal of religion, and so felt the imperative need of being instructed by a man who had seen God.

In his eagerness he went to Devendranath, the venerable leader of the Brahmo Samaj, and asked him, even before the latter had uttered a word, 'Sir, have you seen God?' Devendranath was embarrassed and replied: 'My boy, you have the eyes of a yogi. You should practise meditation.' The youth was disappointed and felt that this teacher was not the man to help him in his spiritual struggle. But he received no better answer from the leaders of other religious sects.

Then he remembered having heard the name of Ramakrishna Paramahamsa from Professor Hastie, who while lecturing his class on Wordsworth's poem The Excursion, had spoken of trances, remarking that such religious ecstasies were the result of purity and concentration. He had said, further, that an exalted experience of this kind was a rare phenomenon, especially in modern times.

'I have known,' he had said, 'only one person who has realized that blessed state, and he is Ramakrishna of Dakshineswar. You will understand trances if you visit the saint.'

Narendra had also heard about Sri Ramakrishna from a relative, Ramchandra Datta, who was one of the foremost householder disciples of the Master. Learning of Narendra's unwillingness to marry and ascribing it to his desire to lead a spiritual life, Ramchandra had said to him, 'If you really want to cultivate spirituality, then visit Ramakrishna at Dakshineswar.'

Narendra met Ramakrishna for the first time in November 1881 at the house of the Master's devotee Surendranath Mitra, the young man having been invited there to entertain the visitors with his melodious music. The Paramahamsa was much impressed by his sincerity and devotion, and after a few inquiries asked him to visit him at Dakshineswar. Narendra accepted. He wished to learn if Ramakrishna was the man to help him in his spiritual quest.

LIFE AND TEACHINGS OF VIVEKANANDA

Swami Vivekananda, known in his pre-monastic life as Narendra Nath Datta, was born in an affluent family in Kolkata on 12 January 1863. His father, Vishwanath Datta, was a successful attorney with interests in a wide range of subjects, and his mother, Bhuvaneshwari Devi, was endowed with deep devotion, strong character and other qualities. A precocious boy, Narendra excelled in music, gymnastics and studies. By the time he graduated from Calcutta University, he had acquired a vast knowledge of different subjects, especially Western philosophy and history. Born with a yogic temperament, he used to practise meditation even from his boyhood, and was associated with Brahmo Movement for some time.

With Sri Ramakrishna

At the threshold of youth Narendra had to pass through a period of spiritual crisis when he was assailed by doubts about the existence of God. It was at that time he first heard about Sri Ramakrishna from one of his English professors at college. One day in November 1881, Narendra went to meet Sri Ramakrishna who was staying at the Kali Temple in Dakshineshwar. He straightaway asked the Master a question which he had put to several others but had received no satisfactory answer: "Sir, have you seen God?" Without a moment's hesitation, Sri Ramakrishna replied: "Yes, I have. I see Him as clearly as I see you, only in a much intenser sense."

Apart from removing doubts from the mind of Narendra, Sri Ramakrishna won him over through his pure, unselfish love. Thus began a guru-disciple relationship which is quite unique in the history of spiritual masters. Narendra now became a frequent visitor to Dakshineshwar and, under the guidance of the Master, made rapid strides on the spiritual path. At Dakshineshwar, Narendra also met several young men who were devoted to Sri Ramakrishna, and they all became close friends.

Difficult Situations

After a few years two events took place which caused Narendra considerable distress. One was the sudden death of his father in 1884. This left the family penniless, and Narendra had to bear the burden of supporting his mother, brothers and sisters. The second event was the illness of Sri Ramakrishna which was diagnosed to be cancer of the throat. In September 1885 Sri Ramakrishna was moved to a house at Shyampukur, and a few months later to a rented villa at Cossipore. In these two places the young disciples nursed the Master with devoted care. In spite of poverty at home and inability to find a job for himself, Narendra joined the group as its leader.

Beginnings of a Monastic Brotherhood

Sri Ramakrishna instilled in these young men the spirit of renunciation and brotherly love for one another. One day he distributed ochre robes among them and sent them out to beg food. In this way he himself laid the foundation for a new monastic order. He gave specific instructions to Narendra about the formation of the new monastic Order. In the small hours of 16 August 1886 Sri Ramakrishna gave up his mortal body. After the Master's passing, fifteen of his young disciples (one more joined them later) began to live together in a dilapidated building at Baranagar in North Kolkata. Under the leadership of Narendra, they formed a new monastic brotherhood, and in 1887 they took the formal vows of sannyasa, thereby assuming new names. Narendra now became Swami Vivekananda (although this name was actually assumed much later.)

Awareness of Life's Mission

After establishing the new monastic order, Vivekananda heard the inner call for a greater mission in his life. While most of the followers of Sri Ramakrishna thought of him in relation to their own personal lives, Vivekananda thought of the Master in relation to India and the rest of the world. As the prophet of the present age, what was Sri Ramakrishna's message to the modern world and to India in particular? This question and the awareness of his own inherent powers urged Swamiji to go out alone into the wide world. So in the middle of 1890, after receiving the blessings of Sri Sarada Devi, the divine consort of Sri Ramakrishna, known to the world as Holy Mother, who was then staying in Kolkata, Swamiji left Baranagar Math and embarked on a long journey of exploration and discovery of India.

Discovery of Real India

During his travels all over India, Swami Vivekananda was deeply moved to see the appalling poverty and backwardness of the masses. He was the first religious leader in India to understand and openly declare that the real cause of India's downfall was the neglect of the masses. The immediate need was to provide food and other bare necessities of life to the hungry millions. For this they should be taught improved methods of agriculture, village industries, etc. It was in this context that Vivekananda grasped the crux of the problem of poverty in India (which had escaped the attention of social reformers of his days): owing to centuries of oppression, the downtrodden masses had lost faith in their capacity to improve their lot.

It was first of all necessary to infuse into their minds faith in themselves. For this they needed a life-giving, inspiring message. Swamiji found this message in the principle of the Atman, the doctrine of the potential divinity of the soul, taught in Vedanta, the ancient system of religious philosophy of India. He saw that, in spite of poverty, the masses clung to religion, but they had never been taught the life-giving, ennobling principles of Vedanta and how to apply them in practical life. Thus the masses needed two kinds of knowledge: secular knowledge to improve their economic condition, and spiritual knowledge to infuse in them faith in themselves and strengthen their moral sense. The next question was, how to spread these two kinds of knowledge among the masses? Through education – this was the answer that Swamiji found.

Need for an Organization

One thing became clear to Swamiji: to carry out his plans for the spread of education and for the uplift of the poor masses, and also of women, an efficient organization of dedicated people was needed. As he said later on, he wanted "to set in motion a machinery which will bring noblest ideas to the doorstep of even the poorest and the meanest." It was to serve as this 'machinery' that Swamiji founded the Ramakrishna Mission a few years later.

Decision to attend the Parliament of Religions

It was when these ideas were taking shape in his mind in the course of his wanderings that Swami Vivekananda heard about the World's Parliament of Religions to be held in Chicago in 1893. His friends and admirers in India wanted him to attend the Parliament. He too felt that the Parliament would provide the right forum to present his Master's message to the world, and so he decided to go to America. Another reason which prompted Swamiji to go to America was to seek financial help for his project of uplifting the masses.

Swamiji, however, wanted to have an inner certitude and divine call regarding his mission. Both of these he got while he sat in deep meditation on the rock-island at Kanyakumari. With the funds partly collected by his Chennai disciples and partly provided by the Raja of Khetri, Swami Vivekananda left for America from Mumbai on 31 May 1893.

Belur Math

In early 1898 Swami Vivekananda acquired a big plot of land on the western bank of the Ganga at a place called Belur to have a permanent abode for the monastery and monastic Order originally started at Baranagar, and got it registered as Ramakrishna Math after a couple of years. Here Swamiji established a new, universal pattern of monastic life which adapts ancient monastic ideals to the conditions of modern life, which gives equal importance to personal illumination and social service, and which is open to all men without any distinction of religion, race or caste.

Disciples

It may be mentioned here that in the West many people were influenced by Swami Vivekananda's life and message. Some of them became his disciples or devoted friends. Among them the names of Margaret Noble (later known as Sister Nivedita), Captain and Mrs Sevier, Josephine McLeod and Sara Ole Bull, deserve special mention. Nivedita dedicated her life to educating girls in Kolkata. Swamiji had many Indian disciples also, some of whom joined Ramakrishna Math and became sannyasins.

WORK AND ITS SECRET

One of the greatest lessons I have learnt in my life is to pay as much attention to the means of work as to its end. He was a great man from whom I learnt it, and his own life was a practical demonstration of this great principle I have been always learning great lessons from that one principle, and it appears to me that all the secret of success is there; to pay as much attention to the means as to the end. Our great defect in life is that we are so much drawn to the ideal, the goal is so much more enchanting, so much more alluring, so much bigger in our mental horizon, that we lose sight of the details altogether.

But whenever failure comes, if we analyse it critically, in ninety-nine per cent of cases we shall find that it was because we did not pay attention to the means. Proper attention to the finishing, strengthening, of the means is what we need. With the means all right, the end must come. We forget that it is the cause that produces the effect; the effect cannot come by itself; and unless the causes are exact, proper, and powerful, the effect will not be produced. Once the ideal is chosen and the means determined, we may almost let go the ideal, because we are sure it will be there, when the means are perfected. When the cause is there, there is no more difficulty about the effect, the effect is bound to come. If we take care of the cause, the effect will take care of itself. The realization of the ideal is the effect. The means are the cause: attention to the means, therefore, is the great secret of life. We also read this in the Gita and learn that we have to work, constantly work with all our power; to put our whole mind in the work, whatever it be, that we are doing. At the same time, we must not be attached. That is to say, we must not be drawn away from the work by anything else; still, we must be able to quit the work whenever we like.

If we examine our own lives, we find that the greatest cause of sorrow is this: we take up something, and put our whole energy on it — perhaps it is a failure and yet we cannot give it up. We know that it is hurting us, that any further clinging to it is simply bringing misery on us; still, we cannot tear ourselves away from it. The bee came to sip the honey, but its feet stuck to the honey-pot and it could not get away. Again and again, we are finding ourselves in that state. That is the whole secret of existence. Why are we here? We came here to sip the honey, and we find our hands and feet sticking to it. We are caught, though we came to catch. We came to enjoy; we are being enjoyed. We came to rule; we are being ruled. We came to work; we are being worked. All the time, we find that. And this comes into every detail of our life. We are being worked upon by other minds, and we are always struggling to work on other minds. We want to enjoy the pleasures of life; and they eat into our vitals. We want to get everything from nature, but we find in the long run that nature takes everything from us — depletes us, and casts us aside.

Had it not been for this, life would have been all sunshine. Never mind! With all its failures and successes, with all its joys and sorrows, it can be one succession of sunshine, if only we are not caught. That is the one cause of misery: we are attached, we are being caught.

Therefore says the Gita: Work constantly; work, but be not attached; be not caught. Reserve unto yourself the power of detaching yourself from everything, however beloved, however much the soul might yearn for it, however great the pangs of misery you feel if you were going to leave it; still, reserve the power of leaving it whenever you want. The weak have no place here, in this life or in any other life. Weakness leads to slavery. Weakness leads to all kinds of misery, physical and mental. Weakness is death. There are hundreds of thousands of microbes surrounding us, but they cannot harm us unless we become weak, until the body is ready and predisposed to receive them. There may be a million microbes of misery, floating about us. Never mind! They dare not approach us, they have no power to get a hold on us, until the mind is weakened. This is the great fact: strength is life, weakness is death. Strength is felicity, life eternal, immortal; weakness is constant strain and misery: weakness is death. Attachment is the source of all our pleasures now.

We are attached to our friends, to our relatives; we are attached to our intellectual and spiritual works; we are attached to external objects, so that we get pleasure from them. What, again, brings misery but this very attachment? We have to detach ourselves to earn joy. If only we had power to detach ourselves at will, there would not be any misery. That man alone will be able to get the best of nature, who, having the power of attaching himself to a thing with all his energy, has also the power to detach himself when he should do so. The difficulty is that there must be as much power of attachment as that of detachment. There are men who are never attracted by anything. They can never love, they are hard-hearted and apathetic; they escape most of the miseries of life. But the wall never feels misery, the wall never loves, is never hurt; but it is the wall, after all. Surely it is better to be attached and caught, than to be a wall. Therefore the man who never loves, who is hard and stony, escaping most of the miseries of life, escapes also its joys. We do not want that. That is weakness, that is death. That soul has not been awakened that never feels weakness, never feels misery. That is a callous state. We do not want that.

At the same time, we not only want this mighty power of love, this mighty power of attachment, the power of throwing our whole soul upon a single object, losing ourselves and letting ourselves be annihilated, as it were, for other souls — which is the power of the gods — but we want to be higher even than the gods. The perfect man can put his whole soul upon that one point of love, yet he is unattached. How comes this? There is another secret to learn.

The beggar is never happy. The beggar only gets a dole with pity and scorn behind it, at least with the thought behind that the beggar is a low object. He never really enjoys what he gets. We are all beggars. Whatever we do, we want a return. We are all traders. We are traders in life, we are traders in virtue, we are traders in religion. And alas! we are also traders in love. If you come to trade, if it is a question of give-and-take, if it is a question of buy-and-sell, abide by the laws of buying and selling. There is a bad time and there is a good time; there is a rise and a fall in prices: always you expect the blow to come. It is like looking at the mirrors Your face is reflected: you make a grimace — there is one in the mirror; if you laugh, the mirror laughs. This is buying and selling, giving and taking.

We get caught. How? Not by what we give, but by what we expect. We get misery in return for our love; not from the fact that we love, but from the fact that we want love in return. There is no misery where there is no want. Desire, want, is the father of all misery. Desires are bound by the laws of success and failure. Desires must bring misery. The great secret of true success, of true happiness, then, is this: the man who asks for no return, the perfectly unselfish man, is the most successful. It seems to be a paradox. Do we not know that every man who is unselfish in life gets cheated, gets hurt? Apparently, yes. "Christ was unselfish, and yet he was crucified." True, but we know that his unselfishness is the reason, the cause of a great victory — the crowning of millions upon millions of lives with the blessings of true success.

Ask nothing; want nothing in return. Give what you have to give; it will come back to you — but do not think of that now, it will come back multiplied a thousandfold — but the attention must not be on that. Yet have the power to give: give, and there it ends. Learn that the whole of life is giving, that nature will force you to give. So, give willingly. Sooner or later you will have to give up. You come into life to accumulate. With clenched hands, you want to take. But nature puts a hand on your throat and makes your hands open. Whether you will it or not, you have to give. The moment you say, "I will not", the blow comes; you are hurt. None is there but will be compelled, in the long run, to give up everything. And the more one struggles against this law, the more miserable one feels. It is because we dare not give, because we are not resigned enough to accede to this grand demand of nature, that we are miserable. The forest is gone, but we get heat in return. The sun is taking up water from the ocean, to return it in showers. You are a machine for taking and giving: you take, in order to give. Ask, therefore, nothing in return; but the more you give, the more will come to you. The quicker you can empty the air out of this room, the quicker it will be filled up by the external air; and if you close all the doors and every aperture, that which is within will remain, but that which is outside will never come in, and that which is within will stagnate, degenerate, and become poisoned. A river is continually emptying itself into the ocean and is continually filling up again. Bar not the exit into the ocean. The moment you do that, death seizes you.

Be, therefore, not a beggar; be unattached This is the most terrible task of life! You do not calculate the dangers on the path. Even by intellectually recognising the difficulties, we really do not know them until we feel them. From a distance we may get a general view of a park: well, what of that? We feel and really know it when we are in it. Even if our every attempt is a failure, and we bleed and are torn asunder, yet, through all this, we have to preserve our heart — we must assert our Godhead in the midst of all these difficulties. Nature wants us to react, to return blow for blow, cheating for cheating, lie for lie, to hit back with all our might. Then it requires a superdivine power not to hit back, to keep control, to be unattached.

Every day we renew our determination to be unattached. We cast our eyes back and look at the past objects of our love and attachment, and feel how every one of them made us miserable. We went down into the depths of despondency because of our "love"! We found ourselves mere slaves in the hands of others, we were dragged down and down! And we make a fresh determination: "Henceforth, I will be master of myself; henceforth, I will have control over myself." But the time comes, and the same story once more! Again the soul is caught and cannot get out. The bird is in a net, struggling and fluttering. This is our life.

I know the difficulties. Tremendous they are, and ninety per cent of us become discouraged and lose heart, and in our turn, often become pessimists and cease to believe in sincerity, love, and all that is grand and noble. So, we find men who in the freshness of their lives have been forgiving, kind, simple, and guileless, become in old age lying masks of men. Their minds are a mass of intricacy. There may be a good deal of external policy, possibly. They are not hot-headed, they do not speak, but it would be better for them to do so; their hearts are dead and, therefore, they do not speak. They do not curse, not become angry; but it would be better for them to be able to be angry, a thousand times better, to be able to curse. They cannot. There is death in the heart, for cold hands have seized upon it, and it can no more act, even to utter a curse, even to use a harsh word.

All this we have to avoid: therefore I say, we require superdivine power. Superhuman power is not strong enough. Superdivine strength is the only way, the one way out. By it alone we can pass through all these intricacies, through these showers of miseries, unscathed. We may be cut to pieces, torn asunder, yet our hearts must grow nobler and nobler all the time.

It is very difficult, but we can overcome the difficulty by constant practice. We must learn that nothing can happen to us, unless we make ourselves susceptible to it. I have just said, no disease can come to me until the body is ready; it does not depend alone on the germs, but upon a certain predisposition which is already in the body. We get only that for which we are fitted. Let us give up our pride and understand this, that never is misery undeserved. There never has been a blow undeserved: there never has been an evil for which I did not pave the way with my own hands. We ought to know that. Analyse yourselves and you will find that every blow you have received, came to you because you prepared yourselves for it. You did half, and the external world did the other half: that is how the blow came. That will sober us down. At the same time, from this very analysis will come a note of hope, and the note of hope is: "I have no control of the external world, but that which is in me and nearer unto me, my own world, is in my control. If the two together are required to make a failure, if the two together are necessary to give me a blow, I will not contribute the one which is in my keeping; and how then can the blow come? If I get real control of myself, the blow will never come."

We are all the time, from our childhood, trying to lay the blame upon something outside ourselves. We are always standing up to set right other people, and not ourselves. If we are miserable, we say, "Oh, the world is a devil's world." We curse others and say, "What infatuated fools!" But why should we be in such a world, if we really are so good? If this is a devil's world, we must be devils also; why else should we be here? "Oh, the people of the world are so selfish!" True enough; but why should we be found in that company, if we be better? Just think of that. We only get what we deserve. It is a lie when we say, the world is bad and we are good. It can never be so. It is a terrible lie we tell ourselves. This is the first lesson to learn: be determined not to curse anything outside, not to lay the blame upon any one outside, but be a man, stand up, lay the blame on yourself. You will find, that is always true. Get hold of yourself.

Is it not a shame that at one moment we talk so much of our manhood, of our being gods — that we know everything, we can do everything, we are blameless, spotless, the most unselfish people in the world; and at the next moment a little stone hurts us, a little anger from a little Jack wounds us — any fool in the street makes "these gods" miserable! Should this be so if we are such gods? Is it true that the world is to blame? Could God, who is the purest and the noblest of souls, be made miserable by any of our tricks? If you are so unselfish, you are like God. What world can hurt you? You would go through the seventh hell unscathed, untouched. But the very fact that you complain and want to lay the blame upon the external world shows that you feel the external world — the very fact that you feel shows that you are not what you claim to be. You only make your offence greater by heaping misery upon misery, by imagining that the external world is hurting you, and crying out, "Oh, this devil's world! This man hurts me; that man hurts me! " and so forth. It is adding lies to misery.

We are to take care of ourselves — that much we can do — and give up attending to others for a time. Let us perfect the means; the end will take care of itself. For the world can be good and pure, only if our lives are good and pure. It is an effect, and we are the means. Therefore, let us purify ourselves. Let us make ourselves perfect.

WORLDWIDE SPIRITUAL REGENERATION

Swami Vivekananda warned us of the dire consequences we face by forgetting the spiritual unity of all beings and things and called for a recovery of our true Self – the bond of all unity. If we fail to heed this call, our civilization will face the unforgiving law of history. Vivekananda reminded us: "You may not believe in the vengeance of God, but you must believe in the vengeance of history." Vivekananda is looked upon by many as the world teacher who shows us the way to regain our human dignity. Today there are millions of thoughtful people throughout the world who derive inspiration from his life and teachings. His message has found its way into the spiritual current of our times. His all-encompassing, universal message has paved the way for a new generation of spiritual seekers who are interested not merely in religion but in attaining genuine peace and self-fulfilment.

Vivekananda is regarded as a great prophet, both in India and abroad. His birthday is observed throughout India as a national holiday. The present government of India, by an act of Parliament, has established an all India university in his name – the first time that the secular government of India has created a university in the name of a religious personality. There is no leader in India on whom his shadow hasn't fallen. His message is the model of education and training presented for the new generation to discover where we fail and how to rise to the need of our time.

Vivekananda's message gives us hope for the future. His love for humanity gave him the mandate for his message, and his innate purity gave him an irresistible power that nobody could match. The same love that was born as Buddha, the Compassionate One, once again assumed human form as Vivekananda. Though he lived only 39 years, he strides like a colossus across the whole of modern history and culture. A versatile genius, Vivekananda's contribution to world thought is immense. His major contributions to world religious thought have been his *spiritual democracy, spiritual humanism,* and an *enduring bond of world unity*.

Vivekananda's teachings foster *spiritual democracy.* Vivekananda offers an infinite variety of ideals and paths to choose from in order to reach the same ultimate goal – Self-knowledge or God-consciousness. Lacking this freedom of spiritual democracy, religion becomes authoritarian and oppressive, insisting upon blind obedience to rigid doctrines and dogmas and unquestioning belief in ceremonials and creeds. Spiritual freedom insures individuality, critical inquiry, honest doubt, free choice of the path, and verification of truth through personal experience. The ideas of exclusive salvation, a jealous God, and a chosen people are all alien to Vivekananda's thought.

Vivekananda promoted *spiritual humanism,* as opposed to secular humanism. Spiritual humanism is not simply doing good to others but rendering loving service to the Divine, seeing its presence in all beings. Spiritual humanism embraces the whole of humanity, regardless of race, culture, country, religion, or social affiliation.

World unity based on political considerations, economic interest, cultural ties, or humanitarian principles is never enduring. The bonds of such kinds of unity are too fragile to withstand the stresses and strains of social diversities. Unity of the world body, in order to be real, must be organic – and this requires a world soul that embraces countless diversities of human experience and human aspirations. Such a world soul must be the soul of all beings. "The God in you is the God in all" Vivekananda says. "If you have not known this, you have known nothing." Unity of the world-soul includes not only human beings, but also animals, plants, and every form of life.

The essential teachings of Swami Vivekananda as a world teacher can be summarized as follows:

The fall of a country or culture is caused by its spiritual bankruptcy. In the same way, its rise depends upon spiritual awakening. Spiritual fall brings in its wake moral fall, moral fall brings intellectual blindness, and intellectual blindness brings material downfall.

The meaning of spirituality is the manifestation of the divinity already in a person. "Religion is realization – not talk or doctrines or theories, however beautiful they may be. It is being and becoming – not hearing or acknowledging. It is the whole soul's becoming changed into what it believes." Direct perception of this innate divinity is the core of spirituality. Doctrines, dogmas, theologies, and philosophies are secondary details.

The ultimate reality of the universe is nondual, designated by various traditions by various names. Believers in time call it time; believers in God call it God; believers in consciousness call it consciousness. We attribute names and epithets to this reality for our convenience, and they are symbolic. "Each soul is a star," wrote Swami Vivekananda, "and all stars are set in the infinite azure, the eternal sky – the Lord. There is the root, the reality, the real individuality, of each and all. Religion began with a search after some of the stars which had passed beyond our horizon, and ended in finding them all in God, with ourselves in the same place." God is not only absolute reality but also the sum total of all souls. When this ultimate reality is ignored or forgotten by us, we confront it in our everyday life in the form of sorrow and suffering. When it is recognized, realized, and adored by us, we overcome all laws of material relative existence.

The unity of religions is based on direct perception of ultimate reality. The paths are different but the goal remains the same. Even if the whole world becomes converted to one religion or another, it will not enhance the cause of unity. Unity in diversity is the plan of the universe. Unity of religions calls for our paying attention to the basic teachings of all faiths, which provide us with the common ground where we are all rooted. Our scientific age is forcing us to find this common unity. Either we remain in our individual religious ghettos or we accept the fact of the innate spiritual unity of all faiths.

Realization of the spiritual unity of humankind begins with ourselves. We may not be able to change the whole world but we can change ourselves. "For the world can be good and pure only if our lives are good and pure. It is an effect, and we are the means. Therefore let us purify ourselves. Let us make ourselves perfect." Unless we begin to see God within, we will never see God without. Again, unless we see God in the hearts of all beings, we will never see God inside ourselves. To serve the less fortunate and think of their wellbeing is a sacred duty of all human beings. This is the basis of all ethics and morality. When we discover the Self and look upon every being as the embodiment of that Self, we attain the goal of life and become blessed. Swami Vivekananda tells us that we are not living in the final days of our destiny. We can change our destiny by our knowledge and awareness of our true Self and by our selfless work and spiritual humanism. Vivekananda says, "The education which does not help the common mass of people to equip themselves for the struggle for life, which does not bring out strength of character, a spirit of philanthropy, and the courage of a lion – is it worth the name?" Regaining our spiritual balance may seem hard or impossible but Vivekananda assures us that it is attainable by our determined effort.

Vivekananda's teachings are based on four fundamental principles: *nonduality of ultimate reality, divinity of the soul, unity of existence,* and *harmony of religions.*

Ultimate reality is always *nondual,* and the call for overcoming human separateness and human finitude is innate and irresistible in all beings. *Divinity of the soul* is the most vital aspect of our lives. We do not become divine by making pilgrimages, bathing in sacred waters, or meticulously performing ceremonies and rituals. The foundation of religion is an implicit faith in our own divinity. Ceremonies and rituals only heighten our faith in this divinity. The difference between a saint and a sinner is that the saint has faith in his saintliness and the sinner has faith in his sins. *Unity of existence* is the law of the universe. Individual selfishness and greed disrupt this unity and endanger even one's own existence. *Harmony of religions* is the corollary of the first three principles. When religion loses its spiritual content all dissentions begin – not before that. Unity of religions cannot be promoted merely by lectures and discourses, conferences and workshops. Until we learn the essence of the teachings of all religions, find a common ground, and live according to these principles, harmony and unity will be a far cry.

The world today faces a serious crisis, and Swami Vivekananda points out that this crisis is essentially spiritual. Vivekananda the world teacher appeals to thinking people of the world to rise to the occasion and bring about a change and a worldwide spiritual regeneration. "That society is the greatest," he says, "where the highest truths become practical. That is my opinion. And if society is not fit for the highest truths, make it so – and the sooner, the better. Stand up, men and women, in this spirit, dare to believe in the truth, dare to practice the truth!"

2

Visit to America

At Cape Comorin the Swami became as excited as a child. He rushed to the temple to worship the Divine Mother. He prostrated himself before the Virgin Goddess. As he came out and looked at the sea his eyes fell on a rock. Swimming to the islet through shark-infested waters, he sat on a stone. His heart thumped with emotion. His great journey from the snow-capped Himalayas to the 'Land's End' was completed. He had travelled the whole length of the Indian subcontinent, his beloved motherland, which, together with his earthly mother, was 'superior to heaven itself.'

Sitting on the stone, he recalled what he had seen with his own eyes: the pitiable condition of the Indian masses, victims of the unscrupulous whims of their rulers, landlords, and priests. The tyranny of caste had sapped their last drop of blood. In most of the so-called leaders who shouted from the housetops for the liberation of the people, he had seen selfishness personified. And now he asked himself what his duty was in this situation. Should he regard the world as a dream and go into solitude to commune with God? He had tried this several times, but without success. He remembered that, as a sannyasin, he had taken the vow to dedicate himself to the service of God; but this God, he was convinced, was revealed through humanity. And his own service to this God must begin, therefore, with the humanity of India. 'May I be born again and again,' he exclaimed, 'and suffer a thousand miseries, if only I may worship the only God in whom I believe, the sum total of all souls, and above all, my God the wicked, my God the afflicted, my God the poor of all races!' Through austerity and self-control the Swami had conserved great spiritual power. His mind had been filled with the wisdom of the East and the West. He had received in abundance Sri Ramakrishna's blessings. He also had many spiritual experiences of his own. He must use all of these assets, he concluded, for the service of God in man.

But what was to be the way? The clear-eyed prophet saw that religion was the backbone of the Indian nation. India would rise through a renewal and restoration of that highest spiritual consciousness which had made her, at all times, the cradle of nations and the cradle of faith. He totally disagreed with foreign critics and their Indian disciples who held that religion was the cause of India's downfall. The Swami blamed, rather, the falsehood, superstition, and hypocrisy that were practised in the name of religion. He himself had discovered that the knowledge of God's presence in man was the source of man's strength and wisdom. He was determined to awaken this sleeping divinity. He knew that the Indian culture had been created and sustained by the twin ideals of renunciation and service, which formed the core of Hinduism. And he believed that if the national life could be intensified through these channels, everything else would take care of itself. The workers for India's regeneration must renounce selfishness, jealousy, greed, and lust for power, and they must dedicate themselves to the service of the poor, the illiterate, the hungry, and the sick, seeing in them the tangible manifestations of the Godhead. People required education, food, health, and the knowledge of science and technology to raise their standard of living. The attempt to teach metaphysics to empty stomachs was sheer madness. The masses everywhere were leading the life of animals on account of ignorance and poverty; therefore these conditions should be removed.

But where would the Swami find the fellow workers to help him in this gigantic task? He wanted whole-time servants of God; workers without worldly ties or vested interests. And he wanted them by thousands. His eyes fell upon the numerous monks who had renounced the world in search of God. But alas, in present-day India most of these led unproductive lives. He would have to infuse a new spirit into them, and they in their turn would have to dedicate themselves to the service of the people. He hit upon a plan, which he revealed later in a letter to a friend. 'Suppose,' the Swami wrote, 'some disinterested sannyasins, bent on doing good to others, went from village to village, disseminating education and seeking in various ways to better the condition of all, down to the untouchable, through oral teaching and by means of maps, magic lanterns, globes, and other accessories - would that not bring forth good in time? All these plans I cannot write out in this brief letter. The long and short of it is that if the mountain does not come to Mahomet, Mahomet must go to the mountain. The poor are too poor to go to schools; they will gain nothing by reading poetry and all that sort of thing. We, as a nation, have lost our individuality. We have to give back to the nation its lost individuality and raise the masses.'

Verily, the Swami, at Kanyakumari, was the patriot and prophet in one. There he became, as he declared later to a Western disciple, 'a condensed India.' But where were the resources to come from, to help him realize his great vision? He himself was a sannyasin, a penniless beggar. The rich of the country talked big and did nothing. His admirers were poor. Suddenly a heroic thought entered his mind: he must approach the outside world and appeal to its conscience. But he was too proud to act like a beggar. He wanted to tell the West that the health of India and the sickness of India were the concern of the whole world. If India sank, the whole world would sink with her. For the outside world, in turn, needed India, her knowledge of the Soul and of God, her spiritual heritage, her ideal of genuine freedom through detachment and renunciation; it needed these in order to extricate itself from the sharp claws of the monster of materialism.

Then to the Swami, brooding alone and in silence on that point of rock off the tip of India, the vision came; there flashed before his mind the new continent of America, a land of optimism, great wealth, and unstinted generosity. He saw America as a country of unlimited opportunities, where people's minds were free from the encumbrance of castes or classes. He would give the receptive Americans the ancient wisdom of India and bring back to his motherland, in exchange, the knowledge of science and technology. If he succeeded in his mission to America, he would not only enhance India's prestige in the Occident, but create a new confidence among his own people. He recalled the earnest requests of his friends to represent India in the forthcoming Parliament of Religions in Chicago. And in particular, he remembered the words of the friends in Kathiawar who had been the first to encourage him to go to the West: 'Go and take it by storm, and then return!'

He swam back to the continent of India and started northwards again, by the eastern coast. It may be mentioned here that during the Swami's trip across the country, just described, there had taken place may incidents that strengthened his faith in God, intensified his sympathy for the so-called lower classes, and broadened his general outlook on life and social conventions.

Several times, when he had nothing to eat, food had come to him unsought, from unexpected quarters. The benefactors had told him that they were directed by God. Then, one day, it had occurred to the Swami that he had no right to lead the life of a wandering monk, begging his food from door to door, and thus depriving the poor of a few morsels which they could otherwise share with their families. Forthwith he entered a deep forest and walked the whole day without eating a grain of food. At nightfall he sat down under a tree, footsore and hungry, and waited to see what would happen next. Presently he saw a tiger approaching. 'Oh,' he said, 'this is right; both of us are hungry. As this body of mine could not be of any service to my fellow men, let it at least give some satisfaction to this hungry animal.' He sat there calmly, but the tiger for some reason or other changed its mind and went off in another direction. The Swami spent the whole night in the forest, meditating on God's inscrutable ways. In the morning he felt a new surge of power.

During his wanderings in the Himalayas, he was once the guest of a Tibetan family and was scandalized to see that polyandry was practised by its members; six brothers sharing a common wife. To the Swami's protest, the eldest brother replied that a Tibetan would consider it selfishness to enjoy a good thing all by himself and not share it with his brothers. After deep thought the Swami realized the relativity of ethics. He saw that many so-called good and evil practices had their roots in the traditions of society. One might argue for or against almost anything. The conventions of a particular society should be judged by its own standards. After that experience, the Swami was reluctant to condemn hastily the traditions of any social group.

One day Swamiji was sharing a railway compartment with two Englishmen, who took him for an illiterate beggar and began to crack jokes in English at his expense. At the next station they were astonished to hear him talking with the station-master in perfect English. Embarrassed, they asked him why he had not protested against their rude words. With a smile, the Swami replied, 'Friends, this is not the first time that I have seen fools.' The Englishmen became angry and wanted a fight. But looking at the Swami's strong body, they thought that discretion was the better part of valour, and apologized. In a certain place in Rajputana, the Swami was busy for three days and nights by people seeking religious instruction. Nobody cared about his food or rest. After they left, a poor man belonging to a low caste offered him, with great hesitation, some uncooked food, since he, being an untouchable, was afraid to give him a prepared meal. The

Swami, however, persuaded the kind-hearted man to prepare the meal for him and ate it with relish. Shedding tears of gratitude, the Swami said to himself, 'Thousands of such good people live in huts, and we despise them as untouchables!'

In Central India he had to pass many hard days without food or shelter, and it was during this time that he lived with a family of outcaste sweepers and discovered the many priceless spiritual virtues of those people, who cowered at the feet of society. Their misery choked him and he sobbed: 'Oh, my country! Oh, my country!'

To resume the story of Swamiji's wandering life: From Cape Comorin he walked most of the way to Madras, stopping at Ramnad and Pondicherry. His fame had already spread to the premier city of South India, and he was greeted by a group of enthusiastic young men. In Madras he publicly announced his intention of going to America. His devotees here collected funds for the trip, and it was through them that he later started his Indian work in an organized form.

Here, in Madras, he poured his whole soul into the discussion of religion, philosophy, science, literature, and history. He would blaze up at people who, for lack of time or zeal, did not practise meditation. 'What!' he thundered at a listener. 'Those giants of old, the ancient rishis, who never walked but strode, standing by whose side you would shrivel into a moth - they, sir, had time for meditation and devotions, and you have none!'

To a scoffer he said: 'How dare you criticize your venerable forefathers in such a fashion? A little learning has muddled your brain. Have you tested the wisdom of the rishis? Have you even as much as read the Vedas? There is a challenge thrown by the rishis. If you dare oppose them, take it up.' At Hyderabad, the capital of the Nizam's State, he gave his first public lecture, the subject being 'My Mission to the West.' The audience was impressed and the Swami was pleased to see that he could hold his own in this new field of activity.

When the devotees in Madras brought him the money for his voyage to America, he refused to accept it and asked them to distribute it among the poor. How was he to know that the Lord wanted him to go to America? Perhaps he was being carried away by his own ambition. He began to pray intensely for divine guidance. Again money was offered to him by some of his wealthy friends, and again he refused. He said to his disciples: 'If it is the Mother's wish that I should go to the West, then let us collect money from the people. It is for them that I am going to the West - for the people and the poor!'

The Swami one day had a symbolic dream, in which he saw Sri Ramakrishna walking into the water of the ocean and beckoning him to follow. He also heard the authoritative word 'Go!' In response to a letter that he had written to Sarada Devi, the Holy Mother, she gave him her blessings for the fulfilment of his desire, knowing that it was Ramakrishna's wish that he should undertake the journey to America. And now, at last, he felt sure of his call.

When everything was arranged for the departure, there suddenly arrived in Madras the private secretary of Swamiji's disciple the Raja of Khetri, bearing the happy news of the birth of a royal son. The Swami was earnestly desired to bless the heir apparent. He consented, and the Raja was overjoyed to see him. At Khetri an incident occurred that the Swami remembered all his life. He was invited by the Maharaja to a musical entertainment in which a nautch-girl was to sing, and he refused to come, since he was a monk and not permitted to enjoy secular pleasures. The singer was hurt and sang in a strain of lamentation. Her words reached the Swami's ears:

Look not, O Lord, upon my sins!

Is not Same-sightedness Thy name?

One piece of iron is used

Inside the holy shrine,

Another for the knife

Held in the butcher's hand;
Yet both of these are turned to gold
When touched by the philosophers' stone.
Sacred the Jamuna's water,
Foul the water in the ditch;
Yet both alike are sanctified
Once they have joined the Ganga's stream.
So, Lord, look not upon my sins!
Is not Same-sightedness Thy name?

The Swami was deeply moved. This girl, whom society condemned as impure, had taught him a great lesson: Brahman, the Ever Pure, Ever Free, and Ever Illumined, is the essence of all beings. Before God there is no distinction of good and evil, pure and impure. Such pairs of opposites become manifest only when the light of Brahman is obscured by maya. A sannyasin ought to look at all things from the standpoint of Brahman. He should not condemn anything, even a so-called impure person. The Swami then joined the party and with tears in his eyes said to the girl: 'Mother, I am guilty. I was about to show you disrespect by refusing to come to this room. But your song awakened my consciousness.' The Swami assumed at the Raja's request the name of Vivekananda, and the Raja accompanied him as far as Jaipur when he departed for Bombay. On his way to Bombay the Swami stopped at the Abu Road station and met Brahmananda and Turiyananda. He told them about his going to America. The two brother disciples were greatly excited. He explained to them the reason for his going: it was India's suffering. 'I travelled,' he said, 'all over India. But alas, it was agony to me, my brothers, to see with my own eyes the terrible poverty of the masses, and I could not restrain my tears! It is now my firm conviction that to preach religion amongst them, without first trying to remove their poverty and suffering, is futile. It is for this reason - to find means for the salvation of the poor of India - that I am going to America.'

Addressing Turiyananda, he said, 'Brother, I cannot understand your so-called religion.' His face was red with his rising blood. Shaking with emotion, he placed his hand on his heart, and said: 'But my heart has grown much, much larger, and I have learnt to feel. Believe me, I feel it very sadly.' He was choked, and then fell silent. Tears rolled down his cheeks. Many years later Turiyananda said, while describing the incident: 'You can imagine what went through my mind when I heard these pathetic words and saw the majestic sadness of Swamiji. "Were not these," I thought, "the very words and feelings of Buddha?"' And he remembered that long ago Naren had visited Bodh-Gaya and in deep meditation had felt the presence of Buddha.

Another scene of the same nature, though it occurred much later, may be recounted here. Swami Turiyananda called on his illustrious brother disciple, after the latter's triumphant return from America, at the Calcutta home of Balaram Bose, and found him pacing the veranda alone. Deep in thought, he did not notice Turiyananda's presence. He began to hum under his breath a celebrated song of Mirabai, and tears welled up in his eyes. He stopped and leaned against the balustrade, and hid his face in his palms. He sang in an anguished voice, repeating several times: 'Oh, nobody understands my sorrow!' And again: 'Only he who suffers knows the depth of my sorrow!' The whole atmosphere became heavy with sadness. The voice pierced Swami Turiyananda's heart like an arrow; but he could not understand the cause of Vivekananda's suffering. Then he suddenly realized that it was a tremendous universal sympathy with the suffering and oppressed everywhere that often made him shed tears of burning blood; and of these the world would never know.

The Swami arrived in Bombay accompanied by the private secretary to the Raja of Khetri, the Prince having provided him with a robe of orange silk, an ochre turban, a handsome purse, and a first-class ticket on the S.S. 'Peninsular' of the Peninsular and Orient Company, which would be sailing on May 31, 1893. The Raja had also bestowed on him the name by which he was to become famous and which was destined to raise India in the estimation of the world.

The ship steamed out of the harbour on the appointed day, and one can visualize the Swami standing on its deck, leaning against the rail and gazing at the fast fading landscape of his beloved motherland. What a multitude of pictures must have raced, at that time, through his mind: the image of Sri Ramakrishna, the Holy Mother, and the brother disciples, either living at the Baranagore monastery or wandering through the plains and hills of India! What a burden of memories this lad of twenty-nine was carrying! The legacy of his noble parents, the blessings of his Master, the wisdom learnt from the Hindu scriptures, the knowledge of the West, his own spiritual experiences, India's past greatness, her present sorrow, and the dream of her future glory, the hopes and aspirations of the millions of India's brown men toiling in their brown fields under the scorching tropical sun, the devotional stories of the Puranas, the dizzy heights of Buddhist philosophy, the transcendental truths of Vedanta, the subtleties of the Indian philosophical systems, the soul-stirring songs of the Indian poets and mystics, the stone-carvings and the frescoes of the Ellora and Ajanta caves, the heroic tales of the Rajput and Mahratta fighters, the hymns of the South Indian Alwars, the snow peaks of the towering Himalayas, the murmuring music of the Ganga - all these and many such thoughts fused together to create in the Swami's mind the image of Mother India, a universe in miniature, whose history and society were the vivid demonstration of her philosophical doctrine of unity in diversity. And could India have sent a son worthier than Vivekananda to represent her in the Parliament of Religions - a son who had learnt his spiritual lessons at the feet of a man whose very life was a Parliament of Religions - a son whose heart was big enough to embrace the whole of humanity and to feel for all in its universal compassion? Soon the Swami adjusted himself to the new life on board the ship - a life completely different from that of a wandering monk. He found it a great nuisance to look after his suitcases, trunk, valise, and wardrobe. His orange robe aroused the curiosity of many fellow passengers, who, however, were soon impressed by his serious nature and deep scholarship. The vessel ploughed through the blue sea, pausing at various ports on the way, and the Swami enjoyed the voyage with the happy excitement of a child, devouring eagerly all he saw.

In Colombo he visited the monasteries of the Hinayana Buddhists. On the way to Singapore he was shown the favourite haunts of the Malay pirates, whose descendants now, as the Swami wrote to an Indian friend, under the 'leviathan guns of modern turreted battleships, have been forced to look about for more peaceful pursuits.' He had his first glimpse of China in the busy port of Hongkong, where hundreds of junks and dinghies moved about, each with the wife of its boatman at the helm, for a whole family lived in each floating craft. The traveller was amused to notice the Chinese babies, most of whom were tied to the backs of their mothers, while the latter were busy either pushing heavy loads or jumping with agility from one craft to another. And there was a rush of boats and steam launches coming in and going out.

'Baby John,' the Swami wrote humorously to the same friend, 'is every moment in danger of having his little head pulverized, pigtail and all, but he does not care a fig. The busy life seems to have no charm for him, and he is quite content to learn the anatomy of a bit of rice-cake given to him by the madly busy mother. The Chinese child is quite a little philosopher and calmly goes to work at the age when your Indian boy can hardly crawl on all fours. He has learnt the philosophy of necessity too well, from his extreme poverty.'

At Canton, in a Buddhist monastery, the Swami was received with respect as a great yogi from India. He saw in China, and later in Japan, many temples with manuscripts written in the ancient Bengali script. This made him realize the extent of the influence of India outside her own borders and strengthened his conviction about the spiritual unity of Asia.

Next the boat reached Japan, and the Swami visited Yokohama, Osaka, Kyoto, and Tokyo. The broad streets, the cage-like little houses, the pine-covered hills, and the gardens with shrubs, grass-plots, artificial pools, and small bridges impressed him with the innate artistic nature of the Japanese people. On the other hand, the thoroughly organized Japanese army equipped with guns made in Japan, the expanding navy, the merchant marine, and the industrial factories revealed to him the scientific skill of a newly awakened Asiatic nation. But he was told that the Japanese regarded India as the 'dreamland of everything noble and great.'

His thoughts always returned to India and her people. He wrote to a disciple in Madras: 'Come out and be men! India wants the sacrifice of at least a thousand of her young men - men, mind you, and not brutes. How many men - unselfish and thoroughgoing men - is Madras ready to supply, who will struggle unto death to bring about a new state of things - sympathy for the poor, bread for hungry mouths, enlightenment for the people at large, who have been brought to the level of beasts by the tyranny of your forefathers?'

From Yokohama he crossed the Pacific Ocean and arrived in Vancouver, British Columbia. Next he travelled by train to Chicago, the destination of his journey and the meeting-place of the Parliament of Religions. The first sight of Chicago, the third largest city of the New Continent, the great civic queen of the Middle West, enthroned on the shore of Lake Michigan, with its teeming population and strange way of life - a mixture of the refinement of the Eastern coast and the crudities of the backwoods - must have bewildered, excited, and terrified the young visitor from India. Swami Vivekananda walked through the spacious grounds of the World's Fair and was speechless with amazement. He marvelled at what the Americans had achieved through hard work, friendly co-operation with one another, and the application of scientific knowledge. Not too many years before, Chicago had consisted of only a few fishermen's huts, and now at the magic touch of human ingenuity, it was turned into a fairyland. Never before had the Swami seen such an accumulation of wealth, power, and inventive genius in a nation. In the fairgrounds he attracted people's notice. Lads ran after him, fascinated by his orange robe and turban. Shopkeepers and porters regarded him as a Maharaja from India and tried to impose upon him. On the Swami's part, his first feeling was one of unbounded admiration. But a bitter disillusionment was to come.

Soon after his arrival in Chicago, he went one day to the information bureau of the Exposition to ask about the forthcoming Parliament of Religions. He was told that it had been put off until the first week of September (it was then only the end of July) and that no one without credentials from a bona fide organization would be accepted as a delegate. He was told also that it was then too late for him to be registered as a delegate. All this had been unexpected by the Swami; for not one of his friends in India - the enthusiastic devotees of Madras, the Raja of Khetri, the Raja of Ramnad, and the Maharaja of Mysore, the Ministers of the native states, and the disciples who had arranged his trip to America - had taken the trouble to make any inquiries concerning the details of the Parliament. No one had known what were to be the dates of the meetings or the conditions of admission. Nor had the Swami brought with him any letter of authority from a religious organization. All had felt that the young monk would need no letter of authorization, his personality being testimonial enough.

'The Swami himself,' as his Irish disciple, Sister Nivedita, wrote some years later, 'was as simple in the ways of the world as his disciples, and when he was once sure that he was divinely called to make this attempt, he could see no difficulties in the way. Nothing could have been more typical of the lack of organizedness of Hinduism itself than this going forth of its representative unannounced, and without formal credentials, to enter the strongly guarded door of the world's wealth and power.' In the meantime, the purse that the Swami had carried from India was dwindling; for things were much more expensive in America than he or his friends had thought. He did not have enough to maintain him in Chicago until September. In a frantic mood he asked help from the Theosophical Society, which professed warm friendship for India. He was told that he would have to subscribe to the creed of the Society; but this he refused to do because he did not believe in most of the Theosophical doctrines. Thereupon the leader declined to give him any help. The Swami became desperate and cabled to his friends in Madras for money.

Finally, however, someone advised him to go to Boston, where the cost of living was cheaper, and in the train his picturesque dress, no less than his regal appearance, attracted a wealthy lady who resided in the suburbs of the city. She cordially invited him to be her guest, and he accepted, to save his dwindling purse. He was lodged at 'Breezy Meadows,' in Metcalf, Massachusetts, and his hostess, Miss Kate Sanborn, was delighted to display to her inquisitive friends this strange curiosity from the Far East. The Swami met a number of people, most of whom annoyed him by asking queer questions regarding Hinduism and the social customs of India, about which they had read in the tracts of Christian missionaries and sensational writers. However, there came to him a few serious-minded people, and among these were Mrs. Johnson, the lady superintendent of a women's prison, and J.H. Wright, a professor of Greek at Harvard University. On the invitation of the superintendent, he visited the prison and was impressed by the humanitarian attitude of its workers towards the inmates. At once there came to his mind the sad plight of the masses of India and he wrote to a friend on August 20, 1893:

How benevolently the inmates are treated, how they are reformed and sent back as useful members of society - how grand, how beautiful, you must see to believe! And oh, how my heart ached to think of what we think of poor, the low, in

India. They have no chance, no escape, no way to climb up. They sink lower and lower every day, they feel the blows showered upon them by a cruel society, and they do not know whence the blows come. They have forgotten that they too are men. And the result is slavery. ... Ah, tyrants! You do not know that the obverse is tyranny and the reverse, slavery.

Swami Vivekananda had no friends in this foreign land, yet he did not lose faith. For had not a kind Providence looked after him during the uncertain days of his wandering life? He wrote in the same letter: 'I am here amongst the children of the Son of Mary, and the Lord Jesus will help me.'

The Swami was encouraged by Professor Wright to represent Hinduism in the Parliament of Religions, since that was the only way he could be introduced to the nation at large. When he announced, however, that he had no credentials, the professor replied, 'To ask you, Swami, for your credentials is like asking the sun about its right to shine.' He wrote about the Swami to a number of important people connected with the Parliament, especially to the chairman of the committee on selection of delegates, who was one of his friends, and said, 'Here is a man more learned than all our learned professors put together.' Professor Wright bought the Swami railroad ticket for Chicago.

The train bearing Vivekananda to Chicago arrived late in the evening, and he had mislaid, unfortunately, the address of the committee in charge of the delegates. He did not know where to turn for help, and no one bothered to give information to this foreigner of strange appearance. Moreover the station was located in a part of the city inhabited mostly by Germans, who could hardly under stand his language. He knew he was stranded there, and looking around saw a huge empty wagon in the railroad freightyard. In this he spent the night without food or a bed.

In the morning he woke up 'smelling fresh water,' to quote his own words, and he walked along the fashionable Lake Shore Drive, which was lined with the mansions of the wealthy, asking people the way to the Parliament grounds. But he was met with indifference. Hungry and weary, he knocked at several doors for food and was rudely treated by the servants. His soiled clothes and unshaven face gave him the appearance of a tramp. Besides, he had forgotten that he was in a land that knew thousands of ways of earning the 'almighty dollar,' but was unfamiliar with Franciscan poverty or the ways of religious vagabonds. He sat down exhausted on the sidewalk and was noticed from an opposite window. The mistress of the house sent for him and asked the Swami if he was a delegate to the Parliament of Religions. He told her of his difficulties. The lady, Mrs. George W. Hale, a society woman of Chicago, gave him breakfast and looked after his needs. When he had rested, she accompanied him to the offices of the Parliament and presented him to Dr. J.H. Barrows, the President of the Parliament, who was one of her personal friends. The Swami was thereupon cordially accepted as a representative of Hinduism and lodged in the house of Mr. and Mrs. John B. Lyons. Mr. and Mrs. Hale and their children as well as the Lyons, became his lifelong friends. Once again the Swami had been strengthened in his conviction that the Lord was guiding his footsteps, and he prayed incessantly to be a worthy instrument of His will.

CHICAGO PARLIAMENT OF RELIGIONS ON 19TH SEPTEMBER, 1893

Three religions now stand in the world which have come down to us from time prehistoric — Hinduism, Zoroastrianism and Judaism. They have all received tremendous shocks and all of them prove by their survival their internal strength. But while Judaism failed to absorb Christianity and was driven out of its place of birth by its all-conquering daughter, and a handful of Parsees is all that remains to tell the tale of their grand religion, sect after sect arose in India and seemed to shake the religion of the Vedas to its very foundations, but like the waters of the seashore in a tremendous earthquake it receded only for a while, only to return in an all-absorbing flood, a thousand times more vigorous, and when the tumult of the rush was over, these sects were all sucked in, absorbed, and assimilated into the immense body of the mother faith. From the high spiritual flights of the Vedanta philosophy, of which the latest discoveries of science seem like echoes, to the low ideas of idolatry with its multifarious mythology, the agnosticism of the Buddhists, and the atheism of the Jains, each and all have a place in the Hindu's religion.

Where then, the question arises, where is the common centre to which all these widely diverging radii converge? Where is the common basis upon which all these seemingly hopeless contradictions rest? And this is the question I shall attempt to answer. The Hindus have received their religion through revelation, the Vedas. They hold that the Vedas are without beginning and without end. It may sound ludicrous to this audience, how a book can be without beginning or end. But by the Vedas no books are meant. They mean the accumulated treasury of spiritual laws discovered by different persons in different times. Just as the law of gravitation existed before its discovery, and would exist if all humanity forgot it, so is it with the laws that govern the spiritual world. The moral, ethical, and spiritual relations between soul and soul and between individual spirits and the Father of all spirits, were there before their discovery, and would remain even if we forgot them.

The discoverers of these laws are called Rishis, and we honour them as perfected beings. I am glad to tell this audience that some of the very greatest of them were women. Here it may be said that these laws as laws may be without end, but they must have had a beginning. The Vedas teach us that creation is without beginning or end. Science is said to have proved that the sum total of cosmic energy is always the same. Then, if there was a time when nothing existed, where was all this manifested energy? Some say it was in a potential form in God. In that case God is sometimes potential and sometimes kinetic, which would make Him mutable. Everything mutable is a compound, and everything compound must undergo that change which is called destruction. So God would die, which is absurd. Therefore there never was a time when there was no creation.

Creation and Creator

If I may be allowed to use a simile, creation and creator are two lines, without beginning and without end, running parallel to each other. God is the ever active providence, by whose power systems after systems are being evolved out of chaos, made to run for a time and again destroyed. This is what the Brahmin boy repeats every day: "The sun and the moon, the Lord created like the suns and moons of previous cycles." And this agrees with modern science. Here I stand and if I shut my eyes, and try to conceive my existence, "I", "I", "I", what is the idea before me? The idea of a body. Am I, then, nothing but a combination of material substances? The Vedas declare, "No". I am a spirit living in a body. I am not the body. The body will die, but I shall not die. Here am I in this body; it will fall, but I shall go on living. I had also a past. The soul was not created, for creation means a combination which means a certain future dissolution. If then the soul was created, it must die. Some are born happy, enjoy perfect health, with beautiful body, mental vigour and all wants supplied. Others are born miserable, some are without hands or feet, others again are idiots and only drag on a wretched existence. Why, if they are all created, why does a just and merciful God create one happy and another unhappy, why is He so partial? Nor would it mend matters in the least to hold that those who are miserable in this life will be happy in a future one. Why should a man be miserable even here in the reign of a just and merciful God?

In the second place, the idea of a creator God does not explain the anomaly, but simply expresses the cruel fiat of an all-powerful being. There must have been causes, then, before his birth, to make a man miserable or happy and those were his past actions. Are not all the tendencies of the mind and the body accounted for by inherited aptitude? Here are two parallel lines of existence — one of the mind, the other of matter. If matter and its transformations answer for all that we have, there is no necessity for supposing the existence of a soul. But it cannot be proved that thought has been evolved out of matter, and if a philosophical monism is inevitable, spiritual monism is certainly logical and no less desirable than a materialistic monism; but neither of these is necessary here.

We cannot deny that bodies acquire certain tendencies from heredity, but those tendencies only mean the physical configuration, through which a peculiar mind alone can act in a peculiar way. There are other tendencies peculiar to a soul caused by its past actions. And a soul with a certain tendency would by the laws of affinity take birth in a body which is the fittest instrument for the display of that tendency. This is in accord with science, for science wants to explain everything by habit, and habit is got through repetitions. So repetitions are necessary to explain the natural habits of a new-born soul. And since they were not obtained in this present life, they must have come down from past lives.

There is another suggestion. Taking all these for granted, how is it that I do not remember anything of my past life ? This can be easily explained. I am now speaking English. It is not my mother tongue, in fact no words of my mother tongue are now present in my consciousness; but let me try to bring them up, and they rush in. That shows that consciousness is only the surface of the mental ocean, and within its depths are stored up all our experiences. Try and struggle, they would come up and you would be conscious even of your past life.

This is direct and demonstrative evidence. Verification is the perfect proof of a theory, and here is the challenge thrown to the world by the Rishis. We have discovered the secret by which the very depths of the ocean of memory can be stirred up — try it and you would get a complete reminiscence of your past life.

Hindu Believes

So then the Hindu believes that he is a spirit. Him the sword cannot pierce — him the fire cannot burn — him the water cannot melt — him the air cannot dry. The Hindu believes that every soul is a circle whose circumference is nowhere, but whose centre is located in the body, and that death means the change of this centre from body to body. Nor is the soul bound by the conditions of matter. In its very essence it is free, unbounded, holy, pure, and perfect. But somehow or other it finds itself tied down to matter, and thinks of itself as matter. Why should the free, perfect, and pure being be thus under the thraldom of matter, is the next question. How can the perfect soul be deluded into the belief that it is imperfect? We have been told that the Hindus shirk the question and say that no such question can be there. Some thinkers want to answer it by positing one or more quasi-perfect beings, and use big scientific names to fill up the gap. But naming is not explaining. The question remains the same. How can the perfect become the quasi-perfect; how can the pure, the absolute, change even a microscopic particle of its nature? But the Hindu is sincere. He does not want to take shelter under sophistry. He is brave enough to face the question in a manly fashion; and his answer is: "I do not know. I do not know how the perfect being, the soul, came to think of itself as imperfect, as joined to and conditioned by matter." But the fact is a fact for all that. It is a fact in everybody's consciousness that one thinks of oneself as the body. The Hindu does not attempt to explain why one thinks one is the body. The answer that it is the will of God is no explanation. This is nothing more than what the Hindu says, "I do not know."

Well, then, the human soul is eternal and immortal, perfect and infinite, and death means only a change of centre from one body to another. The present is determined by our past actions, and the future by the present. The soul will go on evolving up or reverting back from birth to birth and death to death. But here is another question: Is man a tiny boat in a tempest, raised one moment on the foamy crest of a billow and dashed down into a yawning chasm the next, rolling to and fro at the mercy of good and bad actions — a powerless, helpless wreck in an ever-raging, ever-rushing, uncompromising current of cause and effect; a little moth placed under the wheel of causation which rolls on crushing everything in its way and waits not for the widow's tears or the orphan's cry?

The heart sinks at the idea, yet this is the law of Nature. Is there no hope? Is there no escape? — was the cry that went up from the bottom of the heart of despair. It reached the throne of mercy, and words of hope and consolation came down and inspired a Vedic sage, and he stood up before the world and in trumpet voice proclaimed the glad tidings: "Hear, ye children of immortal bliss! even ye that reside in higher spheres! I have found the Ancient One who is beyond all darkness, all delusion: knowing Him alone you shall be saved from death over again." "Children of immortal bliss" — what a sweet, what a hopeful name! Allow me to call you, brethren, by that sweet name — heirs of immortal bliss — yea, the Hindu refuses to call you sinners. Ye are the Children of God, the sharers of immortal bliss, holy and perfect beings. Ye divinities on earth — sinners! It is a sin to call a man so; it is a standing libel on human nature. Come up, O lions, and shake off the delusion that you are sheep; you are souls immortal, spirits free, blest and eternal; ye are not matter, ye are not bodies; matter is your servant, not you the servant of matter. Thus it is that the Vedas proclaim not a dreadful combination of unforgiving laws, not an endless prison of cause and effect, but that at the head of all these laws, in and through every particle of matter and force, stands One "by whose command the wind blows, the fire burns, the clouds rain, and death stalks upon the earth."

And what is His nature? He is everywhere, the pure and formless One, the Almighty and the All-merciful. "Thou art our father, Thou art our mother, Thou art our beloved friend, Thou art the source of all strength; give us strength. Thou art He that beareth the burdens of the universe; help me bear the little burden of this life." Thus sang the Rishis of the Vedas. And how to worship Him? Through love. "He is to be worshipped as the one beloved, dearer than everything in this and the next life."

This is the doctrine of love declared in the Vedas, and let us see how it is fully developed and taught by Krishna, whom the Hindus believe to have been God incarnate on earth. He taught that a man ought to live in this world like a lotus leaf, which grows in water but is never moistened by water; so a man ought to live in the world — his heart to God and his hands to work.

It is good to love God for hope of reward in this or the next world, but it is better to love God for love's sake, and the prayer goes: "Lord, I do not want wealth, nor children, nor learning. If it be Thy will, I shall go from birth to birth, but grant me this, that I may love Thee without the hope of reward — love unselfishly for love's sake." One of the disciples of Krishna, the then Emperor of India, was driven from his kingdom by his enemies and had to take shelter with his queen in a forest in the Himalayas, and there one day the queen asked him how it was that he, the most virtuous of men, should suffer so much misery. Yudhishthira answered, "Behold, my queen, the Himalayas, how grand and beautiful they are; I love them. They do not give me anything, but my nature is to love the grand, the beautiful, therefore I love them. Similarly, I love the Lord. He is the source of all beauty, of all sublimity. He is the only object to be loved; my nature is to love Him, and therefore I love. I do not pray for anything; I do not ask for anything. Let Him place me wherever He likes. I must love Him for love's sake. I cannot trade in love."

The Vedas teach that the soul is divine, only held in the bondage of matter; perfection will be reached when this bond will burst, and the word they use for it is therefore, Mukti — freedom, freedom from the bonds of imperfection, freedom from death and misery. And this bondage can only fall off through the mercy of God, and this mercy comes on the pure. So purity is the condition of His mercy. How does that mercy act? He reveals Himself to the pure heart; the pure and the stainless see God, yea, even in this life; then and then only all the crookedness of the heart is made straight. Then all doubt ceases. He is no more the freak of a terrible law of causation. This is the very centre, the very vital conception of Hinduism. The Hindu does not want to live upon words and theories. If there are existences beyond the ordinary sensuous existence, he wants to come face to face with them. If there is a soul in him which is not matter, if there is an all-merciful universal Soul, he will go to Him direct. He must see Him, and that alone can destroy all doubts. So the best proof a Hindu sage gives about the soul, about God, is: "I have seen the soul; I have seen God." And that is the only condition of perfection. The Hindu religion does not consist in struggles and attempts to believe a certain doctrine or dogma, but in realising — not in believing, but in being and becoming.

Thus the whole object of their system is by constant struggle to become perfect, to become divine, to reach God and see God, and this reaching God, seeing God, becoming perfect even as the Father in Heaven is perfect, constitutes the religion of the Hindus.

And what becomes of a man when he attains perfection? He lives a life of bliss infinite. He enjoys infinite and perfect bliss, having obtained the only thing in which man ought to have pleasure, namely God, and enjoys the bliss with God. So far all the Hindus are agreed. This is the common religion of all the sects of India; but, then, perfection is absolute, and the absolute cannot be two or three. It cannot have any qualities. It cannot be an individual. And so when a soul becomes perfect and absolute, it must become one with Brahman, and it would only realise the Lord as the perfection, the reality, of its own nature and existence, the existence absolute, knowledge absolute, and bliss absolute. We have often and often read this called the losing of individuality and becoming a stock or a stone.

"He jests at scars that never felt a wound." I tell you it is nothing of the kind. If it is happiness to enjoy the consciousness of this small body, it must be greater happiness to enjoy the consciousness of two bodies, the measure of happiness increasing with the consciousness of an increasing number of bodies, the aim, the ultimate of happiness being reached when it would become a universal consciousness.

Therefore, to gain this infinite universal individuality, this miserable little prison-individuality must go. Then alone can death cease when I am alone with life, then alone can misery cease when I am one with happiness itself, then alone can all errors cease when I am one with knowledge itself; and this is the necessary scientific conclusion. Science has proved to me that physical individuality is a delusion, that really my body is one little continuously changing body in an unbroken ocean of matter; and Advaita (unity) is the necessary conclusion with my other counterpart, soul.

Science is nothing but the finding of unity. As soon as science would reach perfect unity, it would stop from further progress, because it would reach the goal. Thus Chemistry could not progress farther when it would discover one element out of which all other could be made. Physics would stop when it would be able to fulfil its services in discovering one energy of which all others are but manifestations, and the science of religion become perfect when it would discover Him who is the one life in a universe of death, Him who is the constant basis of an ever-changing world. One who is the only Soul of which all souls are but delusive manifestations. Thus is it, through multiplicity and duality, that the ultimate unity is reached. Religion can go no farther. This is the goal of all science. All science is bound to come to this conclusion in the long run. Manifestation, and not creation, is the word of science today, and the Hindu is only glad that what he has been cherishing in his bosom for ages is going to be taught in more forcible language, and with further light from the latest conclusions of science.

Descend we now from the aspirations of philosophy to the religion of the ignorant. At the very outset, I may tell you that there is no polytheism in India. In every temple, if one stands by and listens, one will find the worshippers applying all the attributes of God, including omnipresence, to the images. It is not polytheism, nor would the name henotheism explain the situation. "The rose called by any other name would smell as sweet." Names are not explanations.

I remember, as a boy, hearing a Christian missionary preach to a crowd in India. Among other sweet things he was telling them was that if he gave a blow to their idol with his stick, what could it do? One of his hearers sharply answered, "If I abuse your God, what can He do?" "You would be punished," said the preacher, "when you die." "So my idol will punish you when you die," retorted the Hindu. The tree is known by its fruits. When I have seen amongst them that are called idolaters, men, the like of whom in morality and spirituality and love I have never seen anywhere, I stop and ask myself, "Can sin beget holiness?"

Superstition is a great enemy of man, but bigotry is worse. Why does a Christian go to church? Why is the cross holy? Why is the face turned toward the sky in prayer? Why are there so many images in the Catholic Church? Why are there so many images in the minds of Protestants when they pray? My brethren, we can no more think about anything without a mental image than we can live without breathing. By the law of association, the material image calls up the mental idea and vice versa. This is why the Hindu uses an external symbol when he worships. He will tell you, it helps to keep his mind fixed on the Being to whom he prays. He knows as well as you do that the image is not God, is not omnipresent. After all, how much does omnipresence mean to almost the whole world? It stands merely as a word, a symbol. Has God superficial area? If not, when we repeat that word "omnipresent", we think of the extended sky or of space, that is all.

As we find that somehow or other, by the laws of our mental constitution, we have to associate our ideas of infinity with the image of the blue sky, or of the sea, so we naturally connect our idea of holiness with the image of a church, a mosque, or a cross. The Hindus have associated the idea of holiness, purity, truth, omnipresence, and such other ideas with different images and forms. But with this difference that while some people devote their whole lives to their idol of a church and never rise higher, because with them religion means an intellectual assent to certain doctrines and doing good to their fellows, the whole religion of the Hindu is centred in realisation. Man is to become divine by realising the divine. Idols or temples or churches or books are only the supports, the helps, of his spiritual childhood: but on and on he must progress.

He must not stop anywhere. "External worship, material worship," say the scriptures, "is the lowest stage; struggling to rise high, mental prayer is the next stage, but the highest stage is when the Lord has been realised." Mark, the same earnest man who is kneeling before the idol tells you, "Him the Sun cannot express, nor the moon, nor the stars, the lightning cannot express Him, nor what we speak of as fire; through Him they shine." But he does not abuse any one's idol or call its worship sin. He recognises in it a necessary stage of life. "The child is father of the man." Would it be right for an old man to say that childhood is a sin or youth a sin?

If a man can realise his divine nature with the help of an image, would it be right to call that a sin? Nor even when he has passed that stage, should he call it an error. To the Hindu, man is not travelling from error to truth, but from truth to truth, from lower to higher truth. To him all the religions, from the lowest fetishism to the highest absolutism, mean so many attempts of the human soul to grasp and realise the Infinite, each determined by the conditions of its birth and association, and each of these marks a stage of progress; and every soul is a young eagle soaring higher and higher, gathering more and more strength, till it reaches the Glorious Sun.

Plan of Nature

Unity in variety is the plan of nature, and the Hindu has recognised it. Every other religion lays down certain fixed dogmas, and tries to force society to adopt them. It places before society only one coat which must fit Jack and John and Henry, all alike. If it does not fit John or Henry, he must go without a coat to cover his body. The Hindus have discovered that the absolute can only be realised, or thought of, or stated, through the relative, and the images, crosses, and crescents are simply so many symbols — so many pegs to hang the spiritual ideas on. It is not that this help is necessary for every one, but those that do not need it have no right to say that it is wrong. Nor is it compulsory in Hinduism.

One thing I must tell you. Idolatry in India does not mean anything horrible. It is not the mother of harlots. On the other hand, it is the attempt of undeveloped minds to grasp high spiritual truths. The Hindus have their faults, they sometimes have their exceptions; but mark this, they are always for punishing their own bodies, and never for cutting the throats of their neighbours. If the Hindu fanatic burns himself on the pyre, he never lights the fire of Inquisition. And even this cannot be laid at the door of his religion any more than the burning of witches can be laid at the door of Christianity. To the Hindu, then, the whole world of religions is only a travelling, a coming up, of different men and women, through various conditions and circumstances, to the same goal. Every religion is only evolving a God out of the material man, and the same God is the inspirer of all of them. Why, then, are there so many contradictions? They are only apparent, says the Hindu. The contradictions come from the same truth adapting itself to the varying circumstances of different natures.

It is the same light coming through glasses of different colours. And these little variations are necessary for purposes of adaptation. But in the heart of everything the same truth reigns. The Lord has declared to the Hindu in His incarnation as Krishna, "I am in every religion as the thread through a string of pearls. Wherever thou seest extraordinary holiness and extraordinary power raising and purifying humanity, know thou that I am there." And what has been the result? I challenge the world to find, throughout the whole system of Sanskrit philosophy, any such expression as that the Hindu alone will be saved and not others. Says Vyasa, "We find perfect men even beyond the pale of our caste and creed." One thing more. How, then, can the Hindu, whose whole fabric of thought centres in God, believe in Buddhism which is agnostic, or in Jainism which is atheistic?

The Buddhists or the Jains do not depend upon God; but the whole force of their religion is directed to the great central truth in every religion, to evolve a God out of man. They have not seen the Father, but they have seen the Son. And he that hath seen the Son hath seen the Father also. This, brethren, is a short sketch of the religious ideas of the Hindus. The Hindu may have failed to carry out all his plans, but if there is ever to be a universal religion, it must be one which will have no location in place or time; which will be infinite like the God it will preach, and whose sun will shine upon the followers of Krishna and of Christ, on saints and sinners alike; which will not be Brahminic or Buddhistic, Christian or Mohammedan, but the sum total of all these, and still have infinite space for development; which in its catholicity will embrace in its infinite arms, and find a place for, every human being, from the lowest grovelling savage not far removed from the brute, to the highest man towering by the virtues of his head and heart almost above humanity, making society stand in awe of him and doubt his human nature. It will be a religion which will have no place for persecution or intolerance in its polity, which will recognise divinity in every man and woman, and whose whole scope, whose whole force, will be created in aiding humanity to realise its own true, divine nature.

Offer such a religion, and all the nations will follow you. Ashoka's council was a council of the Buddhist faith. Akbar's, though more to the purpose, was only a parlour-meeting. It was reserved for America to proclaim to all quarters of the globe that the Lord is in every religion.

May He who is the Brahman of the Hindus, the Ahura-Mazda of the Zoroastrians, the Buddha of the Buddhists, the Jehovah of the Jews, the Father in Heaven of the Christians, give strength to you to carry out your noble idea! The star arose in the East; it travelled steadily towards the West, sometimes dimmed and sometimes effulgent, till it made a circuit of the world; and now it is again rising on the very horizon of the East, the borders of the Sanpo,* a thousandfold more effulgent than it ever was before. Hail, Columbia, motherland of liberty! It has been given to thee, who never dipped her hand in her neighbour's blood, who never found out that the shortest way of becoming rich was by robbing one's neighbours, it has been given to thee to march at the vanguard of civilisation with the flag of harmony.

Swami Vivekananda on 26th September, 1893 in America

I am not a Buddhist, as you have heard, and yet I am. If China, or Japan, or Ceylon follow the teachings of the Great Master, India worships him as God incarnate on earth. You have just now heard that I am going to criticise Buddhism, but by that I wish you to understand only this. Far be it from me to criticise him whom I worship as God incarnate on earth. But our views about Buddha are that he was not understood properly by his disciples. The relation between Hinduism (by Hinduism, I mean the religion of the Vedas) and what is called

Buddhism at the present day is nearly the same as between Judaism and Christianity. Jesus Christ was a Jew, and Shakya Muni was a Hindu. The Jews rejected Jesus Christ, nay, crucified him, and the Hindus have accepted Shakya Muni as God and worship him. But the real difference that we Hindus want to show between modern Buddhism and what we should understand as the teachings of Lord Buddha lies principally in this: Shakya Muni came to preach nothing new. He also, like Jesus, came to fulfil and not to destroy. Only, in the case of Jesus, it was the old people, the Jews, who did not understand him, while in the case of Buddha, it was his own followers who did not realise the import of his teachings. As the Jew did not understand the fulfilment of the Old Testament, so the Buddhist did not understand the fulfilment of the truths of the Hindu religion. Again, I repeat, Shakya Muni came not to destroy, but he was the fulfilment, the logical conclusion, the logical development of the religion of the Hindus.

The religion of the Hindus is divided into two parts: the ceremonial and the spiritual. The spiritual portion is specially studied by the monks. In that there is no caste. A man from the highest caste and a man from the lowest may become a monk in India, and the two castes become equal. In religion there is no caste; caste is simply a social institution. Shakya Muni himself was a monk, and it was his glory that he had the large-heartedness to bring out the truths from the hidden Vedas and through them broadcast all over the world. He was the first being in the world who brought missionarising into practice — nay, he was the first to conceive the idea of proselytising.

The great glory of the Master lay in his wonderful sympathy for everybody, especially for the ignorant and the poor. Some of his disciples were Brahmins. When Buddha was teaching, Sanskrit was no more the spoken language in India. It was then only in the books of the learned. Some of Buddha's Brahmins disciples wanted to translate his teachings into Sanskrit, but he distinctly told them, "I am for the poor, for the people; let me speak in the tongue of the people." And so to this day the great bulk of his teachings are in the vernacular of that day in India.

Whatever may be the position of philosophy, whatever may be the position of metaphysics, so long as there is such a thing as death in the world, so long as there is such a thing as weakness in the human heart, so long as there is a cry going out of the heart of man in his very weakness, there shall be a faith in God.

On the philosophic side the disciples of the Great Master dashed themselves against the eternal rocks of the Vedas and could not crush them, and on the other side they took away from the nation that eternal God to which every one, man or woman, clings so fondly. And the result was that Buddhism had to die a natural death in India. At the present day there is not one who calls oneself a Buddhist in India, the land of its birth.

But at the same time, Brahminism lost something — that reforming zeal, that wonderful sympathy and charity for everybody, that wonderful heaven which Buddhism had brought to the masses and which had rendered Indian society so great that a Greek historian who wrote about India of that time was led to say that no Hindu was known to tell an untruth and no Hindu woman was known to be unchaste.

Hinduism cannot live without Buddhism, nor Buddhism without Hinduism. Then realise what the separation has shown to us, that the Buddhists cannot stand without the brain and philosophy of the Brahmins, nor the Brahmin without the heart of the Buddhist. This separation between the Buddhists and the Brahmins is the cause of the downfall of India. That is why India is populated by three hundred millions of beggars, and that is why India has been the slave of conquerors for the last thousand years. Let us then join the wonderful intellect of the Brahmins with the heart, the noble soul, the wonderful humanising power of the Great Master.

Chicago world parliament of religions on 27th September, 1893

The World's Parliament of Religions has become an accomplished fact, and the merciful Father has helped those who laboured to bring it into existence, and crowned with success their most unselfish labour.

My thanks to those noble souls whose large hearts and love of truth first dreamed this wonderful dream and then realised it. My thanks to the shower of liberal sentiments that has overflowed this platform.

My thanks to his enlightened audience for their uniform kindness to me and for their appreciation of every thought that tends to smooth the friction of religions. A few jarring notes were heard from time to time in this harmony. My special thanks to them, for they have, by their striking contrast, made general harmony the sweeter.

Much has been said of the common ground of religious unity. I am not going just now to venture my own theory. But if any one here hopes that this unity will come by the triumph of any one of the religions and the destruction of the others, to him I say, "Brother, yours is an impossible hope." Do I wish that the Christian would become Hindu? God forbid. Do I wish that the Hindu or Buddhist would become Christian? God forbid.

The seed is put in the ground, and earth and air and water are placed around it. Does the seed become the earth; or the air, or the water? No. It becomes a plant, it develops after the law of its own growth, assimilates the air, the earth, and the water, converts them into plant substance, and grows into a plant.

Similar is the case with religion. The Christian is not to become a Hindu or a Buddhist, nor a Hindu or a Buddhist to become a Christian. But each must assimilate the spirit of the others and yet preserve his individuality and grow according to his own law of growth. If the Parliament of Religions has shown anything to the world it is this: It has proved to the world that holiness, purity and charity are not the exclusive possessions of any church in the world, and that every system has produced men and women of the most exalted character.

In the face of this evidence, if anybody dreams of the exclusive survival of his own religion and the destruction of the others, I pity him from the bottom of my heart, and point out to him that upon the banner of every religion will soon be written, in spite of resistance: "Help and not Fight," "Assimilation and not Destruction," "Harmony and Peace and not Dissension."

3

Swami Vivekananda on Nationalism

Swami Vivekananda is measured as one of the prophets of the Indian nationalism because he tried to awaken Indian people who were lying in deep slumber. He wanted to see the emergence of a strong and self-confident India which would provide the message of the Vedanta to the world. He maintained that the Indians should be proud of their history, civilization and religion and should attempt their stage best to reform them - in the light of the demands of time. The awakening of the spirit of India was the goal for young people. Hence, he asked them to "arise, awake and stop not till the goal is reached."

Vivekananda was highly critical of the British rule in India because he held that due to their rule, Indians lost confidence, famines engulfed the land, farmers and artisans were reduced to poverty and penury. The British were exploiting Indians in all the spheres of economic action. They had let loose the reign of terror and struck fear in the minds of the people. Due to exploitative economic policies of the British government, Indians could not develop their natural possessions and her productive potential was sapped. It was imperative that Indians should know the evil effects of the British rule in India.

Vivekananda was of the opinion that the national regeneration of India would begin when people became fearless and started demanding their rights. Also, he asked the Indians to develop solidarity and oneness of the spirit through the eradication of social evils, superstitions and caste-arrogance. He was of the opinion that caste system divided the Indian society into classes and created the feeling of inferiority, and superiority in the middle of them.

He held that though there was a diversity of races, languages, religions and cultures in India, there lived a general ground flanked by Indian people. There was a general religious custom which could be depended upon to build national spirit. Just as to Europe, the foundation of national unity was political thoughts but in Asia, religion shaped the foundation of it. It was not necessarily a scrupulous religion as such, but all religions would help us develop the national integration. For the Indians, religion was a unifying force as the spirituality was blood in the life of India. All differences melted in it. Indians preserved their faith in the mainly hard circumstances.

It was the duty of the educated Indians to create its knowledge accessible to the people in their oneness and solidarity. He exhorted Indians not to get involved in the divisive issues of race and language and imbibe the spirit of unity. He said that Hindus should not blame Muslims for their numerous invasions because the Muslim conquest came as a salvation to the downtrodden masses in India. One fifth of India did not become Muslim because of sword but because of their egalitarian message. So, national unity could not be fostered through caste disagreement but it would be secured through raising the lower to the stage of higher classes and not through bringing the upper to the lower stage. The privileges of classes should cease and it was the duty of every aristocracy to dig its own grave and the sooner it did so the better. The more it delayed, the more it would fester and died worse death. India should be of one mind and of one resolve. Hence, we necessity revive the whole of India. India necessity conquers the world not with the help of gun, but with the help of spirituality.

For the growth of national spirit in India, independence of mind was necessary. India should expose herself to the outside world but she should not get scared of any one because her freedom would come through heroism and bravery. Indians should be proud of their country and declare that all Indians, despite their dissimilar castes and religions, are brothers. Therefore in Vivekananda's theory of nationalism, there were four significant components which were as follows:

There was unity and oneness of the Indian people despite their outward diversity. It was necessary to remove caste differences to inculcate the spirit of social solidarity societies. National spirit in India could be urbanized through young people through devoting their life to social service and national awakening.

WORKS OF SWAMI VIVEKANANDA

His books (compiled from lectures given around the world) on the four are very influential and still seen as fundamental texts for anyone interested in the Hindu practice of Yoga. His letters are of great literary and spiritual value. He was also a very good singer and a poet. He had composed many songs including his favorite "Kali the Mother".

He used humor for his teachings and was also an excellent cook. His language is very free flowing and much of the charms of his original English letters have been destroyed by copybookish translation into Bengali. His own Bengali writings stand testimony to the fact that he believed that words - spoken or written should be for making things easier to understand rather than show off the speaker or writer's knowledge.

Interaction with contemporary giants

Many years after his death, Rabindranath Tagore (a prominent member of the Brahmo Samaj) had said: *If you want to know India, study Vivekananda. In him everything is positive and nothing negative*. Incidentally, in the earlier years Tagore did not have much respect for Swami Vivekananda for his idol-worshipping.

On the other hand, *Swamiji* was not particularly impressed by Tagore, though he had been interacting with Tagore's father Maharshi Debendra Nath. *Swamiji* was a very good singer and used to sing lots of *Bhajans*, including about twelve written and composed by Tagore.

Another contemporary Sri Aurobindo, actually considered *Swamiji* as his mentor. While in Alipore Jail, Sri Aurobindo used to be visited by Swami Vivekananda in his meditation. *Swamiji* guided Sri Aurobindo's yoga.

Mahatma Gandhi who strived for a lot of reform in Hinduism himself, said: *Swami Vivekananda's writings need no introduction from anybody. They make their own irresistible appeal*.

Abroad, he has had some interactions with Max Mueller and Romain Rolland. The latter also wrote a book in 1930 entitled *Vie de Vivekananda (Life of Vivekananda)*.

Quotes of Swami Vivekananda

"Each soul is potentially divine. The goal is to manifest this divinity within, by controlling nature, external and internal. Do this either by work, or worship, or psychic control, or philosophy - by one, or more, or all of these - and be free. This is the whole of religion. Doctrines, or dogmas, or rituals, or books, or temples, or forms, are but secondary details."

"The one theme of the Vedanta philosophy is the search after unity. The Hindu mind does not care for the particular; it is always after the general, nay, the universal. "what is it that by knowing which everything else is to be known." That is the one search."

"Look upon every man, woman, and everyone as God. You cannot help anyone, you can only serve: serve the children of the Lord, serve the Lord Himself, if you have the privilege."

"It may be that I shall find it good to get outside of my body — to cast it off like a disused garment. But I shall not cease to work! I shall inspire men everywhere, until the world shall know that it is one with God." "Mankind ought to be taught that religions are but the varied expressions of THE RELIGION, which is Oneness, so that each may choose the path that suits him best."

SWAMI VIVEKANANDA ON DEMOCRACY

Vivekananda was a great advocate of democracy and he wanted to awaken the young people to set up free and democratic government in India. For him, the principle of liberty was significant because he held that there could not be growth in society as well as that of an individual without liberty, He said that every one should have liberty of thought, discussion, food, marriage and dress. He wanted to democratize the Indian society through abolishing caste privileges, through opposing cunning of priest craft and social tyranny.

Vivekananda was a supporter of equality of all men and pleaded for the abolition of caste and class privileges. He thought that the spirit of equality in India could be inculcated through the spread of knowledge and education. Caste system was a hindrance to the development of India into a strong nation. He held that in democracy, power rested with the people. He was of the view that for the democratization of the country, the western thinkers tried to perfect the political and social order but the Eastern thinkers laid more stress on perfection of individual. For, sound social and political institutions were ultimately rooted in the goodness of individuals. For him, religious tolerance was crucial for the growth of democracy because that alone could promote the cause of liberty, equality and fraternity.

SWAMI VIVEKANANDA ON SOCIAL CHANGE

Vivekananda wanted an overall development of India and the eradication of poverty and degeneration of the people. He was an opponent of aristocracy and feudalism. He pleaded for bridging the gap flanked by the rich and the poor. For that purpose, he wanted to awaken the toiling masses of the country. He was of the view that in future, the Shudras or those who were toiling hard would become the rulers of the country. The socialist and anarchist movements in the Western countries indicated this. Vivekananda urbanized his own theory of social change to explain this.

Vivekananda's theory of social change was based on the Indian concept of history. It was a theory of political cycle that visualized periodic and circular change in the regimes on the foundation of law of change, with the help of historical evidences from the history of Greece, Rome and India. He held that in every individual, there prevailed three qualities of Sattva (Knowledge) Rajas (Valour) and Tamas (ignorance) and in every society and in every civilization, there lived four classes of the people. All societies which had urbanized division of labour had four classes of Brahmins, Kshatriyas, Vaishyas and Shudras. Just as to Swami Vivekananda, on the foundation of historical examples and law of nature, each of this class in every society governed the country, one after another in succession.

Vivekananda was of the opinion that in the first stage of human development in approximately all ancient civilizations of the world, the power was in the hands of the Brahmin or a priest. He ruled with the help of magic. His power was overthrown through the Kshatriyas or warriors who shaped monarchical or oligarchic governments. But the power of this class was overthrown through the Vaishyas or traders. In mainly of the contemporary nations, such as England, the power of controlling society was in the hands of Vaishyas, who amassed wealth through carrying out commerce and trade. They became powerful only in the 18th and 19th centuries. Several a kingly crowns had to kiss the ground due to the rising power of commercial classes. Now, the Vaishyas had enormous power in their hands. So, the conquest of India was not the conquest through Christianity but it was a conquest through the commercial classes, whose flag was a factory chimney, whose warriors were merchant men and whose battlefields were the market spaces of the world. It was the opinion of Vivekananda that the power of the Vaishyas would be overthrown through the Shudras.

Just as to Vivekananda, as per the law of nature, wherever there was an awakening of new and stronger life, there it tried to conquer and take the lay of the old and the decaying. Nature favored the dying of the unfit and the survival of the fittest. The power of the Kshatriyas was brought down because of its dictatorship. He maintained that the real power of the society rested with the Shudras who produced wealth with the help of their labour power. But they were treated harshly through the ruling classes. But they would gather strength and overthrow the rule of commercial classes. The Shudras would become great not through acquiring the qualities of Brahmins, Kshatriyas or Vaishyas, but through retaining their own qualities as producers of wealth. In the Western world, we had seen that the ranks of the Shudras were rising and with the augment in their awakening, they would capture power. The last stage of social change was the victory of Shudras and the capture of political power through them. The rise of Socialist and anarchist movements in Europe substantiated this.

Therefore , in the political theory of Vivekananda, the awakening and freedom of India was synchronized with the rise of Shudras and workers and peasants to political power. He was a supporter of nationalism and provided the foundation of Neo-Vedanta to it. He used religion and civilization in the cause of nationalism.

4

Fulfilment of Hindu Religion

Swami Vivekananda said: "The Jews rejected Jesus Christ, nay, crucified him, and the Hindus have accepted Shakya Muni as God and worship him. But the real difference that we Hindus want to show between modern Buddhism and what we should understand as the teachings of Lord Buddha lies principally in this: Shakya Muni came to preach nothing new. He also, like Jesus, came to fulfil and not to destroy. Only, in the case of Jesus, it was the old people, the Jews, who did not understand him, while in the case of Buddha, it was his own followers who did not realize the import of his teachings. As the Jew did not understand the fulfilment of the Old Testament, so the Buddhist did not understand the fulfilment of the truths of the Hindu religion. Again, I repeat, Shakya Muni came not to destroy, but he was the fulfilment, the logical conclusion, the logical development of the religion of the Hindus."

Swami Vivekananda wrote: "The Buddhas and the Christs that we know are but second-rate heroes in comparison with the greatest men of whom the world knows nothing. Hundreds of these unknown heroes have lived in every country working silently. Silently they live and silently they pass away; and in time their thoughts find expression in Buddhas or Christs, and it is these latter that become known to us." (Emphasis mine.)

Further he wrote: "The highest kind of men silently collect true and noble ideas, and others — the Buddhas and Christs — go from place to place preaching them and working for them. In the life of Gautama Buddha we notice him constantly saying that he is the twenty-fifth Buddha. The twenty-four before him are unknown to history, although the Buddha known to history must have built upon foundations laid by them. The highest men are calm, silent, and unknown." (Emphasis mine.)

Buddha, Christ and Krishna: A Drop of Mother (Kali): In the Complete Works of Swami Vivekananda, Volume 7, in his speech titled The Divine Mother, recorded by Miss S E Waldo, a disciple dated July 2, 1895, Swami Vivekananda said: "A bit of Mother, a drop was Krishna, another was Buddha, and another was Christ. The worship of even one spark of Mother in our earthly mother leads to greatness. Worship Her if you want love and wisdom." (Emphasis mine.)

Mother is the Greatest and Next is Buddha and Christ: In the Complete Works of Swami Vivekananda, Volume 7, in his speech recorded by Miss S E Waldo, a disciple dated July 3, 1895, Swami Vivekananda said: "The Absolute cannot be worshipped, so we must worship a manifestation, such a one as has our nature. Jesus had our nature; he became the Christ; so can we, and so must we. Christ and Buddha were the names of a state to be attained; Jesus and Gautama were the persons to manifest it. "Mother" is the first and highest manifestation, next the Christs and Buddhas." (Emphasis mine.)

Buddha and Christ – Inferior to Krishna: In the Complete Works of Swami Vivekananda, Volume 9, Gita Class, Sister Nivedita's notes of a New York Bhagavad-Gita class, recorded in a June 16, 1900 letter to Miss Josephine MacLeod, records the speech of Swami Vivekananda thus: "There was an implication throughout the talk that Christ and Buddha were inferior to Krishna — in the grasp of problems — inasmuch as they preached the highest ethics as a world path, whereas

Krishna saw the right of the whole, in all its parts — to its own differing ideals." (Emphasis mine.)

Shri Ramakrishna Greater than Christ, Buddha and Krishna: In the Complete Works of Swami Vivekananda, Volume 5, Econcilation of Jnana and Bhakti-Sat-Chit-Ananda-how sectarianism originates-bring in sharddha and the worship of shakti and avatars-the ideal of hero we want now, not the Madhura Bhava-Shri Ramakrishna avatars, Swami Vivekananda said to his disciple:

"Swamiji: Tell me first — what do you mean by an Avatara? Disciple: Why, I mean one like Shri Ramachandra, Shri Krishna, Shri Gauranga, Buddha, Jesus, and others.

Swamiji: I know Bhagavan Shri Ramakrishna to be even greater than those you have just named. What to speak of believing, which is a petty thing — I know! Let us, however, drop the subject now; more of it another time." (Emphasis mine.)

Buddhism a Rebel Child, Christianity a Patchy Imitation of Hinduism: In the Complete Works of Swami Vivekananda, Volume 3, the work before us: Delivered at the Triplicane Literary Society, Madras, Swami Vivekananda said: "Before even the Buddhists were born, there are evidences accumulating every day that Indian thought penetrated the world. Before Buddhism, Vedanta had penetrated into China, into Persia, and the Islands of the Eastern Archipelago. Again when the mighty mind of the Greek had linked the different parts of the Eastern world together there came Indian thought; and Christianity with all its boasted civilisation is but a collection of little bits of Indian thought. Ours is the religion of which Buddhism with all its greatness is a rebel child, and of which Christianity is a very patchy imitation. One of these cycles has again arrived." (Emphasis mine.)

Buddha a Demon who Ruined India, Christ Ruined Greece and Rome : In the Complete Works of Swami Vivekananda, Volume 5, the East and the West, Swami Vivekananda called

Buddha as a demon. However, the editor of the Complete works added in the parenthesis that Swami Vivekananda later changed this view in 1902. The question that remains is – if the change happened in 1902, what about the message at the Parliament of Religions in 1893, where he mentioned that Buddha was the fulfilment of Hinduism? Let the readers make a conclusion about such contrary stands at different times. The quote is given below:

"On the advent of Buddhism, Dharma was entirely neglected, and the path of Moksha alone became predominant. Hence, we read in the Agni Purana, in the language of similes, that the demon Gayasura — that is, Buddha (Swamiji afterwards changed this view with reference to Buddha, as is evident from the letter dated Varanasi, the 9th February, 1902, in this volume.) — tried to destroy the world by showing the path of Moksha to all; and therefore the Devas held a council and by stratagem set him at rest for ever." (Emphasis mine.)

Further in the same work, Swami Vivekananda wrote: "It is only the Vedic religion which considers ways and means and lays down rules for the fourfold attainment of man, comprising Dharma, Artha, Kama, and Moksha. Buddha ruined us, and so did Christ ruin Greece and Rome! Then, in due course of time, fortunately, the Europeans became Protestants, shook off the teachings of Christ as represented by Papal authority, and heaved a sigh of relief. In India, Kumarila again brought into currency the Karma-Marga, the way of Karma only, and Shankara and Ramanuja firmly re-established the Eternal Vedic religion, harmonizing and balancing in due proportions Dharma, Artha, Kama, and Moksha." (Emphasis mine.)

Muhammad-The Danger of Being Not a Trained Yogi: In the Complete Works of Swami Vivekananda, Volume 1, Raja Yoga, CHAPTER VII: Dhyana and Samadhi, Swami Vivekananda wrote: "The Yogi says there is a great danger in stumbling upon this state. In a good many cases there is the danger of the brain being deranged, and, as a rule, you will find that all those men, however great they were, who had stumbled upon this superconscious state without understanding it, groped in the dark, and generally had, along with their knowledge, some quaint superstition. They opened themselves to hallucinations. Mohammed claimed that the Angel Gabriel came to him in a cave one day and took him on the heavenly horse, Harak, and he visited the heavens. But with all that, Mohammed spoke some wonderful truths. If you read the Koran, you find the most wonderful truths mixed with superstitions. How will you explain it? That man was inspired, no doubt, but that inspiration was, as it were, stumbled upon. He was not a trained Yogi, and did not know the reason of what he was doing. Think of the good Mohammed did to the world, and think of the great evil that has been done through his fanaticism! Think of the millions massacred through his teachings, mothers bereft of their children, children made orphans, whole countries destroyed, millions upon millions of people killed!" (Emphasis mine.)

Brahmo Samaj and Arya Samaj-Apology to the English Masters: In the Complete Works of Swami Vivekananda, Volume 8, in his letter from Ridgely Manor, dated, 30th October, 1899 and addressed to 'dear optimist,' Swami Vivekananda wrote: "As for religious sects — the Brahmo Samaj, the Arya Samaj, and other sects have been useless mixtures; they were only voices of apology to our English masters to allow us to live! We have started a new India — a growth — waiting to see what comes. We believe in new ideas only when the nation wants them, and what will be true for us. The test of truth for this Brahmo Samaj is "what our masters approve"; with us, what the Indian reasoning and experience approves. The struggle has begun — not between the Brahmo Samaj and us, for they are gone already, but a harder, deeper, and more terrible one." (Emphasis mine.)

Why the Contradictory Stances?

The question that arises is-why did Swami Vivekananda speak contradictory things on the same subject? Is it because

Swami Vivekananda himself evolved over a period of time in his thoughts? Or was he practicing a clever tactic to promote Hinduism? Though one can never be sure of the reasons, the evidence seems to be indicating the later. For example, while submitting the sayings of Shri Ramakrishna to Prof. Max Muller, Swami Vivekananda instructed to avoid anything that contradicts the supposedly universal aspects of Hinduism.

Swami Vivekananda wrote: "Max Müller wants all the sayings of Shri Ramakrishna classified, that is, all on Karma in one place, on Vairagya in another place, so on Bhakti, Jnana, etc., etc. You must undertake to do this forthwith.... We must take care to present only the universal aspect of his teachings." (Emphasis mine.)

Further, in admitting non-Hindu boys to Ashramam, Swami Vivekananda again instructed to teach only the universal side of religion.

Swami Vivekananda wrote: "Admit boys of all religions — Hindu, Mohammedan, Christian, or anything; but begin rather gently — I mean, see that they get their food and drink a little separately, and teach them only the universal side of religion." (Emphasis mine.)

An Appeal to Hindus: Love and Respect Does Not Mean Uncritical Acceptance of Views, As Christians we love and respect our Hindu brothers and sisters. However this does not mean that we accept everything that a Hindu says. We will critically evaluate it and test everything.

A group of Christians in Thessalonica were accepting everything that Apostle Paul says. Even though it was an Apostle who was speaking, the Holy Spirit did not appreciate that. In Acts 17:11 we read: "Now the Bereans were of more noble character than the Thessalonians, for they received the message with great eagerness and examined the Scriptures every day to see if what Paul said was true." In fact, the Holy Spirit commanded the same Thessalonians through the same Apostle in I Thessalonians 5.21: "Test everything. Hold on to the good." That is the rigor which is expected of a Christian from our God.

Now a few Hindus might it find it difficult to accept. Should we test everything that is in the realm of faith? Should we be critical of each other? If you find it difficult to accept, then read the following quotes from Swami Vivekananda who wrote this in another context.

In the Complete Works of Swami Vivekananda, Volume 3, in the work titled My Plan of Campaign, Delivered at the Victoria Hall, Madras, Swami Vivekananda said: "For that, the eternal gratitude of every trueborn Indian is hers (Mrs. Besant), and all blessings be on her and hers for ever. But that is one thing — and joining the Society of the Theosophists is another. Regard and estimation and love are one thing, and swallowing everything any one has to say, without reasoning, without criticizing, without analyzing, is quite another." (Emphasis and words in parenthesis are mine.)

Can a Christian also say that I respect and love Hindus but that does not mean that I will accept everything that they say as correct? How can a Christian be accused of hate and intolerance when he says the same thing? Is it not sophistry to say "How can they preach of love who cannot bear another man to follow a different path from their own? If that is love, what is hatred? We have no quarrel with any religion in the world, whether it teaches men to worship Christ, Buddha, or Mohammed, or any other prophet" and in the same breath write "Regard and estimation and love are one thing, and swallowing everything any one has to say, without reasoning, without criticizing, without analyzing, is quite another."

In fact, after examining the veracity of the Holy Bible, we believe in the supremacy of the Holy Bible. If anything in the Vedas or Puranas or any Hindu literature agrees with the Holy Bible, then we will accept those as true. If anything in the Vedas or Puranas or any Hindu literature contradicts with the Holy Bible, then we will reject those as false. If any Hindu finds this as offensive, arrogant and as an attitude of intolerance, then read the following quote from Swami Vivekananda. Swami Vivekananda wrote: "Sutras are subordinate to the authority of the Vedas. They are the words of the Rishis, our forefathers, and you have to believe them if you want to become a Hindu. You may even believe the most peculiar ideas about the Godhead, but if you deny the authority of the Vedas, you are a Nastika. Therein lies the difference between the scriptures of the Christians or the Buddhists and ours; theirs are all Puranas, and not scriptures, because they describe the history of the deluge, and the history of kings and reigning families, and record the lives of great men, and so on. This is the work of the Puranas, and so far as they agree with the Vedas, they are good. So far as the Bible and the scriptures of other nations agree with the Vedas, they are perfectly good, but when they do not agree, they are no more to be accepted. So with the Koran. There are many moral teachings in these, and so far as they agree with the Vedas they have the authority of the Puranas, but no more." (Emphasis mine.)

Since both Hindus and Christians believe that their respective texts are standard to measure each other, there are a lot of issues which we will consider each other as in error. What are we going to do with those? Leave those as matters of faith? No. That is against the command to test everything. We have to discuss those and give reasons. Those reasons should include not only the hair splitting logical coherence but also the empirical evidence and the existential relevance.

In the following series of articles, I will be presenting the Christian case against many of Swami Vivekananda's misinterpretations and allegations against the Biblical faith. This is with the intention that Hindus might consider accepting Jesus Christ as their LORD and Saviour as revealed in the Holy Bible. I hope that this statement will no longer be treated as arrogant and intolerant and thus ignored but will be critically examined to see the veracity of its truth.

THE HINDU RELIGION

My religion is to learn. I read my Bible better in the light of your Bible and the dark prophecies of my religion become brighter when compared with those of your prophets. Truth has always been universal. If I alone were to have six fingers on my hand while all of you had only five, you would not think that my hand was the true intent of nature, but rather that it was abnormal and diseased. Just so with religion. If one creed alone were to be true and all the others untrue, you would have a right to say that that religion was diseased; if one religion is true, all the others must be true. Thus the Hindu religion is your property as well as mine. Of the two hundred and ninety millions of people inhabiting India, only two millions are Christians, sixty millions Mohammedans and all the rest are Hindus.

The Hindus found their creed upon the ancient Vedas, a word derived from Vid, "to know". These are a series of books which, to our minds, contain the essence of all religion; but we do not think they alone contain the truths. They teach us the immortality of the soul. In every country and every human breast there is a natural desire to find a stable equilibrium — something that does not change. We cannot find it in nature, for all the universe is nothing but an infinite mass of changes. But to infer from that that nothing unchanging exists is to fall into the error of the Southern school of Buddhists and the Charvakas, which latter believe that all is matter and nothing mind, that all religion is a cheat, and morality and goodness, useless superstitions. The Vedanta philosophy teaches that man is not bound by his five senses. They only know the present, and neither the future nor the past; but as the present signifies both past and future, and all three are only demarcations of time, the present also would be unknown if it were not for something above the senses, something independent of time, which unifies the past and the future in the present. But what is independent? Not our body, for it depends upon outward conditions; nor our mind, because the thoughts of which it is composed are caused. It is our soul. The Vedas say the whole world is a mixture of independence and dependence, of freedom and slavery, but through it all shines the soul independent, immortal, pure, perfect, holy. For if it is independent, it cannot perish, as death is but a change, and depends upon conditions; if independent, it must be perfect, for imperfection is again but a condition, and therefore dependent. And this immortal and perfect soul must be the same in the highest God as well as in the humblest man, the difference between them being only in the degree in which this soul manifests itself.

But why should the soul take to itself a body? For the same reason that I take a looking-glass — to see myself. Thus, in the body, the soul is reflected. The soul is God, and every human being has a perfect divinity within himself, and each one must show his divinity sooner or later. If I am in a dark room, no amount of protestation will make it any brighter — I must light a match. Just so, no amount of grumbling and wailing will make our imperfect body more perfect.

But the Vedanta teaches — call forth your soul, show your divinity. Teach your children that they are divine, that religion is a positive something and not a negative nonsense; that it is not subjection to groans when under oppression, but expansion and manifestation. Every religion has it that man's present and future are modified by the past, and that the present is but the effect of the past. How is it, then, that every child is born with an experience that cannot be accounted for by hereditary transmission? How is it that one is born of good parents, receives a good education and becomes a good man, while another comes from besotted parents and ends on the gallows? How do you explain this inequality without implicating God? Why should a merciful Father set His child in such conditions which must bring forth misery? It is no explanation to say God will make amends; later on — God has no blood-money. Then, too, what becomes of my liberty, if this be my first birth? Coming into this world without the experience of a former life, my independence would be gone, for my path would be marked out by the experience of others. If I cannot be the maker of my own fortune, then I am not free. I take upon myself the blame for the misery of this existence, and say I will unmake the evil I have done in another existence. This, then, is our philosophy of the migration of the soul. We come into this life with the experience of another, and the fortune or misfortune of this existence is the result of our acts in a former existence, always becoming better, till at last perfection is reached.

We believe in a God, the Father of the universe, infinite and omnipotent. But if our soul at last becomes perfect, it also must become infinite. But there is no room for two infinite unconditional beings, and hence we believe in a Personal God, and we ourselves are He. These are the three stages which every religion has taken. First we see God in the far beyond, then we come nearer to Him and give Him omnipresence so that we live in Him; and at last we recognise that we are He. The idea of an Objective God is not untrue — in fact, every idea of God, and hence every religion, is true, as each is but a different stage in the journey, the aim of which is the perfect conception of the Vedas. Hence, too, we not only tolerate, but we Hindus accept every religion, praying in the mosque of the Mohammedans, worshipping before the fire of the Zoroastrians, and kneeling before the cross of the Christians, knowing that all the religions, from the lowest fetishism to the highest absolutism, mean so many attempts of the human soul to grasp and realise the infinite, each determined by the conditions of its birth and association, and each of them marking a stage of progress. We gather all these flowers and bind them with the twine of love, making a wonderful bouquet of worship.

If I am God, then my soul is a temple of the Highest, and my every motion should be a worship — love for love's sake, duty for duty's sake, without hope of reward or fear of punishment. Thus my religion means expansion, and expansion means realisation and perception in the highest sense — no mumbling words or genuflections. Man is to become divine, realising the divine more and more from day to day in an endless progress.

VEDIC RELIGIOUS IDEALS

What concerns us most is the religious thought — on soul and God and all that appertains to religion. We will take the Samhitas. These are collections of hymns forming, as it were, the oldest Aryan literature, properly speaking, the oldest literature in the world. There may have been some scraps of literature of older date here and there, older than that even, but not books, or literature properly so called. As a collected book, this is the oldest the world has, and herein is portrayed the earliest feeling of the Aryans, their aspirations, the questions that arose about their manners and methods, and so on. At the very outset we find a very curious idea. These hymns are sung in praise of different gods, Devas as they are called, the bright ones. There is quite a number of them. One is called Indra, another Varuna, another Mitra, Parjanya, and so on. Various mythological and allegorical figures come before us one after the other — for instance, Indra the thunderer, striking the serpent who has withheld the rains from mankind. Then he lets fly his thunderbolt, the serpent is killed, and rain comes down in showers. The people are pleased, and they worship Indra with oblations. They make a sacrificial pyre, kill some animals, roast their flesh upon spits, and offer that meat to Indra. And they had a popular plant called Soma. What plant it was nobody knows now; it has entirely disappeared, but from the books we gather that, when crushed, it produced a sort of milky juice, and that was fermented; and it can also be gathered that this fermented Soma juice was intoxicating. This also they offered to Indra and the other gods, and they also drank it themselves. Sometimes they drank a little too much, and so did the gods. Indra on occasions got drunk. There are passages to show that Indra at one time drank so much of this Soma juice that he talked irrelevant words. So with Varuna. He is another god, very powerful, and is in the same way protecting his votaries, and they are praising him with their libations of Soma. So is the god of war, and so on. But the popular idea that strikes one as making the mythologies of the Samhitas entirely different from the other mythologies is, that along with every one of these gods is the idea of an infinity. This infinite is abstracted, and sometimes described as Aditya.

At other times it is affixed, as it were, to all the other gods. Take, for example, Indra. In some of the books you will find that Indra has a body, is very strong, sometimes is wearing golden armour, and comes down, lives and eats with his votaries, fights the demons, fights the snakes, and so on. Again, in one hymn we find that Indra has been given a very high position; he is omnipresent and omnipotent, and Indra sees the heart of every being. So with Varuna. This Varuna is god of the air and is in charge of the water, just as Indra was previously; and then, all of a sudden, we find him raised up and said to be omnipresent, omnipotent, and so on. I will read one passage about this Varuna in his highest form, and you will understand what I mean. It has been translated into English poetry, so it is better that I read it in that form.

The mighty Lord on high our deeds, as if at hand, espies; The gods know all men do, though men would fain their acts disguise; Whoever stands, whoever moves, or steals from place to place, Or hides him in his secret cell — the gods his movements trace. Wherever two together plot, and deem they are alone, King Varuna is there, a third, and all their schemes are known. This earth is his, to him belong those vast and boundless skies; Both seas within him rest, and yet in that small pool he lies, Whoever far beyond the sky should think his way to wing. He could not there elude the grasp of Varuna the King. His spies, descending from the skies, glide all this world around; Their thousand eyes all-scanning sweep to earth's remotest bound.

So we can multiply examples about the other gods; they all come, one after the other, to share the same fate — they first begin as gods, and then they are raised to this conception as the Being in whom the whole universe exists, who sees every heart, who is the ruler of the universe. And in the case of Varuna, there is another idea, just the germ of one idea which came, but was immediately suppressed by the Aryan mind, and that was the idea of fear.

In another place we read they are afraid they have sinned and ask Varuna for pardon. These ideas were never allowed, for reasons you will come to understand later on, to grow on Indian soil, but the germs were there sprouting, the idea of fear, and the idea of sin. This is the idea, as you all know, of what is called monotheism. This monotheism, we see, came to India at a very early period. Throughout the Samhitas, in the first and oldest part, this monotheistic idea prevails, but we shall find that it did not prove sufficient for the Aryans; they threw it aside, as it were, as a very primitive sort of idea and went further on, as we Hindus think. Of course in reading books and criticisms on the Vedas written by Europeans, the Hindu cannot help smiling when he reads, that the writings of our authors are saturated with this previous education alone. Persons who have sucked in as their mother's milk the idea that the highest ideal of God is the idea of a Personal God, naturally dare not think on the lines of these ancient thinkers of India, when they find that just after the Samhitas, the monotheistic idea with which the Samhita portion is replete was thought by the Aryans to be useless and not worthy of philosophers and thinkers, and that they struggled hard for a more philosophical and transcendental idea.

The monotheistic idea was much too human for them, although they gave it such descriptions as "The whole universe rests in Him," and "Thou art the keeper of all hearts." The Hindus were bold, to their great credit be it said, bold thinkers in all their ideas, so bold that one spark of their thought frightens the so-called bold thinkers of the West. Well has it been said by Prof. Max Müller about these thinkers that they climbed up to heights where their lungs only could breathe, and where those of other beings would have burst. These brave people followed reason wherever it led them, no matter at what cost, never caring if all their best superstitions were smashed to pieces, never caring what society would think about them, or talk about them; but what they thought was right and true, they preached and they talked.

Before going into all these speculations of the ancient Vedic sages, we will first refer to one or two very curious instances in the Vedas. The peculiar fact — that these gods are taken up, as it were, one after the other, raised and sublimated, till each has assumed the proportions of the infinite Personal God of the Universe — calls for an explanation. Prof. Max Müller creates for it a new name, as he thinks it peculiar to the Hindus: he calls it "Henotheism". We need not go far for the explanation. It is within the book. A few steps from the very place where we find those gods being raised and sublimated, we find the explanation also.

The question arises how the Hindu mythologies should be so unique, so different from all others. In Babylonian or Greek mythologies we find one god struggling upwards, and he assumes a position and remains there, while the other gods die out. Of all the Molochs, Jehovah becomes supreme, and the other Molochs are forgotten, lost for ever; he is the God of gods. So, too, of all the Greek gods, Zeus comes to the front and assumes big proportions, becomes the God of the Universe, and all the other gods become degraded into minor angels. This fact was repeated in later times. The Buddhists and the Jains raised one of their prophets to the Godhead, and all the other gods they made subservient to Buddha, or to Jina. This is the worldwide process, but there we find an exception, as it were.

One god is praised, and for the time being it is said that all the other gods obey his commands, and the very one who is said to be raised up by Varuna, is himself raised up, in the next book, to the highest position. They occupy the position of the Personal God in turns. But the explanation is there in the book, and it is a grand explanation, one that has given the theme to all subsequent thought in India, and one that will be the theme of the whole world of religions: "Ekam Sat Vipra Bahudha Vadanti — That which exists is One; sages call It by various names." In all these cases where hymns were written about all these gods, the Being perceived was one and the same; it was the perceiver who made the difference.

It was the hymnist, the sage, the poet, who sang in different languages and different words, the praise of one and the same Being. "That which exists is One; sages call It by various names." Tremendous results have followed from that one verse. Some of you, perhaps, are surprised to think that India is the only country where there never has been a religious persecution, where never was any man disturbed for his religious faith. Theists or atheists, monists, dualists, monotheists are there and always live unmolested.

Materialists were allowed to preach from the steps of Brahminical temples, against the gods, and against God Himself; they went preaching all over the land that the idea of God was a mere superstition, and that gods, and Vedas, and religion were simply superstitions invented by the priests for their own benefit, and they were allowed to do this unmolested. And so, wherever he went, Buddha tried to pull down every old thing sacred to the Hindus to the dust, and Buddha died of ripe old age. So did the Jains, who laughed at the idea of God. "How can it be that there is a God?" they asked; "it must be a mere superstition."

So on, endless examples there are. Before the Mohammedan wave came into India, it was never known what religious persecution was; the Hindus had only experienced it as made by foreigners on themselves. And even now it is a patent fact how much Hindus have helped to build Christian churches, and how much readiness there is to help them. There never has been bloodshed. Even heterodox religions that have come out of India have been likewise affected; for instance, Buddhism. Buddhism is a great religion in some respects, but to confuse Buddhism with Vedanta is without meaning; anyone may mark just the difference that exists between Christianity and the Salvation Army. There are great and good points in Buddhism, but these great points fell into hands which were not able to keep them safe. The jewels which came from philosophers fell into the hands of mobs, and the mobs took up their ideas. They had a great deal of enthusiasm, some marvellous ideas, great and humanitarian ideas, but, after all, there is something else that is necessary — thought and intellect — to keep everything safe. Wherever you see the most humanitarian ideas fall into the hands of the multitude, the first result, you may notice, is degradation. It is learning and intellect that keep things sure. Now this Buddhism went as the first missionary religion to the world, penetrated the whole of the civilised world as it existed at that time, and never was a drop of blood shed for that religion. We read how in China the Buddhist missionaries were persecuted, and thousands were massacred by two or three successive emperors, but after that, fortune favoured the Buddhists, and one of the emperors offered to take vengeance on the persecutors, but the missionaries refused. All that we owe to this one verse. That is why I want you to remember it: "Whom they call Indra, Mitra, Varuna — That which exists is One; sages call It by various names."

It was written, nobody knows at what date, it may be 8,000 years ago, in spite of all modern scholars may say, it may be 9,000 years ago. Not one of these religious speculations is of modern date, but they are as fresh today as they were when they were written, or rather, fresher, for at that distant date man was not so civilised as we know him now. He had not learnt to cut his brother's throat because he differed a little in thought from himself; he had not deluged the world in blood, he did not become demon to his own brother. In the name of humanity he did not massacre whole lots of mankind then.

Therefore these words come to us today very fresh, as great stimulating, life-giving words, much fresher than they were when they were written: "That which exists is One; sages call It by various names." We have to learn yet that all religions, under whatever name they may be called, either Hindu, Buddhist, Mohammedan, or Christian, have the same God, and he who derides any one of these derides his own God.

That was the solution they arrived at. But, as I have said, this ancient monotheistic idea did not satisfy the Hindu mind. It did not go far enough, it did not explain the visible world: a ruler of the world does not explain the world — certainly not. A ruler of the universe does not explain the universe, and much less an external ruler, one outside of it. He may be a moral guide, the greatest power in the universe, but that is no explanation of the universe; and the first question that we find now arising, assuming proportions, is the question about the universe: "Whence did it come?" "How did it come?" "How does it exist?" Various hymns are to be found on this question struggling forward to assume form, and nowhere do we find it so poetically, so wonderfully expressed as in the following hymn:

"Then there was neither aught nor naught, nor air, nor sky, nor anything. What covered all? Where rested all? Then death was not, nor deathlessness, nor change to night and day." The translation loses a good deal of the poetical beauty. "Then death was not, nor deathlessness, nor change to night and day;" the very sound of the Sanskrit is musical. "That existed, that breath, covering as it were, that God's existence; but it did not begin to move." It is good to remember this one idea that it existed motionless, because we shall find how this idea sprouts up afterwards in the cosmology, how according to the Hindu metaphysics and philosophy, this whole universe is a mass of vibrations, as it were, motions; and there are periods when this whole mass of motions subsides and becomes finer and finer, remaining in that state for some time. That is the state described in this hymn. It existed unmoved, without vibration, and when this creation began, this began to vibrate and all this creation came out of it, that one breath, calm, self-sustained, naught else beyond it.

"Gloom existed first." Those of you who have ever been in India or any tropical country, and have seen the bursting of the monsoon, will understand the majesty of these words. I remember three poets' attempts to picture this. Milton says, "No light, but rather darkness visible." Kalidasa says, "Darkness which can be penetrated with a needle," but none comes near this Vedic description, "Gloom hidden in gloom." Everything is parching and sizzling, the whole creation seems to be burning away, and for days it has been so, when one afternoon there is in one corner of the horizon a speck of cloud, and in less than half an hour it has extended unto the whole earth, until, as it were, it is covered with cloud, cloud over cloud, and then it bursts into a tremendous deluge of rain. The cause of creation was described as will. That which existed at first became changed into will, and this will began to manifest itself as desire. This also we ought to remember, because we find that this idea of desire is said to be the cause of all we have. This idea of will has been the cornerstone of both the Buddhist and the Vedantic system, and later on, has penetrated into German philosophy and forms the basis of Schopenhauer's system of philosophy. It is here we first hear of it.

"Now first arose desire, the primal seed of mind. Sages, searching in their hearts by wisdom, found the bond, Between existence and non-existence."

It is a very peculiar expression; the poet ends by saying that "perhaps He even does not know." We find in this hymn, apart from its poetical merits, that this questioning about the universe has assumed quite definite proportions, and that the minds of these sages must have advanced to such a state, when all sorts of common answers would not satisfy them. We find that they were not even satisfied with this Governor above. There are various other hymns where the same idea, comes in, about how this all came, and just as we have seen, when they were trying to find a Governor of the universe, a Personal God, they were taking up one Deva after another, raising him up to that position, so now we shall find that in various hymns one or other idea is taken up, and expanded infinitely and made responsible for everything in the universe.

One particular idea is taken as the support, in which everything rests and exists, and that support has become all this. So on with various ideas. They tried this method with Prana, the life principle. They expanded the idea of the life principle until it became universal and infinite. It is the life principle that is supporting everything; not only the human body, but it is the light of the sun and the moon, it is the power moving everything, the universal motive energy. Some of these attempts are very beautiful, very poetical. Some of them as, "He ushers the beautiful morning," are marvellously lyrical in the way they picture things. Then this very desire, which, as we have just read, arose as the first primal germ of creation, began to be stretched out, until it became the universal God. But none of these ideas satisfied.

Here the idea is sublimated and finally abstracted into a personality. "He alone existed in the beginning; He is the one Lord of all that exists; He supports this universe; He who is the author of souls, He who is the author of strength, whom all the gods worship, whose shadow is life, whose shadow is death; whom else shall we worship? Whose glory the snow-tops of the Himalayas declare, whose glory the oceans with all their waters proclaim." So on it goes, but, as I told you just now, this idea did not satisfy them. At last we find a very peculiar position. The Aryan mind had so long been seeking an answer to the question from outside. They questioned everything they could find, the sun, the moon, and stars, and they found all they could in this way.

The whole of nature at best could teach them only of a personal Being who is the Ruler of the universe; it could teach nothing further. In short, out of the external world we can only get the idea of an architect, that which is called the Design

Theory. It is not a very logical argument, as we all know; there is something childish about it, yet it is the only little bit of anything we can know about God from the external world, that this world required a builder. But this is no explanation of the universe. The materials of this world were before Him, and this God wanted all these materials, and the worst objection is that He must be limited by the materials.

The builder could not have made a house without the materials of which it is composed. Therefore he was limited by the materials; he could only do what the materials enabled him to. Therefore the God that the Design Theory gives is at best only an architect, and a limited architect of the universe; He is bound and restricted by the materials; He is not independent at all. That much they had found out already, and many other minds would have rested at that. In other countries the same thing happened; the human mind could not rest there; the thinking, grasping minds wanted to go further, but those that were backward got hold of them and did not allow them to grow. But fortunately these Hindu sages were not the people to be knocked on the head; they wanted to get a solution, and now we find that they were leaving the external for the internal. The first thing that struck them was, that it is not with the eyes and the senses that we perceive that external world, and know anything about religion; the first idea, therefore, was to find the deficiency, and that deficiency was both physical and moral, as we shall see.

You do not know, says one of these sages, the cause of this universe; there has arisen a tremendous difference between you and me — why? Because you have been talking sense things and are satisfied with sense-objects and with the mere ceremonials of religion, while I have known the Purusha beyond.

Along with this progress of spiritual ideas that I am trying to trace for you, I can only hint to you a little about the other factor in the growth, for that has nothing to do with our subject, therefore I need not enlarge upon it — the growth of rituals. As those spiritual ideas progressed in arithmetical progression, so the ritualistic ideas progressed in geometrical progression. The old superstitions had by this time developed into a tremendous mass of rituals, which grew and grew till it almost killed the Hindu life And it is still there, it has got hold of and permeated every portion of our life and made us born slaves. Yet, at the same time, we find a fight against this advance of ritual from the very earliest days. The one objection raised there is this, that love for ceremonials, dressing at certain times, eating in a certain way, and shows and mummeries of religion like these are only external religion, because you are satisfied with the senses and do not want to go beyond them. This is a tremendous difficulty with us, with every human being. At best when we want to hear of spiritual things our standard is the senses; or a man hears things about philosophy, and God, and transcendental things, and after hearing about them for days, he asks: After all, how much money will they bring, how much sense-enjoyment will they bring? For his enjoyment is only in the senses, quite naturally. But that satisfaction in the senses, says our sage, is one of the causes which have spread the veil between truth and ourselves. Devotion to ceremonials, satisfaction in the senses, and forming various theories, have drawn a veil between ourselves and truth. This is another great landmark, and we shall have to trace this ideal to the end, and see how it developed later on into that wonderful theory of Maya of the Vedanta, how this veil will be the real explanation of the Vedanta, how the truth was there all the time, it was only this veil that had covered it.

Thus we find that the minds of these ancient Aryan thinkers had begun a new theme. They found out that in the external world no search would give an answer to their question. They might seek in the external world for ages, but there would be no answer to their questions. So they fell back upon this other method; and according to this, they were taught that these desires of the senses, desires for ceremonials and externalities have caused a veil to come between themselves and the truth, and that this cannot be removed by any ceremonial. They had to fall back on their own minds, and analyse the mind to find the truth in themselves. The outside world failed and they turned back upon the inside world, and then it became the real philosophy of the Vedanta; from here the Vedanta philosophy begins. It is the foundation-stone of Vedanta philosophy. As we go on, we find that all its inquiries are inside. From the very outset they seemed to declare — look not for the truth in any religion; it is here in the human soul, the miracle of all miracles in the human soul, the emporium of all knowledge, the mine of all existence — seek here. What is not here cannot be there. And they found out step by step that that which is external is but a dull reflection at best of that which is inside. We shall see how they took, as it were, this old idea of God, the Governor of the universe, who is external to the universe, and first put Him inside the universe. He is not a God outside, but He is inside; and they took Him from there into their own hearts. Here He is in the heart of man, the Soul of our souls, the Reality in us.

Several great ideas have to be understood, in order to grasp properly the workings of the Vedanta philosophy. In the first place it is not philosophy in the sense we speak of the philosophy of Kant and Hegel. It is not one book, or the work of one man. Vedanta is the name of a series of books written at different times. Sometimes in one of these productions there will be fifty different things. Neither are they properly arranged; the thoughts, as it were, have been jotted down. Sometimes in the midst of other extraneous things, we find some wonderful idea. But one fact is remarkable, that these ideas in the Upanishads would be always progressing. In that crude old language, the working of the mind of every one of the sages has been, as it were, painted just as it went; how the ideas are at first very crude, and they become finer and finer till they reach the goal of the Vedanta, and this goal assumes a philosophical name. Just at first it was a search after the Devas, the bright ones, and then it was the origin of the universe, and the very same search is getting another name, more philosophical, clearer — the unity of all things — "Knowing which everything else becomes known."

PAPER ON HINDUISM

Three religions now stand in the world which have come down to us from time prehistoric — Hinduism, Zoroastrianism and Judaism. They have all received tremendous shocks and all of them prove by their survival their internal strength. But while Judaism failed to absorb Christianity and was driven out of its place of birth by its all-conquering daughter, and a handful of Parsees is all that remains to tell the tale of their grand religion, sect after sect arose in India and seemed to shake the religion of the Vedas to its very foundations, but like the waters of the seashore in a tremendous earthquake it receded only for a while, only to return in an all-absorbing flood, a thousand times more vigorous, and when the tumult of the rush was over, these sects were all sucked in, absorbed, and assimilated into the immense body of the mother faith. From the high spiritual flights of the Vedanta philosophy, of which the latest discoveries of science seem like echoes, to the low ideas of idolatry with its multifarious mythology, the agnosticism of the Buddhists, and the atheism of the Jains, each and all have a place in the Hindu's religion. Where then, the question arises, where is the common centre to which all these widely diverging radii converge? Where is the common basis upon which all these seemingly hopeless contradictions rest? And this is the question I shall attempt to answer.

The Hindus have received their religion through revelation, the Vedas. They hold that the Vedas are without beginning and without end. It may sound ludicrous to this audience, how a book can be without beginning or end. But by the Vedas no books are meant. They mean the accumulated treasury of spiritual laws discovered by different persons in different times.

Just as the law of gravitation existed before its discovery, and would exist if all humanity forgot it, so is it with the laws that govern the spiritual world. The moral, ethical, and spiritual relations between soul and soul and between individual spirits and the Father of all spirits, were there before their discovery, and would remain even if we forgot them. The discoverers of these laws are called Rishis, and we honour them as perfected beings. I am glad to tell this audience that some of the very greatest of them were women. Here it may be said that these laws as laws may be without end, but they must have had a beginning. The Vedas teach us that creation is without beginning or end. Science is said to have proved that the sum total of cosmic energy is always the same. Then, if there was a time when nothing existed, where was all this manifested energy? Some say it was in a potential form in God. In that case God is sometimes potential and sometimes kinetic, which would make Him mutable. Everything mutable is a compound, and everything compound must undergo that change which is called destruction. So God would die, which is absurd. Therefore there never was a time when there was no creation.

If I may be allowed to use a simile, creation and creator are two lines, without beginning and without end, running parallel to each other. God is the ever active providence, by whose power systems after systems are being evolved out of chaos, made to run for a time and again destroyed. This is what the Brahmin boy repeats every day: "The sun and the moon, the Lord created like the suns and moons of previous cycles." And this agrees with modern science. Here I stand and if I shut my eyes, and try to conceive my existence, "I", "I", "I", what is the idea before me? The idea of a body. Am I, then, nothing but a combination of material substances? The Vedas declare, "No". I am a spirit living in a body. I am not the body. The body will die, but I shall not die. Here am I in this body; it will fall, but I shall go on living. I had also a past. The soul was not created, for creation means a combination which means a certain future dissolution. If then the soul was created, it must die. Some are born happy, enjoy perfect health, with beautiful body, mental vigour and all wants supplied.

Others are born miserable, some are without hands or feet, others again are idiots and only drag on a wretched existence. Why, if they are all created, why does a just and merciful God create one happy and another unhappy, why is He so partial ? Nor would it mend matters in the least to hold that those who are miserable in this life will be happy in a future one. Why should a man be miserable even here in the reign of a just and merciful God? In the second place, the idea of a creator God does not explain the anomaly, but simply expresses the cruel fiat of an all-powerful being. There must have been causes, then, before his birth, to make a man miserable or happy and those were his past actions.

Are not all the tendencies of the mind and the body accounted for by inherited aptitude? Here are two parallel lines of existence — one of the mind, the other of matter. If matter and its transformations answer for all that we have, there is no necessity for supposing the existence of a soul. But it cannot be proved that thought has been evolved out of matter, and if a philosophical monism is inevitable, spiritual monism is certainly logical and no less desirable than a materialistic monism; but neither of these is necessary here. We cannot deny that bodies acquire certain tendencies from heredity, but those tendencies only mean the physical configuration, through which a peculiar mind alone can act in a peculiar way. There are other tendencies peculiar to a soul caused by its past actions. And a soul with a certain tendency would by the laws of affinity take birth in a body which is the fittest instrument for the display of that tendency. This is in accord with science, for science wants to explain everything by habit, and habit is got through repetitions. So repetitions are necessary to explain the natural habits of a new-born soul. And since they were not obtained in this present life, they must have come down from past lives.

There is another suggestion. Taking all these for granted, how is it that I do not remember anything of my past life ? This can be easily explained. I am now speaking English. It is not my mother tongue, in fact no words of my mother tongue are now present in my consciousness; but let me try to bring them up, and they rush in. That shows that consciousness is only the surface of the mental ocean, and within its depths are stored up all our experiences. Try and struggle, they would come up and you would be conscious even of your past life. This is direct and demonstrative evidence. Verification is the perfect proof of a theory, and here is the challenge thrown to the world by the Rishis. We have discovered the secret by which the very depths of the ocean of memory can be stirred up — try it and you would get a complete reminiscence of your past life.

Science is nothing but the finding of unity. As soon as science would reach perfect unity, it would stop from further progress, because it would reach the goal. Thus Chemistry could not progress farther when it would discover one element out of which all other could be made. Physics would stop when it would be able to fulfil its services in discovering one energy of which all others are but manifestations, and the science of religion become perfect when it would discover Him who is the one life in a universe of death, Him who is the constant basis of an ever-changing world. One who is the only Soul of which all souls are but delusive manifestations. Thus is it, through multiplicity and duality, that the ultimate unity is reached. Religion can go no farther. This is the goal of all science.

All science is bound to come to this conclusion in the long run. Manifestation, and not creation, is the word of science today, and the Hindu is only glad that what he has been cherishing in his bosom for ages is going to be taught in more forcible language, and with further light from the latest conclusions of science. Descend we now from the aspirations of philosophy to the religion of the ignorant. At the very outset, I may tell you that there is no polytheism in India. In every temple, if one stands by and listens, one will find the worshippers applying all the attributes of God, including omnipresence, to the images. It is not polytheism, nor would the name henotheism explain the situation. "The rose called by any other name would smell as sweet." Names are not explanations.

I remember, as a boy, hearing a Christian missionary preach to a crowd in India. Among other sweet things he was telling them was that if he gave a blow to their idol with his stick, what could it do? One of his hearers sharply answered, "If I abuse your God, what can He do?" "You would be punished," said the preacher, "when you die." "So my idol will punish you when you die," retorted the Hindu. The tree is known by its fruits. When I have seen amongst them that are called idolaters, men, the like of whom in morality and spirituality and love I have never seen anywhere, I stop and ask myself, "Can sin beget holiness?" Superstition is a great enemy of man, but bigotry is worse. Why does a Christian go to church? Why is the cross holy? Why is the face turned toward the sky in prayer? Why are there so many images in the Catholic Church? Why are there so many images in the minds of Protestants when they pray? My brethren, we can no more think about anything without a mental image than we can live without breathing. By the law of association, the material image calls up the mental idea and vice versa. This is why the Hindu uses an external symbol when he worships. He will tell you, it helps to keep his mind fixed on the Being to whom he prays. He knows as well as you do that the image is not God, is not omnipresent. After all, how much does omnipresence mean to almost the whole world? It stands merely as a word, a symbol. Has God superficial area? If not, when we repeat that word "omnipresent", we think of the extended sky or of space, that is all.

5

Teaching and Training

It is hard to say when Naren actually accepted Sri Ramakrishna as his guru. As far as the master was concerned, the spiritual relationship was established at the first meeting at Dakshineswar, when he had touched Naren, stirring him to his inner depths. From that moment he had implicit faith in the disciple and bore him a great love. But he encouraged Naren in the independence of his thinking. The love and faith of the Master acted as a restraint upon the impetuous youth and became his strong shield against the temptations of the world. By gradual steps the disciple was then led from doubt to certainty, and from anguish of mind to the bliss of the Spirit. This, however, was not an easy attainment.

Sri Ramakrishna, perfect teacher that he was, never laid down identical disciplines for disciples of diverse temperaments. He did not insist that Narendra should follow strict rules about food, nor did he ask him to believe in the reality of the gods and goddesses of Hindu mythology. It was not necessary for Narendra's philosophic mind to pursue the disciplines of concrete worship. But a strict eye was kept on Naren's practice of discrimination, detachment, self-control, and regular meditation. Sri Ramakrishna enjoyed Naren's vehement arguments with the other devotees regarding the dogmas and creeds of religion and was delighted to hear him tear to shreds their unquestioning beliefs. But when, as often happened, Naren teased the gentle Rakhal for showing reverence to the Divine Mother Kali, the Master would not tolerate these attempts to unsettle the brother disciple's faith in the forms of God.

As a member of the Brahmo Samaj, Narendra accepted its doctrine of monotheism and the Personal God. He also believed in the natural depravity of man. Such doctrines of non-dualistic Vedanta as the divinity of the soul and the oneness of existence he regarded as blasphemy; the view that man is one with God appeared to him pure nonsense. When the master warned him against thus limiting God's infinitude and asked him to pray to God to reveal to him His true nature, Narendra smiled. One day he was making fun of Sri Ramakrishna's non-dualism before a friend and said, 'What can be more absurd than to say that this jug is God, this cup is God, and that we too are God?' Both roared with laughter.

Just then the Master appeared. Coming to learn the cause of their fun, he gently touched Naren and plunged into deep samadhi. The touch produced a magic effect, and Narendra entered a new realm of consciousness.

He saw the whole universe permeated by the Divine Spirit and returned home in a daze. While eating his meal, he felt the presence of Brahman in everything - in the food, and in himself too. While walking in the street, he saw the carriages, the horses, the crowd, and himself as if made of the same substance. After a few days the intensity of the vision lessened to some extent, but still he could see the world only as a dream. While strolling in a public park of Calcutta, he struck his head against the iron railing, several times, to see if they were real or a mere illusion of the mind. Thus he got a glimpse of non-dualism, the fullest realization of which was to come only later, at the Cossipore garden.

Sri Ramakrishna was always pleased when his disciples put to the test his statements or behaviour before accepting his teachings. He would say: 'Test me as the money-changers test their coins. You must not believe me without testing me thoroughly.' The disciples often heard him say that his nervous system had undergone a complete change as a result of his spiritual experiences, and that he could not bear the touch of any metal, such as gold or silver. One day, during his absence in Calcutta, Narendra hid a coin under Ramakrishna's bed. After his return when the Master sat on the bed, he started up in pain as if stung by an insect. The mattress was examined and the hidden coin was found. Naren, on the other hand, was often tested by the Master. One day, when he entered the Master's room, he was completely ignored. Not a word of greeting was uttered. A week later he came back and met with the same indifference, and during the third and fourth visits saw no evidence of any thawing of the Master's frigid attitude.

At the end of a month Sri Ramakrishna said to Naren, 'I have not exchanged a single word with you all this time, and still you come.'

The disciple replied: 'I come to Dakshineswar because I love you and want to see you. I do not come here to hear your words.'

The Master was overjoyed. Embracing the disciple, he said: 'I was only testing you. I wanted to see if you would stay away on account of my outward indifference. Only a man of your inner strength could put up with such indifference on my part. Anyone else would have left me long ago.'

On one occasion Sri Ramakrishna proposed to transfer to Narendranath many of the spiritual powers that he had acquired as a result of his ascetic disciplines and visions of God. Naren had no doubt concerning the Master's possessing such powers. He asked if they would help him to realize God. Sri Ramakrishna replied in the negative but added that they might assist him in his future work as a spiritual teacher. 'Let me realize God first,' said Naren, 'and then I shall perhaps know whether or not I want supernatural powers. If I accept them now, I may forget God, make selfish use of them, and thus come to grief.' Sri Ramakrishna was highly pleased to see his chief disciple's single-minded devotion.

Several factors were at work to mould the personality of young Narendranath. Foremost of these were his inborn spiritual tendencies, which were beginning to show themselves under the influence of Sri Ramakrishna, but against which his rational mind put up a strenuous fight. Second was his habit of thinking highly and acting nobly, disciplines acquired from a mother steeped in the spiritual heritage of India. Third were his broadmindedness and regard for truth wherever found, and his sceptical attitude towards the religious beliefs and social conventions of the Hindu society of his time. These he had learnt from his English-educated father, and he was strengthened in them through his own contact with Western culture.

With the introduction in India of English education during the middle of the nineteenth century, as we have seen, Western science, history, and philosophy were studied in the Indian colleges and universities. The educated Hindu youths, allured by the glamour, began to mould their thought according to this new light, and Narendra could not escape the influence. He developed a great respect for the analytical scientific method and subjected many of the Master's spiritual visions to such scrutiny. The English poets stirred his feelings, especially Wordsworth and Shelley, and he took a course in Western medicine to understand the functioning of the nervous system, particularly the brain and spinal cord, in order to find out the secrets of Sri Ramakrishna's trances. But all this only deepened his inner turmoil.

John Stuart Mill's Three Essays on Religion upset his boyish theism and the easy optimism imbibed from the Brahmo Samaj. The presence of evil in nature and man haunted him and he could not reconcile it at all with the goodness of an omnipotent Creator. Hume's scepticism and Herbert Spencer's doctrine of the Unknowable filled his mind with a settled philosophical agnosticism. After the wearing out of his first emotional freshness and naivete, he was beset with a certain dryness and incapacity for the old prayers and devotions. He was filled with an ennui which he concealed, however, under his jovial nature. Music, at this difficult stage of his life, rendered him great help; for it moved him as nothing else and gave him a glimpse of unseen realities that often brought tears to his eyes.

Narendra did not have much patience with humdrum reading, nor did he care to absorb knowledge from books as much as from living communion and personal experience. He wanted life to be kindled by life, and thought kindled by thought. He studied Shelley under a college friend, Brajendranath Seal, who later became the leading Indian philosopher of his time, and deeply felt with the poet his pantheism, impersonal love, and vision of a glorified millennial humanity. The universe, no longer a mere lifeless, loveless mechanism, was seen to contain a spiritual principle of unity. Brajendranath, moreover, tried to present him with a synthesis of the Supreme Brahman of Vedanta, the Universal Reason of Hegel, and the gospel of Liberty, Equality, and Fraternity of the French Revolution. By accepting as the principle of morals the sovereignty of the Universal Reason and the negation of the individual, Narendra achieved an intellectual victory over scepticism and materialism, but no peace of mind.

Narendra now had to face a new difficulty. The 'ballet of bloodless categories' of Hegel and his creed of Universal Reason required of Naren a suppression of the yearning and susceptibility of his artistic nature and joyous temperament, the destruction of the cravings of his keen and acute senses, and the smothering of his free and merry conviviality. This amounted almost to killing his own true self. Further, he could not find in such a philosophy any help in the struggle of a hot-blooded youth against the cravings of the passions, which appeared to him as impure, gross, and carnal. Some of his musical associates were men of loose morals for whom he felt a bitter and undisguised contempt.

Narendra therefore asked his friend Brajendra if the latter knew the way of deliverance from the bondage of the senses, but he was told only to rely upon Pure Reason and to identify the self with it, and was promised that through this he would experience an ineffable peace.

The friend was a Platonic transcendentalist and did not have faith in what he called the artificial prop of grace, or the mediation of a guru. But the problems and difficulties of Narendra were very different from those of his intellectual friend. He found that mere philosophy was impotent in the hour of temptation and in the struggle for his soul's deliverance. He felt the need of a hand to save, to uplift, to protect - shakti or power outside his rational mind that would transform his impotence into strength and glory. He wanted a flesh-and-blood reality established in peace and certainty, in short, a living guru, who, by embodying perfection in the flesh, would compose the commotion of his soul.

The leaders of the Brahmo Samaj, as well as those of the other religious sects, had failed. It was only Ramakrishna who spoke to him with authority, as none had spoken before, and by his power brought peace into the troubled soul and healed the wounds of the spirit. At first Naren feared that the serenity that possessed him in the presence of the Master was illusory, but his misgivings were gradually vanquished by the calm assurance transmitted to him by Ramakrishna out of his own experience of Satchidananda Brahman - Existence, Knowledge, and Bliss Absolute. (This account of the struggle of Naren's collegiate days summarizes an article on Swami Vivekananda by Brajendranath Seal, published in the Life of Swami Vivekananda by the Advaita Ashrama, Mayavati, India.)

Narendra could not but recognize the contrast of the Sturm und Drang of his soul with the serene bliss in which Sri Ramakrishna was always bathed. He begged the Master to teach him meditation, and Sri Ramakrishna's reply was to him a source of comfort and strength. The Master said: 'God listens to our sincere prayer. I can swear that you can see God and talk with Him as intensely as you see me and talk with me. You can hear His words and feel His touch.' Further the Master declared: 'You may not believe in divine forms, but if you believe in an Ultimate Reality who is the Regulator of the universe, you can pray to Him thus: "O God, I do not know Thee. Be gracious to reveal to me Thy real nature." He will certainly listen to you if your prayer is sincere.'

Narendra, intensifying his meditation under the Master's guidance, began to lose consciousness of the body and to feel an inner peace, and this peace would linger even after the meditation was over. Frequently he felt the separation of the body from the soul. Strange perceptions came to him in dreams, producing a sense of exaltation that persisted after he awoke. The guru was performing his task in an inscrutable manner, Narendra's friends observed only his outer struggle; but the real transformation was known to the teacher alone - or perhaps to the disciple too.

In 1884, when Narendranath was preparing for the B.A. examination, his family was struck by a calamity. His father suddenly died, and the mother and children were plunged into great grief. For Viswanath, a man of generous nature, had lived beyond his means, and his death burdened the family with a heavy debt. Creditors, like hungry wolves, began to prowl about the door, and to make matters worse, certain relatives brought a lawsuit for the partition of the ancestral home. Though they lost it, Narendra was faced, thereafter, with poverty. As the eldest male member of the family, he had to find the wherewithal for the feeding of seven or eight mouths and began to hunt a job. He also attended the law classes. He went about clad in coarse clothes, barefoot, and hungry. Often he refused invitations for dinner from friends, remembering his starving mother, brothers, and sisters at home. He would skip family meals on the fictitious plea that he had already eaten at a friend's house, so that the people at home might receive a larger share of the scanty food. The Datta family was proud and would not dream of soliciting help from outsiders. With his companions Narendra was his usual gay self. His rich friends no doubt noticed his pale face, but they did nothing to help. Only one friend sent occasional anonymous aid, and Narendra remained grateful to him for life. Meanwhile, all his efforts to find employment failed. Some friends who earned money in a dishonest way asked him to join them, and a rich woman sent him an immoral proposal, promising to put an end to his financial distress. But Narendra gave to these a blunt rebuff. Sometimes he would wonder if the world were not the handiwork of the Devil - for how could one account for so much suffering in God's creation?

One day, after a futile search for a job, he sat down, weary and footsore, in the big park of Calcutta in the shadow of the Ochterlony monument. There some friends joined him and one of them sang a song, perhaps to console him, describing God's abundant grace.

Bitterly Naren said: 'Will you please stop that song? Such fancies are, no doubt, pleasing to those who are born with silver spoons in their mouths. Yes, there was a time when I, too, thought like that. But today these ideas appear to me a mockery.'

The friends were bewildered.

One morning, as usual, Naren left his bed repeating God's name, and was about to go out in search of work after seeking divine blessings. His mother heard the prayer and said bitterly: 'Hush, you fool! You have been crying yourself hoarse for God since your childhood. Tell me what has God done for you?' Evidently the crushing poverty at home was too much for the pious mother.

These words stung Naren to the quick. A doubt crept into his mind about God's existence and His Providence.

It was not in Naren's nature to hide his feelings. He argued before his friends and the devotees of Sri Ramakrishna about God's non-existence and the futility of prayer even if God existed. His over-zealous friends thought he had become an atheist and ascribed to him many unmentionable crimes, which he had supposedly committed to forget his misery. Some of the devotees of the Master shared these views. Narendra was angry and mortified to think that they could believe him to have sunk so low. He became hardened and justified drinking and the other dubious pleasures resorted to by miserable people for a respite from their suffering. He said, further, that he himself would not hesitate to follow such a course if he were assured of its efficacy. Openly asserting that only cowards believed in God for fear of hell-fire, he argued the possibility of God's non-existence and quoted Western philosophers in support of his position. And when the devotees of the Master became convinced that he was hopelessly lost, he felt a sort of inner satisfaction.

A garbled report of the matter reached Sri Ramakrishna, and Narendra thought that perhaps the Master, too, doubted his moral integrity. The very idea revived his anger. 'Never mind,' he said to himself. 'If good or bad opinion of a man rests on such flimsy grounds, I don't care.'

But Narendra was mistaken. For one day Bhavanath, a devotee of the master and an intimate friend of Narendra, cast aspersions on the latter's character, and the Master said angrily: 'Stop, you fool! The Mother has told me that it is simply not true. I shan't look at your face if you speak to me again that way.' The fact was that Narendra could not, in his heart of hearts, disbelieve in God. He remembered the spiritual visions of his own boyhood and many others that he had experienced in the company of the Master. Inwardly he longed to understand God and His ways. And one day he gained this understanding. It happened in the following way:

He had been out since morning in a soaking rain in search of employment, having had neither food nor rest for the whole day. That evening he sat down on the porch of a house by the roadside, exhausted. He was in a daze. Thoughts began to flit before his mind, which he could not control. Suddenly he had a strange vision, which lasted almost the whole night. He felt that veil after veil was removed from before his soul, and he understood the reconciliation of God's justice with His mercy. He came to know - but he never told how - that misery could exist in the creation of a compassionate God without impairing His sovereign power or touching man's real self. He understood the meaning of it all and was at peace. Just before daybreak, refreshed both in body and in mind, he returned home.

This revelation profoundly impressed Narendranath. He became indifferent to people's opinion and was convinced that he was not born to lead an ordinary worldly life, enjoying the love of a wife and children and physical luxuries. He recalled how the several proposals of marriage made by his relatives had come to nothing, and he ascribed all this to God's will. The peace and freedom of the monastic life cast a spell upon him. He determined to renounce the world, and set a date for this act. Then, coming to learn that Sri Ramakrishna would visit Calcutta that very day, he was happy to think that he could embrace the life of a wandering monk with his guru's blessings.

When they met, the Master persuaded his disciple to accompany him to Dakshineswar. As they arrived in his room, Sri Ramakrishna went into an ecstatic mood and sang a song, while tears bathed his eyes. The words of the song clearly indicated that the Master knew of the disciple's secret wish. When other devotees asked him about the cause of his grief, Sri Ramakrishna said, 'Oh, never mind, it is something between me and Naren, and nobody else's business.' At night he called Naren to his side and said with great feeling: 'I know you are born for Mother's work. I also know that you will be a monk. But stay in the world as long as I live, for my sake at least.' He wept again. Soon after, Naren procured a temporary job, which was sufficient to provide a hand-to-mouth living for the family.

One day Narendra asked himself why, since Kali, the Divine Mother listened to Sri Ramakrishna prayers, should not the Master pray to Her to relieve his poverty. When he told Sri Ramakrishna about this idea, the latter inquired why he did not pray himself to Kali, adding that Narendranath suffered because he did not acknowledge Kali as the Sovereign Mistress of the universe. 'Today,' the Master continued, 'is a Tuesday, an auspicious day for the Mother's worship. Go to Her shrine in the evening, prostrate yourself before the image, and pray to Her for any boon; it will be granted. Mother Kali is the embodiment of Love and Compassion. She is the Power of Brahman. She gives birth to the world by Her mere wish. She fulfils every sincere prayer of Her devotees.'

At nine o'clock in the evening, Narendranath went to the Kali temple. Passing through the courtyard, he felt within himself a surge of emotion, and his heart leapt with joy in anticipation of the vision of the Divine Mother. Entering the temple, he cast his eyes upon the image and found the stone figure to be nothing else but the living Goddess, the Divine Mother Herself, ready to give him any boon he wanted - either a happy worldly life or the joy of spiritual freedom.

He was in ecstasy. He prayed for the boon of wisdom, discrimination, renunciation, and Her uninterrupted vision, but forgot to ask the Deity for money. He felt great peace within as he returned to the Master's room, and when asked if he had prayed for money, was startled. He said that he had forgotten all about it.

The Master told him to go to the temple again and pray to the Divine Mother to satisfy his immediate needs. Naren did as he was bidden, but again forgot his mission. The same thing happened a third time. Then Naren suddenly realized that Sri Ramakrishna himself had made him forget to ask the Divine Mother for worldly things; perhaps he wanted Naren to lead a life of renunciation. So he now asked Sri Ramakrishna to do something for the family. The master told the disciple that it was not Naren's destiny to enjoy a worldly life, but assured him that the family would be able to eke out a simple existence.

The above incident left a deep impression upon Naren's mind; it enriched his spiritual life, for he gained a new understanding of the Godhead and Its ways in the phenomenal universe. Naren's idea of God had hitherto been confined either to that of a vague Impersonal Reality or to that of an extracosmic Creator removed from the world. He now realized that the Godhead is immanent in the creation, that after projecting the universe from within Itself, It has entered into all created entities as life and consciousness, whether manifest or latent. This same immanent Spirit, or the World Soul, when regarded as a person creating, preserving, and destroying the universe, is called the Personal God, and is worshipped by different religions through such a relationship as that of father, mother, king, or beloved. These relationships, he came to understand, have their appropriate symbols, and Kali is one of them.

Embodying in Herself creation and destruction, love and terror, life and death, Kali is the symbol of the total universe. The eternal cycle of the manifestation and non-manifestation of the universe is the breathing-out and breathing-in of this Divine Mother. In one aspect She is death, without which there cannot be life. She is smeared with blood, since without blood the picture of the phenomenal universe is not complete. To the wicked who have transgressed Her laws, She is the embodiment of terror, and to the virtuous, the benign Mother. Before creation She contains within Her womb the seed of the universe, which is left from the previous cycle.

After the manifestation of the universe She becomes its preserver and nourisher, and at the end of the cycle She draws it back within Herself and remains as the undifferentiated Sakti, the creative power of Brahman. She is non-different from Brahman. When free from the acts of creation, preservation, and destruction, the Spirit, in Its acosmic aspect, is called Brahman; otherwise It is known as the World Soul or the Divine Mother of the universe. She is therefore the doorway to the realization of the Absolute; She is the Absolute. To the daring devotee who wants to see the transcendental Absolute, She reveals that form by withdrawing Her phenomenal aspect. Brahman is Her transcendental aspect. She is the Great Fact of the universe, the totality of created beings. She is the Ruler and the Controller. All this had previously been beyond Narendra's comprehension. He had accepted the reality of the phenomenal world and yet denied the reality of Kali. He had been conscious of hunger and thirst, pain and pleasure, and the other characteristics of the world, and yet he had not accepted Kali, who controlled them all. That was why he had suffered. But on that auspicious Tuesday evening the scales dropped from his eyes. He accepted Kali as the Divine Mother of the universe. He became Her devotee.

Many years later he wrote to an American lady: 'Kali worship is my special fad.' But he did not preach Her in public, because he thought that all that modern man required was to be found in the Upanishads. Further, he realized that the Kali symbol would not be understood by universal humanity.

Narendra enjoyed the company of the Master for six years, during which time his spiritual life was moulded. Sri Ramakrishna was a wonderful teacher in every sense of the word. Without imposing his ideas upon anyone, he taught more by the silent influence of his inner life than by words or even by personal example. To live near him demanded of the disciple purity of thought and concentration of mind. He often appeared to his future monastic followers as their friend and playmate. Through fun and merriment he always kept before them the shining ideal of God-realization. He would not allow any deviation from bodily and mental chastity, nor any compromise with truth and renunciation. Everything else he left to the will of the Divine Mother.

Narendra was his 'marked' disciple, chosen by the Lord for a special mission. Sri Ramakrishna kept a sharp eye on him, though he appeared to give the disciple every opportunity to release his pent-up physical and mental energy. Before him, Naren often romped about like a young lion cub in the presence of a firm but indulgent parent. His spiritual radiance often startled the Master, who saw that maya, the Great Enchantress, could not approach within 'ten feet' of that blazing fire.

Narendra always came to the Master in the hours of his spiritual difficulties. One time he complained that he could not meditate in the morning on account of the shrill note of a whistle from a neighbouring mill, and was advised by the Master to concentrate on the very sound of the whistle. In a short time he overcame the distraction. Another time he found it difficult to forget the body at the time of meditation. Sri Ramakrishna sharply pressed the space between Naren's eyebrows and asked him to concentrate on that sensation. The disciple found this method effective.

Witnessing the religious ecstasy of several devotees, Narendra one day said to the Master that he too wanted to experience it. 'My child,' he was told, 'when a huge elephant enters a small pond, a great commotion is set up, but when it plunges into the Ganga, the river shows very little agitation. These devotees are like small ponds; a little experience makes their feelings flow over the brim. But you are a huge river.' Another day the thought of excessive spiritual fervour frightened Naren.

The Master reassured him by saying: 'God is like an ocean of sweetness; wouldn't you dive into it? Suppose there is a bowl filled with syrup, and you are a fly, hungry for the sweet liquid. How would you like to drink it?' Narendra said that he would sit on the edge of the bowl, otherwise he might be drowned in the syrup and lose his life. 'But,' the Master said, 'you must not forget that I am talking of the Ocean of Satchidananda, the Ocean of Immortality. Here one need not be afraid of death.

Only fools say that one should not have too much of divine ecstasy. Can anybody carry to excess the love of God? You must dive deep in the Ocean of God.' On one occasion Narendra and some of his brother disciples were vehemently arguing about God's nature - whether He was personal or impersonal, whether Divine Incarnation was fact or myth, and so forth and so on. Narendra silenced his opponents by his sharp power of reasoning and felt jubilant at his triumph. Sri Ramakrishna enjoyed the discussion and after it was over sang in an ecstatic mood:

How are you trying, O my mind,
to know the nature of God?
You are groping like a madman
locked in a dark room.
He is grasped through ecstatic love;
how can you fathom Him without it?
Only through affirmation, never negation,
can you know Him;
Neither through Veda nor through Tantra
nor the six darsanas.

All fell silent, and Narendra realized the inability of the intellect to fathom God's mystery.

In his heart of hearts Naren was a lover of God. Pointing to his eyes, Ramakrishna said that only a bhakta possessed such a tender look; the eyes of the jnani were generally dry. Many a time, in his later years, Narendra said, comparing his own spiritual attitude with that of the Master: 'He was a jnani within, but a bhakta without; but I am a bhakta within, and a jnani without.' He meant that Ramakrishna's gigantic intellect was hidden under a thin layer of devotion, and Narendra's devotional nature was covered by a cloak of knowledge.

We have already referred to the great depth of Sri Ramakrishna's love for his beloved disciple. He was worried about the distress of Naren's family and one day asked a wealthy devotee if he could not help Naren financially. Naren's pride was wounded and he mildly scolded the Master. The latter said with tears in his eyes: 'O my Naren! I can do anything for you, even beg from door to door.' Narendra was deeply moved but said nothing. Many days after, he remarked, 'The Master made me his slave by his love for me.'

This great love of Sri Ramakrishna enabled Naren to face calmly the hardships of life. Instead of hardening into a cynic, he developed a mellowness of heart. But, as will be seen later, Naren to the end of his life was often misunderstood by his friends. A bold thinker, he was far ahead of his time. Once he said: 'Why should I expect to be understood? It is enough that they love me. After all, who am I? The Mother knows best. She can do Her own work. Why should I think myself to be indispensable?'

The poverty at home was not an altogether unmitigated evil. It drew out another side of Naren's character. He began to feel intensely for the needy and afflicted. Had he been nurtured in luxury, the Master used to say, he would perhaps have become a different person - a statesman, a lawyer, an orator, or a social reformer. But instead, he dedicated his life to the service of humanity.

Sri Ramakrishna had had the prevision of Naren's future life of renunciation. Therefore he was quite alarmed when he came to know of the various plans made by Naren's relatives for his marriage. Prostrating himself in the shrine of Kali, he prayed repeatedly: 'O Mother! Do break up these plans. Do not let him sink in the quagmire of the world.' He closely watched Naren and warned him whenever he discovered the trace of an impure thought in his mind.

Naren's keen mind understood the subtle implications of Sri Ramakrishna's teachings. One day the Master said that the three salient disciplines of Vaishnavism were love of God's name, service to the devotees, and compassion for all living beings. But he did not like the word compassion and said to the devotees: 'How foolish to speak of compassion! Man is an insignificant worm crawling on the earth - and he to show compassion to others! This is absurd. It must not be compassion, but service to all. Recognize them as God's manifestations and serve them.'

The other devotees heard the words of the Master but could hardly understand their significance. Naren, however fathomed the meaning. Taking his young friends aside, he said that Sri Ramakrishna's remarks had thrown wonderful light on the philosophy of non-dualism with its discipline of non-attachment, and on that of dualism with its discipline of love. The two were not really in conflict. A non-dualist did not have to make his heart dry as sand, nor did he have to run away from the world. As Brahman alone existed in all men, a non-dualist must love all and serve all. Love, in the true sense of the word, is not possible unless one sees God in others. Naren said that the Master's words also reconciled the paths of knowledge and action. An illumined person did not have to remain inactive; he could commune with Brahman through service to other embodied beings, who also are embodiments of Brahman. 'If it be the will of God,' Naren concluded, 'I shall one day proclaim this noble truth before the world at large. I shall make it the common property of all - the wise and the fool, the rich and the poor, the brahmin and the pariah.'

Years later he expressed these sentiments in a noble poem which concluded with the following words:

Thy God is here before thee now,

Revealed in all these myriad forms:

Rejecting them, where seekest thou

His presence? He who freely shares

His love with every living thing

Proffers true service unto God.

It was Sri Ramakrishna who re-educated Narendranath in the essentials of Hinduism. He, the fulfilment of the spiritual aspirations of the three hundred millions of Hindus for the past three thousand years, was the embodiment of the Hindu faith. The beliefs Narendra had learnt on his mother's lap had been shattered by a collegiate education, but the young man now came to know that Hinduism does not consist of dogmas or creeds; it is an inner experience, deep and inclusive, which respects all faiths, all thoughts, all efforts and all realizations.

Unity in diversity is its ideal. Narendra further learnt that religion is a vision which, at the end, transcends all barriers of caste and race and breaks down the limitations of time and space. He learnt from the Master that the Personal God and worship through symbols ultimately lead the devotee to the realization of complete oneness with the Deity. The Master taught him the divinity of the soul, the non-duality of the Godhead, the unity of existence, and the harmony of religions. He showed Naren by his own example how a man in this very life could reach perfection, and the disciple found that the Master had realized the same God-consciousness by following the diverse disciplines of Hinduism, Christianity, and Islam.

One day the Master, in an ecstatic mood, said to the devotees: 'There are many opinions and many ways. I have seen them all and do not like them any more. The devotees of different faiths quarrel among themselves. Let me tell you something. You are my own people. There are no strangers around. I clearly see that God is the whole and I am a part of Him. He is the Lord and I am His servant. And sometimes I think He is I and I am He.'

Narendra regarded Sri Ramakrishna as the embodiment of the spirit of religion and did not bother to know whether he was or not an Incarnation of God. He was reluctant to cast the Master in any theological mould. It was enough for Naren if he could see through the vista of Ramakrishna's spiritual experiences all the aspects of the Godhead.

How did Narendra impress the other devotees of the Master, especially the youngsters? He was their idol. They were awed by his intellect and fascinated by his personality. In appearance he was a dynamic youth, overflowing with vigour and vitality, having a physical frame slightly over middle height and somewhat thickset in the shoulders. He was graceful without being feminine. He had a strong jaw, suggesting his staunch will and fixed determination. The chest was expansive, and the breadth of the head towards the front signified high mental power and development.

But the most remarkable thing about him was his eyes, which Sri Ramakrishna compared to lotus petals. They were prominent but not protruding, and part of the time their gaze was indrawn, suggesting the habit of deep meditation; their colour varied according to the feeling of the moment. Sometimes they would be luminous in profundity, and sometimes they sparkled in merriment. Endowed with the native grace of an animal, he was free in his movements. He walked sometimes with a slow gait and sometimes with rapidity, always a part of his mind absorbed in deep thought. And it was a delight to hear his resonant voice, either in conversation or in music.

But when Naren was serious his face often frightened his friends. In a heated discussion his eyes glowed. If immersed in his own thoughts, he created such an air of aloofness that no one dared to approach him. Subject to various moods, sometimes he showed utter impatience with his environment, and sometimes a tenderness that melted everybody's heart. His smile was bright and infectious. To some he was a happy dreamer, to some he lived in a real world rich with love and beauty, but to all he unfailingly appeared a scion of an aristocratic home.

And how did the Master regard his beloved disciple? To quote his own words:

> *'Narendra belongs to a very high plane - the realm of the Absolute. He has a manly nature. So many devotees come here, but there is no one like him.*
>
> *'Every now and then I take stock of the devotees. I find that some are like lotuses with ten petals, some like lotuses with a hundred petals. But among lotuses Narendra is a thousand-petalled one.*
>
> *'Other devotees may be like pots or pitchers; but Narendra is a huge water-barrel.*
>
> *'Others may be like pools or tanks; but Narendra is a huge reservoir like the Haldarpukur.*

'Among fish, Narendra is a huge red-eyed carp; others are like minnows or smelts or sardines.

'Narendra is a "very big receptacle", one that can hold many things. He is like a bamboo with a big hollow space inside.

'Narendra is not under the control of anything. He is not under the control of attachment or sense pleasures. He is like a male pigeon. If you hold a male pigeon by its beak, it breaks away from you; but the female pigeon keeps still. I feel great strength when Narendra is with me in a gathering.'

Sometime about the middle of 1885 Sri Ramakrishna showed the first symptoms of a throat ailment that later was diagnosed as cancer. Against the advice of the physicians, he continued to give instruction to spiritual seekers, and to fall into frequent trances. Both of these practices aggravated the illness. For the convenience of the physicians and the devotees, he was at first removed to a house in the northern section of Calcutta and then to a garden house at Cossipore, a suburb of the city. Narendra and the other young disciples took charge of nursing him. Disregarding the wishes of their guardians, the boys gave up their studies or neglected their duties at home, at least temporarily, in order to devote themselves heart and soul to the service of the Master. His wife, known among the devotees as the Holy Mother, looked after the cooking; the older devotees met the expenses. All regarded this service to the guru as a blessing and privilege.

Narendra time and again showed his keen insight and mature judgement during Sri Ramakrishna's illness. Many of the devotees, who looked upon the Master as God's Incarnation and therefore refused to see in him any human frailty, began to give a supernatural interpretation of his illness.

They believed that it had been brought about by the will of the Divine Mother or the Master himself to fulfil an inscrutable purpose, and that it would be cured without any human effort after the purpose was fulfilled. Narendra said, however, that since Sri Ramakrishna was a combination of God and man the physical element in him was subject to such laws of nature as birth, growth, decay, and destruction. He refused to give the Master's disease, a natural phenomenon, any supernatural explanation. Nonetheless, he was willing to shed his last drop of blood in the service of Sri Ramakrishna.

Emotion plays an important part in the development of the spiritual life. While intellect removes the obstacles, it is emotion that gives the urge to the seeker to move forward. But mere emotionalism without the disciplines of discrimination and renunciation often leads him astray. He often uses it as a short cut to trance or ecstasy. Sri Ramakrishna, no doubt, danced and wept while singing God's name and experienced frequent trances; but behind his emotion there was the long practice of austerities and renunciation. His devotees had not witnessed the practice of his spiritual disciplines. Some of them, especially the elderly householders, began to display ecstasies accompanied by tears and physical contortions, which in many cases, as later appeared, were the result of careful rehearsal at home or mere imitation of Sri Ramakrishna's genuine trances. Some of the devotees, who looked upon the Master as a Divine Incarnation, thought that he had assumed their responsibilities, and therefore they relaxed their own efforts. Others began to speculate about the part each of them was destined to play in the new dispensation of Sri Ramakrishna. In short, those who showed the highest emotionalism posed as the most spiritually advanced.

Narendra's alert mind soon saw this dangerous trend in their lives. He began to make fun of the elders and warned his young brother disciples about the harmful effect of indulging in such outbursts. Real spirituality, he told them over and over again, was the eradication of worldly tendencies and the development of man's higher nature. He derided their tears and trances as symptoms of nervous disorder, which should be corrected by the power of the will, and, if necessary, by nourishing food and proper medical treatment.

Very often, he said, unwary devotees of God fall victims to mental and physical breakdown. 'Of one hundred persons who take up the spiritual life,' he grimly warned, 'eighty turn out to be charlatans, fifteen insane, and only five, maybe, get a glimpse of the real truth. Therefore, beware.' He appealed to their inner strength and admonished them to keep away from all sentimental nonsense. He described to the young disciples Sri Ramakrishna's uncompromising self-control, passionate yearning for God, and utter renunciation of attachment to the world, and he insisted that those who loved the Master should apply his teachings in their lives.

Sri Ramakrishna, too, coming to realize the approaching end of his mortal existence, impressed it upon the devotees that the realization of God depended upon the giving up of lust and greed. The young disciples became grateful to Narendranath for thus guiding them during the formative period of their spiritual career. They spent their leisure hours together in meditation, study, devotional music, and healthy spiritual discussions.

The illness of Sri Ramakrishna showed no sign of abatement; the boys redoubled their efforts to nurse him, and Narendra was constantly by their side, cheering them whenever they felt depressed. One day he found them hesitant about approaching the Master. They had been told that the illness was infectious. Narendra dragged them to the Master's room. Lying in a corner was a cup containing part of the gruel which Sri Ramakrishna could not swallow. It was mixed with his saliva. Narendra seized the cup and swallowed its contents. This set at rest the boys' misgivings.

Narendra, understanding the fatal nature of Sri Ramakrishna's illness and realizing that the beloved teacher would not live long, intensified his own spiritual practices. His longing for the vision of God knew no limit. One day he asked the Master for the boon of remaining merged in samadhi three or four days at a stretch, interrupting his meditation now and then for a bite of food. 'You are a fool,' said the Master. 'There is a state higher than that. It is you who sing: "O Lord! Thou art all that exists."' Sri Ramakrishna wanted the disciple to see God in all beings and to serve them in a spirit of worship. He often said that to see the world alone, without God, is ignorance, ajnana; to see God alone, without the world, is a kind of philosophical knowledge, jnana; but to see all beings permeated by the spirit of God is supreme wisdom, vijnana. Only a few blessed souls could see God dwelling in all. He wanted Naren to attain this supreme wisdom. So the master said to him, 'Settle your family affairs first, then you shall know a state even higher than samadhi.'

On another occasion, in response to a similar request, Sri Ramakrishna said to Naren: 'Shame on you! You are asking for such an insignificant thing. I thought that you would be like a big banyan tree, and that thousands of people would rest in your shade. But now I see that you are seeking your own liberation.' Thus scolded, Narendra shed profuse tears. He realized the greatness of Sri Ramakrishna's heart.

An intense fire was raging within Narendra's soul. He could hardly touch his college books; he felt it was a dreadful thing to waste time in that way. One morning he went home but suddenly experienced an inner fear. He wept for not having made much spiritual progress, and hurried to Cossipore almost unconscious of the outside world. His shoes slipped off somewhere, and as he ran past a rick of straw some of it stuck to his clothes. Only after entering the Master's room did he feel some inner peace.

Sri Ramakrishna said to the other disciples present: 'Look at Naren's state of mind. Previously he did not believe in the Personal God or divine forms. Now he is dying for God's vision.' The Master then gave Naren certain spiritual instructions about meditation.

Naren was being literally consumed by a passion for God. The world appeared to him to be utterly distasteful. When the Master reminded him of his college studies, the disciple said,

'I would feel relieved if I could swallow a drug and forget all I have learnt' He spent night after night in meditation under the tress in the Panchavati at Dakshineswar, where Sri Ramakrishna, during the days of his spiritual discipline, had contemplated God.

He felt the awakening of the Kundalini (The spiritual energy, usually dormant in man, but aroused by the practice of spiritual disciplines. See glossary.) and had other spiritual visions.

One day at Cossipore Narendra was meditating under a tree with Girish, another disciple. The place was infested with mosquitoes. Girish tried in vain to concentrate his mind. Casting his eyes on Naren, he saw him absorbed in meditation, though his body appeared to be covered by a blanket of the insects.

A few days later Narendra's longing seemed to have reached the breaking-point. He spent an entire night walking around the garden house at Cossipore and repeating Rama's name in a heart-rending manner. In the early hours of the morning Sri Ramakrishna heard his voice, called him to his side, and said affectionately: 'Listen, my child, why are you acting that way? What will you achieve by such impatience?' He stopped for a minute and then continued: 'See, Naren. What you have been doing now, I did for twelve long years. A storm raged in my head during that period. What will you realize in one night?'

But the master was pleased with Naren's spiritual struggle and made no secret of his wish to make him his spiritual heir. He wanted Naren to look after the young disciples. 'I leave them in your care,' he said to him. 'Love them intensely and see that they practise spiritual disciplines even after my death, and that they do not return home.' He asked the young disciples to regard Naren as their leader. It was an easy task for them. Then, one day, Sri Ramakrishna initiated several of the young disciples into the monastic life, and thus himself laid the foundation of the future Ramakrishna Order of monks.

Attendance on the Master during his sickness revealed to Narendra the true import of Sri Ramakrishna's spiritual experiences. He was amazed to find that the Master could dissociate himself from all consciousness of the body by a mere wish, at which time he was not aware of the least pain from his ailment. Constantly he enjoyed an inner bliss, in spite of the suffering of the body, and he could transmit that bliss to the disciples by a mere touch or look. To Narendra, Sri Ramakrishna was the vivid demonstration of the reality of the Spirit and the unsubstantiality of matter.

One day the Master was told by a scholar that he could instantly cure himself of his illness by concentrating his mind on his throat. This Sri Ramakrishna refused to do since he could never withdraw his mind from God. But at Naren's repeated request, the Master agreed to speak to the Divine Mother about his illness. A little later he said to the disciple in a sad voice: 'Yes, I told Her that I could not swallow any food on account of the sore in my throat, and asked Her to do something about it. But the Mother said, pointing to you all, "Why, are you not eating enough through all these mouths?" I felt so humiliated that I could not utter another word.' Narendra realized how Sri Ramakrishna applied in life the Vedantic idea of the oneness of existence and also came to know that only through such realization could one rise above the pain and suffering of the individual life.

To live with Sri Ramakrishna during his illness was in itself a spiritual experience. It was wonderful to witness how he bore with his pain. In one mood he would see that the Divine Mother alone was the dispenser of pleasure and pain and that his own will was one with the Mother's will, and in another mood he would clearly behold, the utter absence of diversity, God alone becoming men, animals, gardens, houses, roads, 'the executioner, the victim, and the slaughter-post,' to use the Master's own words.

Narendra saw in the Master the living explanation of the scriptures regarding the divine nature of the soul and the illusoriness of the body. Further, he came to know that Sri Ramakrishna had attained to that state by the total renunciation of 'woman' and 'gold,' which, indeed, was the gist of his teaching. Another idea was creeping into Naren's mind. He began to see how the transcendental Reality, the Godhead, could embody Itself as the Personal God, and the Absolute become a Divine Incarnation. He was having a glimpse of the greatest of all divine mysteries: the incarnation of the Father as the Son for the redemption of the world. He began to believe that God becomes man so that man may become God. Sri Ramakrishna thus appeared to him in a new light.

Under the intellectual leadership of Narendranath, the Cossipore garden house became a miniature university. During the few moments' leisure snatched from nursing and meditation, Narendra would discuss with his brother disciples religions and philosophies, both Eastern and Western. Along with the teachings of Sankara, Krishna, and Chaitanya, those of Buddha and Christ were searchingly examined.

Narendra had a special affection for Buddha, and one day suddenly felt a strong desire to visit Bodh-Gaya, where the great Prophet had attained enlightenment. With Kali and Tarak, two of the brother disciples, he left, unknown to the others, for that sacred place and meditated for long hours under the sacred Bo-tree.

Once while thus absorbed he was overwhelmed with emotion and, weeping profusely, embraced Tarak. Explaining the incident, he said afterwards that during the meditation he keenly felt the presence of Buddha and saw vividly how the history of India had been changed by his noble teachings; pondering all this he could not control his emotion.

Back in Cossipore, Narendra described enthusiastically to the Master and the brother disciples of Buddha's life, experiences, and teachings. Sri Ramakrishna in turn related some of his own experiences. Narendra had to admit that the Master, after the attainment of the highest spiritual realization, had of his own will kept his mind on the phenomenal plane.

He further understood that a coin, however valuable, which belonged to an older period of history, could not be used as currency at a later date. God assumes different forms in different ages to serve the special needs of the time. Narendra practised spiritual disciplines with unabating intensity. Sometimes he felt an awakening of a spiritual power that he could transmit to others. One night in March 1886, he asked his brother disciple Kali to touch his right knee, and then entered into deep meditation. Kali's hand began to tremble; he felt a kind of electric shock.

Afterwards Narendra was rebuked by the Master for frittering away spiritual powers before accumulating them in sufficient measure. He was further told that he had injured Kali's spiritual growth, which had been following the path of dualistic devotion, by forcing upon the latter some of his own non-dualistic ideas. The Master added, however, that the damage was not serious.

Narendra had had enough of visions and manifestations of spiritual powers, and he now wearied of them. His mind longed for the highest experience of non-dualistic Vedanta, the nirvikalpa samadhi, in which the names and forms of the phenomenal world disappear and the aspirant realizes total non-difference between the individual soul, the universe, and Brahman, or the Absolute.

He told Sri Ramakrishna about it, but the master remained silent. And yet one evening the experience came to him quite unexpectedly.

He was absorbed in his usual meditation when he suddenly felt as if a lamp were burning at the back of his head. The light glowed more and more intensely and finally burst. Narendra was overwhelmed by that light and fell unconscious. After some time, as he began to regain his normal mood, he could feel only his head and not the rest of his body.

In an agitated voice he said to Gopal, a brother disciple who was meditating in the same room, 'Where is my body?'

Gopal answered: 'Why, Naren, it is there. Don't you feel it?'

Gopal was afraid that Narendra was dying, and ran to Sri Ramakrishna's room. He found the Master in a calm but serious mood, evidently aware of what had happened in the room downstairs. After listening to Gopal the Master said, 'Let him stay in that state for a while; he has teased me long enough for it.' For some time Narendra remained unconscious. When he regained his normal state of mind he was bathed in an ineffable peace. As he entered Sri Ramakrishna's room the latter said: 'Now the Mother has shown you everything. But this realization, like the jewel locked in a box, will be hidden away from you and kept in my custody. I will keep the key with me.

Only after you have fulfilled your mission on this earth will the box be unlocked, and you will know everything as you have known now'. The experience of this kind of samadhi usually has a most devastating effect upon the body; Incarnations and special messengers of God alone can survive its impact. By way of advice, Sri Ramakrishna asked Naren to use great discrimination about his food and companions, only accepting the purest.

Later the master said to the other disciples: 'Narendra will give up his body of his own will. When he realizes his true nature, he will refuse to stay on this earth.

Very soon he will shake the world by his intellectual and spiritual powers. I have prayed to the Divine Mother to keep away from him the Knowledge of the Absolute and cover his eyes with a veil of maya. There is much work to be done by him. But the veil, I see, is so thin that it may be rent at any time.'

Sri Ramakrishna, the Avatar of the modern age, was too gentle and tender to labour himself, for humanity's welfare. He needed some sturdy souls to carry on his work.

Narendra was foremost among those around him; therefore Sri Ramakrishna did not want him to remain immersed in nirvikalpa samadhi before his task in this world was finished. The disciples sadly watched the gradual wasting away of Sri Ramakrishna's physical frame. His body became a mere skeleton covered with skin; the suffering was intense. But he devoted his remaining energies to the training of the disciples, especially Narendra. He had been relieved of his worries about Narendra; for the disciple now admitted the divinity of Kali, whose will controls all things in the universe. Naren said later on: 'From the time he gave me over to the Divine Mother, he retained the vigour of his body only for six months. The rest of the time - and that was two long years - he suffered.'

One day the Master, unable to speak even in a whisper, wrote on a piece of paper: 'Narendra will teach others.' The disciple demurred. Sri Ramakrishna replied: 'But you must. Your very bones will do it.' He further said that all the supernatural powers he had acquired would work through his beloved disciple.

A short while before the curtain finally fell on Sri Ramakrishna's earthly life, the Master one day called Naren to his bedside. Gazing intently upon him, he passed into deep meditation. Naren felt that a subtle force, resembling an electric current, was entering his body. He gradually lost outer consciousness. After some time he regained knowledge of the physical world and found the Master weeping. Sri Ramakrishna said to him: 'O Naren, today I have given you everything I possess - now I am no more than a fakir, a penniless beggar. By the powers I have transmitted to you, you will accomplish great things in the world, and not until then will you return to the source whence you have come.'

Narendra from that day became the channel of Sri Ramakrishna's powers and the spokesman of his message.

Two days before the dissolution of the Master's body, Narendra was standing by the latter's bedside when a strange thought flashed into his mind: Was the Master truly an Incarnation of God? He said to himself that he would accept

Sri Ramakrishna's divinity if the Master, on the threshold of death, declared himself to be an Incarnation. But this was only a passing thought. He stood looking intently at the Master face.

Slowly Sri Ramakrishna's lips parted and he said in a clear voice: 'O my Naren, are you still not convinced? He who in the past was born as Rama and Krishna is now living in this very body as Ramakrishna - but not from the standpoint of your Vedanta.' Thus Sri Ramakrishna, in answer to Narendra's mental query, put himself in the category of Rama and Krishna, who are recognized by orthodox Hindus as two of the Avatars, or Incarnations of God.

A few words may be said here about the meaning of the Incarnation in the Hindu religious tradition. One of the main doctrines of Vedanta is the divinity of the soul: every soul, in reality, is Brahman. Thus it may be presumed that there is no difference between an Incarnation and an ordinary man.

To be sure, from the standpoint of the Absolute, or Brahman, no such difference exists. But from the relative standpoint, where multiplicity is perceived, a difference must be admitted. Embodied human beings reflect godliness in varying measure. In an Incarnation this godliness is fully manifest. Therefore an Incarnation is unlike an ordinary mortal or even an illumined saint.

To give an illustration: There is no difference between a clay lion and a clay mouse, from the standpoint of the clay. Both become the same substance when dissolved into clay. But the difference between the lion and the mouse, from the standpoint of form, is clearly seen. Likewise, as Brahman, an ordinary man is identical with an Incarnation. Both become the same Brahman when they attain final illumination. But in the relative state of name and form, which is admitted by Vedanta, the difference between them is accepted.

According to the Bhagavad Gita (IV. 6-8), Brahman in times of spiritual crisis assumes a human body through Its own inscrutable power, called maya. Though birthless, immutable, and the Lord of all beings, yet in every age Brahman appears to be incarnated in a human body for the protection of the good and the destruction of the wicked.

As noted above, the Incarnation is quite different from an ordinary man, even from a saint. Among the many vital differences may be mentioned the fact that the birth of an ordinary mortal is governed by the law of karma, whereas that of an Incarnation is a voluntary act undertaken for the spiritual redemption of the world.

Further, though maya is the cause of the embodiment of both an ordinary mortal and an Incarnation, yet the former is fully under maya's control, whereas the latter always remains its master. A man, though potentially Brahman, is not conscious of his divinity; but an Incarnation is fully aware of the true nature of His birth and mission. The spiritual disciplines practised by an Incarnation are not for His own liberation, but for the welfare of humanity; as far as He is concerned, such terms as bondage and liberation have no meaning, He being ever free, ever pure, and ever illumined. Lastly, an Incarnation can bestow upon others the boon of liberation, whereas even an illumined saint is devoid of such power.

Thus the Master, on his death-bed, proclaimed himself through his own words as the Incarnation or God-man of modern times.

On August 15, 1886, the Master's suffering became almost unbearable. After midnight he felt better for a few minutes. He summoned Naren to his beside and gave him the last instructions, almost in a whisper. The disciples stood around him. At two minutes past one in the early morning of August 16, Sri Ramakrishna uttered three times in a ringing voice the name of his beloved Kali and entered into the final samadhi, from which his mind never again returned to the physical world.

The body was given to the fire in the neighbouring cremation ground on the bank of the Ganga. But to the Holy

Mother, as she was putting on the signs of a Hindu widow, there came these words of faith and reassurance: 'I am not dead. I have just gone from one room to another.'

As the disciples returned from the cremation ground to the garden house, they felt great desolation. Sri Ramakrishna had been more than their earthly father. His teachings and companionship still inspired them. They felt his presence in his room. His words rang in their ears. But they could no longer see his physical body or enjoy his seraphic smile. They all yearned to commune with him.

Within a week of the Master's passing away, Narendra one night was strolling in the garden with a brother disciple, when he saw in front of him a luminous figure.

There was no mistaking: it was Sri Ramakrishna himself. Narendra remained silent, regarding the phenomenon as an illusion. But his brother disciple exclaimed in wonder, 'See, Naren! See!' There was no room for further doubt. Narendra was convinced that it was Sri Ramakrishna who had appeared in a luminous body. As he called to the other brother disciples to behold the Master, the figure disappeared.

SRI RAMAKRISHNA TEACHER

Ramakrishna, the God-man of modern times, was born on February 18, 1836, in the little village of Kamarpukur, in the district of Hooghly in Bengal. How different were his upbringing and the environment of his boyhood from those of Narendranath, who was to become, later, the bearer and interpreter of his message! Ramakrishna's parents, belonging to the brahmin caste, were poor, pious, and devoted to the traditions of their ancient religion. Full of fun and innocent joys, the fair child, with flowing hair and a sweet, musical voice, grew up in a simple countryside of rice-fields, cows, and banyan and mango trees. He was apathetic about his studies and remained practically illiterate all his life, but his innate spiritual tendencies found expression through devotional songs and the company of wandering monks, who fired his boyish imagination by the stories of their spiritual adventures.

At the age of six he experienced a spiritual ecstasy while watching a flight of snow-white cranes against a black sky overcast with rain-clouds. He began to go into trances as he meditated on gods and goddesses. His father's death, which left the family in straitened circumstances, deepened his spiritual mood. And so, though at the age of sixteen he joined his brother in Calcutta, he refused to go on there with his studies; for, as he remarked, he was simply not interested in an education whose sole purpose was to earn mere bread and butter. He felt a deep longing for the realization of God. The floodgate of Ramakrishna's emotion burst all bounds when he took up the duties of a priest in the Kali temple of Dakshineswar, where the Deity was worshipped as the Divine Mother.

Ignorant of the scriptures and of the intricacies of ritual, Ramakrishna poured his whole soul into prayer, which often took the form of devotional songs. Food, sleep, and other physical needs were completely forgotten in an all-consuming passion for the vision of God. His nights were spent in contemplation in the neighbouring woods. Doubt sometimes alternated with hope; but an inner certainty and the testimony of the illumined saints sustained him in his darkest hours of despair. Formal worship or the mere sight of the image did not satisfy his inquiring mind; for he felt that a figure of stone could not be the bestower of peace and immortality. Behind the image there must be the real Spirit, which he was determined to behold. This was not an easy task. For a long time the Spirit played with him a teasing game of hide-and-seek, but at last it yielded to the demand of love on the part of the young devotee. When he felt the direct presence of the Divine Mother, Ramakrishna dropped unconscious to the floor, experiencing within himself a constant flow of bliss. This foretaste of what was to follow made him God-intoxicated, and whetted his appetite for further experience. He wished to see God uninterruptedly, with eyes open as well as closed.

He therefore abandoned himself recklessly to the practice of various extreme spiritual disciplines. To remove from his mind the least trace of the arrogance of his high brahmin caste, he used to clean stealthily the latrine at a pariah's house. Through a stern process of discrimination he effaced all sense of distinction between gold and clay. Purity became the very breath of his nostrils, and he could not regard a woman, even in a dream, in any other way except as his own mother or the Mother of the universe. For years his eyelids did not touch each other in sleep. And he was finally thought to be insane.

Indeed, the stress of his spiritual practice soon told upon Ramakrishna's delicate body and he returned to Kamarpukur to recover his health. His relatives and old friends saw a marked change in his nature; for the gay boy had been transformed into a contemplative young man whose vision was directed to something on a distant horizon. His mother proposed marriage, and finding in this the will of the Divine Mother, Ramakrishna consented. He even indicated where the girl was to be found, namely, in the village of Jayrambati, only three miles away. Here lived the little Saradamani, a girl of five, who was in many respects very different from the other girls of her age. The child would pray to God to make her character as fragrant as the tuberose. Later, at Dakshineswar, she prayed to God to make her purer than the full moon, which, pure as it was, showed a few dark spots. The marriage was celebrated and Ramakrishna, participating, regarded the whole affair as fun or a new excitement.

In a short while he came back to Dakshineswar and plunged again into the stormy life of religious experimentation. His mother, his newly married wife, and his relatives were forgotten. Now, however, his spiritual disciplines took a new course. He wanted to follow the time-honoured paths of the Hindu religion under the guidance of competent teachers, and they came to him one by one, nobody knew from where. One was a woman, under whom he practised the disciplines of Tantra and of the Vaishnava faith and achieved the highest result in an incredibly short time. It was she who diagnosed his physical malady as the manifestation of deep spiritual emotions and described his apparent insanity as the result of an agonizing love for God; he was immediately relieved.

It was she, moreover, who first declared him to be an Incarnation of God, and she proved her statement before an assembly of theologians by scriptural evidence. Under another teacher, the monk Jatadhari, Ramakrishna delved into the mysteries of Rama worship and experienced Rama's visible presence. Further, he communed with God through the divine relationships of Father, Mother, Friend, and Beloved. By an austere sannyasin named Totapuri, he was initiated into the monastic life, and in three days he realized his complete oneness with Brahman, the undifferentiated Absolute, which is the culmination of man's spiritual endeavour. Totapuri himself had had to struggle for forty years to realize this identity.

Ramakrishna turned next to Christianity and Islam, to practise their respective disciplines, and he attained the same result that he had attained through Hinduism. He was thereby convinced that these, too, were ways to the realization of God-consciousness. Finally, he worshipped his own wife - who in the meantime had grown into a young woman of nineteen - as the manifestation of the Divine Mother of the universe and surrendered at her feet the fruit of his past spiritual practices. After this he left behind all his disciplines and struggles. For according to Hindu tradition, when the normal relationship between husband and wife, which is the strongest foundation of the worldly life, has been transcended and a man sees in his wife the divine presence, he then sees God everywhere in the universe. This is the culmination of the spiritual life.

Ramakrishna himself was now convinced of his divine mission on earth and came to know that through him the Divine Mother would found a new religious order comprising those who would accept the doctrine of the Universal Religion which he had experienced. It was further revealed to him that anyone who had prayed to God sincerely, even once, as well as those who were passing through their final birth on earth, would accept him as their spiritual ideal and mould their lives according to his universal teaching.

The people around him were bewildered to see this transformation of a man whom they had ridiculed only a short while ago as insane. The young priest had become God's devotee; the devotee, an ascetic; the ascetic, a saint; the saint, a man of realization; and the man of realization, a new Prophet. Like the full-blown blossom attracting bees, Ramakrishna drew to him men and women of differing faith, intelligence, and social position. He gave generously to all from the inexhaustible store house of divine wisdom, and everyone felt uplifted in his presence. But the Master himself was not completely satisfied. He longed for young souls yet untouched by the world, who would renounce everything for the realization of God and the service of humanity. He was literally consumed with this longing.

The talk of worldly people was tasteless to him. He often compared such people to mixture of milk and water with the latter preponderating, and said that he had become weary of trying to prepare thick milk from the mixture. Evenings, when his anguish reached its limit, he would climb the roof of a building near the temple and cry at the top of his voice: 'Come, my boys! Oh, where are you all? I cannot bear to live without you!' A mother could not feel more intensely for her beloved children, a friend for his dearest friend, or a lover for her sweetheart.

QUALIFICATIONS OF THE ASPIRANT AND THE TEACHER

How are we to know a teacher, then? The sun requires no torch to make him visible, we need not light a candle in order to see him. When the sun rises, we instinctively become aware of the fact, and when a teacher of men comes to help us, the soul will instinctively know that truth has already begun to shine upon it. Truth stands on its own evidence, it does not require any other testimony to prove it true, it is self effulgent. It penetrates into the innermost corners of our nature, and in its presence the whole universe stands up and says, "This is truth." The teachers whose wisdom and truth shine like the light of the sun are the very greatest the world has known, and they are worshipped as God by the major portion of mankind. But we may get help from comparatively lesser ones also; only we ourselves do not possess intuition enough to judge properly of the man from whom we receive teaching and guidance; so there ought to be certain tests, certain conditions, for the teacher to satisfy, as there are also for the taught.

The conditions necessary for the taught are purity, a real thirst after knowledge, and perseverance. No impure soul can be really religious. Purity in thought, speech, and act is absolutely necessary for any one to be religious. As to the thirst after knowledge, it is an old law that we all get whatever we want. None of us can get anything other than what we fix our hearts upon. To pant for religion truly is a very difficult thing, not at all so easy as we generally imagine. Hearing religious talks or reading religious books is no proof yet of a real want felt in the heart; there must be a continuous struggle, a constant fight, an unremitting grappling with our lower nature, till the higher want is actually felt and the victory is achieved. It is not a question of one or two days, of years, or of lives; the struggle may have to go on for hundreds of lifetimes. The success sometimes may come immediately, but we must be ready to wait patiently even for what may look like an infinite length of time. The student who sets out with such a spirit of perseverance will surely find success and realisation at last. In regard to the teacher, we must see that he knows the spirit of the scriptures. The whole world reads Bibles, Vedas, and Korans; but they are all only words, syntax, etymology, philology, the dry bones of religion. The teacher who deals too much in words and allows the mind to be carried away by the force of words loses the spirit. It is the knowledge of the *spirit* of the scriptures alone that constitutes the true religious teacher. The network of the words of the scriptures is like a huge forest in which the human mind often loses itself and finds no way out. — "The network of words is a big forest; it is the cause of a curious wandering of the mind." "The various methods of joining words, the various methods of speaking in beautiful language, the various methods of explaining the diction of the scriptures are only for the disputations and enjoyment of the learned, they do not conduce to the development of spiritual perception"

Those who employ such methods to impart religion to others are only desirous to show off their learning, so that the world may praise them as great scholars. You will find that no one of the great teachers of the world ever went into these various explanations of the text; there is with them no attempt at "text-torturing", no eternal playing upon the meaning of words and their roots. Yet they nobly taught, while others who have nothing to teach have taken up a word sometimes and written a three-volume book on its origin, on the man who used it first, and on what that man was accustomed to eat, and how long he slept, and so on.

Bhagavan Ramakrishna used to tell a story of some men who went into a mango orchard and busied themselves in counting the leaves, the twigs, and the branches, examining their colour, comparing their size, and noting down everything most carefully, and then got up a learned discussion on each of these topics, which were undoubtedly highly interesting to them. But one of them, more sensible than the others, did not care for all these things. and instead thereof, began to eat the mango fruit. And was he not wise? So leave this counting of leaves and twigs and note-taking to others. This kind of work has its proper place, but not here in the spiritual domain. You never see a strong spiritual man among these "leaf counters". Religion, the highest aim, the highest glory of man, does not require so much labour. If you want to be a Bhakta, it is not at all necessary for you to know whether Krishna was born in Mathura or in Vraja, what he was doing, or just the exact date on which he pronounced the teachings of the Gita. You only require to *feel* the craving for the beautiful lessons of duty and love in the Gita. All the other particulars about it and its author are for the enjoyment of the learned. Let them have what they desire. Say "Shantih, Shantih" to their learned controversies, and let *us* "eat the mangoes".

The second condition necessary in the teacher is — sinlessness. The question is often asked, "Why should we look into the character and personality of a teacher? We have only to judge of what he says, and take that up." This is not right. If a man wants to teach me something of dynamics, or chemistry, or any other physical science, he may be anything he likes, because what the physical sciences require is merely an intellectual equipment; but in the spiritual sciences it is impossible from first to last that there can be any spiritual light in the soul that is impure. What religion can an impure man teach? The *sine qua non* of acquiring spiritual truth for one's self or for imparting it to others is the purity of heart and soul. A vision of God or a glimpse of the beyond never comes until the soul is pure. Hence with the teacher of religion we must see first what he *is*, and then what he says. He must be perfectly pure, and then alone comes the value of his words, because he is only then the true "transmitter". What can he transmit if he has not spiritual power in himself? There must be the worthy vibration of spirituality in the mind of the teacher, so that it may be sympathetically conveyed to the mind of the taught. The function of the teacher is indeed an affair of the transference of something, and not one of mere stimulation of the existing intellectual or other faculties in the taught. Something real and appreciable as an influence comes from the teacher and goes to the taught. Therefore the teacher must be pure.

The third condition is in regard to the motile. The teacher must not teach with any ulterior selfish motive — for money, name, or fame; his work must be simply out of love, out of pure love for mankind at large. The only medium through which spiritual force can be transmitted is love. Any selfish motive, such as the desire for gain or for name, will immediately destroy this conveying median. God is love, and only he who has known God as love can be a teacher of godliness and God to man.

When you see that in your teacher these conditions are all fulfilled, you are safe; if they are not, it is unsafe to allow yourself to be taught by him, for there is the great danger that, if he cannot convey goodness to your heart, he may convey wickedness. This danger must by all means be guarded against. — "He who is learned in the scriptures, sinless, unpolluted by lust, and is the greatest knower of the Brahman" is the real teacher.

From what has been said, it naturally follows that we cannot be taught to love, appreciate, and assimilate religion everywhere and by everybody. The "books in the running brooks, sermons in stones, and good in everything" is all very true as a poetical figure: but nothing can impart to a man a single grain of truth unless he has the undeveloped germs of it in himself. To whom do the stones and brooks preach sermons? To the human soul, the lotus of whose inner holy shrine is already quick with life. And the light which causes the beautiful opening out of this lotus comes always from the good and wise teacher. When the heart has thus been opened, it becomes fit to receive teaching from the stones or the brooks, the stars, or the sun, or the moon, or from any thing which has its existence in our divine universe; but the unopened heart will see in them nothing but mere stones or mere brooks. A blind man may go to a museum, but he will not profit by it in any way; his eyes must be opened first, and then alone he will be able to learn what the things in the museum can teach.

This eye-opener of the aspirant after religion is the teacher. With the teacher, therefore, our relationship is the same as that between an ancestor and his descendant. Without faith, humility, submission, and veneration in our hearts towards our religious teacher, there cannot be any growth of religion in us; and it is a significant fact that, where this kind of relation between the teacher and the taught prevails, there alone gigantic spiritual men are growing; while in those countries which have neglected to keep up this kind of relation the religious teacher has become a mere lecturer, the teacher expecting his five dollars and the person taught expecting his brain to be filled with the teacher's words, and each going his own way after this much has been done. Under such circumstances spirituality becomes almost an unknown quantity. There is none to transmit it and none to have it transmitted to. Religion with such people becomes business; they think they can obtain it with their dollars. Would to God that religion could be obtained so easily! But unfortunately it cannot be.

Religion, which is the highest knowledge and the highest wisdom, cannot be bought, nor can it be acquired from books. You may thrust your head into all the corners of the world, you may explore the Himalayas, the Alps, and the Caucasus, you may sound the bottom of the sea and pry into every nook of Tibet and the desert of Gobi, you will not find it anywhere until your heart is ready for receiving it and your teacher has come. And when that divinely appointed teacher comes, serve him with childlike confidence and simplicity, freely open your heart to his influence, and see in him God manifested. Those who come to seek truth with such a spirit of love and veneration, to them the Lord of Truth reveals the most wonderful things regarding truth, goodness, and beauty.

6

Vivekananda's Philosophy

A STUDY OF THE SANKHYA PHILOSOPHY

Prakriti is called by the Sankhya philosophers indiscrete, and defined as the perfect balance of the materials in it; and it naturally follows that in perfect balance there cannot be any motion. In the primal state before any manifestation, when there was no motion but perfect balance, this Prakriti was indestructible, because decomposition or death comes from instability or change. Again, according to the Sankhya, atoms are not the primal state. This universe does not come out of atoms: they may be the secondary or the tertiary state.

The primordial material may form into atoms and become grosser and bigger things; and as far as modern investigations go, they rather point towards the same conclusion. For instance, in the modern theory of ether, if you say ether is atomic, it will not solve anything.

To make it clearer, say that air is composed of atoms, and we know that ether is everywhere, interpenetrating, omnipresent, and that these air atoms are floating, as it were, in ether. If ether again be composed of atoms, there will still be spaces between every two atoms of ether. What fills up these? If you suppose that there is another ether still finer which does this, there will again be other spaces between the atoms of that finer ether which require filling up, and so it will be *regressus ad infinitum,* what the Sankhya philosophers call the "cause leading to nothing" So the atomic theory cannot be final. According to Sankhya, nature is omnipresent, one omnipresent mass of nature, in which are the causes of everything that exists. What is meant by cause? Cause is the fine state of the manifested state; the unmanifested state of that which becomes manifested. What do you mean by destruction?

It is reverting to the cause If you have a piece of pottery and give it a blow, it is destroyed. What is meant by this is that the effects go back to their own nature, they materials out of which the pottery was created go back into their original state. Beyond this idea of destruction, any idea such as annihilation is on the face of it absurd. According to modern physical science, it can be demonstrated that all destruction means that which Kapila said ages ago — simply reverting to the cause. Going back to the finer form is all that is meant by destruction. You know how it can be demonstrated in a laboratory that matter is indestructible. At this present stage of our knowledge, if any man stands up and says that matter or this soul becomes annihilated, he is only making himself, ridiculous; it is only uneducated, silly people who would advance such a proposition; and it is curious that modern knowledge coincides with what those old philosophers taught. It must be so, and that is the proof of truth. They proceeded in their inquiry, taking up mind as the basis; they analysed the mental part of this universe and came to certain conclusions, which we, analysing the physical part, must come to, for they both must lead to the same centre.

You must remember that the first manifestation of this Prakriti in the cosmos is what the Sankhya calls "Mahat". We may call it intelligence — the great principle, its literal meaning. The first change in Prakriti is this intelligence; I would not translate it by self-consciousness, because that would be wrong. Consciousness is only a part of this intelligence.

Mahat is universal. It covers all the grounds of sub-consciousness, consciousness, and super-consciousness; so any one state of consciousness, as applied to this Mahat, would not be sufficient. In nature, for instance, you note certain changes going on before your eyes which you see and understand, but there are other changes, so much finer, that no human perception can catch them. They are from the same cause, the same Mahat is making these changes. Out of Mahat comes universal egoism. These are all substance. There is no difference between matter and mind, except in degree. The substance is the same in finer or grosser form; one changes into the other, and this exactly coincides with the conclusions of modern physiological research. By believing in the teaching that the mind is not separate from the brain, you will be saved from much fighting and struggling. Egoism again changes into two varieties. In one variety it changes into the organs. Organs are of two kinds, organs of sensation and organs of reaction.

They are not the eyes or the ears, but back of those are what you call brain-centres, and nerve-centres, and so on. This egoism, this matter or substance, becomes changed, and out of this material are manufactured these centres. Of the same substance is manufactured the other variety, the Tanmatras, fine particles of matter, which strike our organs of perception and bring about sensations. You cannot perceive them but only know they are there. Out of the Tanmatras is manufactured the gross matter — earth, water, and all the things that we see and feel. I want to impress this on your mind. It is very, hard to grasp it, because in Western countries the ideas are so queer about mind and matter.

It is hard to get those impressions out of our brains. I myself had a tremendous difficulty, being educated in Western philosophy in my boyhood. These are all cosmic things. Think of this universal extension of matter, unbroken, one substance, undifferentiated, which is the first state of everything, and which begins to change in the same way as milk becomes curd. This first change is called Mahat. The substance Mahat changes into the grosser matter called egoism. The third change is manifested as universal sense-organs, and universal fine particles, and these last again combine and become this gross universe which with eyes, nose, and ears, we see, smell, and hear.

This is the cosmic plan according to the Sankhya, and what is in the cosmos must also be microcosmic. Take an individual man. He has first a part of undifferentiated nature in him, and that material nature in him becomes changed into this Mahat, a small particle of this universal intelligence, and this particle of universal intelligence in him becomes changed into egoism, and then into the sense-organs and the fine particles of matter which combine and manufacture his body. I want this to be clear, because it is the stepping-stone to Sankhya, and it is absolutely necessary for you to understand it, because this is the basis of the philosophy of the whole world. There is no philosophy in the world that is not indebted to Kapila. Pythagoras came to India and studied this philosophy, and that was the beginning of the philosophy of the Greeks. Later, it formed the Alexandrian school, and still later, the Gnostic. It became divided into two; one part went to Europe and Alexandria, and the other remained in India; and out of this, the system of Vyasa was developed. The Sankhya philosophy of Kapila was the first rational system that the world ever saw. Every metaphysician in the world must pay homage to him. I want to impress on your mind that we are bound to listen to him as the great father of philosophy. This wonderful man, the most ancient of philosophers, is mentioned even in the Shruti: "O Lord, Thou who produced the sage Kapila in the Beginning." How wonderful his perceptions were, and if there is ant proof required of the extraordinary power of the perception of Yogis, such men are the proof. They had no microscopes or telescopes. Yet how fine their perception was, how perfect and wonderful their analysis of things!

I will here point out the difference between Schopenhauer and the Indian philosophy. Schopenhauer says that desire, or will, is the cause of everything. It is the will to exist that make us manifest, but we deny this. The will is identical with the motor nerves. When I see an object there is no will; when its sensations are carried to the brain, there comes the reaction, which says "Do this", or "Do not do this", and this state of the ego-substance is what is called will. There cannot be a single particle of will which is not a reaction. So many things precede will. It is only a manufactured something out of the ego, and the ego is a manufacture of something still higher — the intelligence — and that again is a modification of the indiscrete nature. That was the Buddhistic idea, that whatever we see is the will. It is psychologically entirely wrong, because will can only be identified with the motor nerves. If you take out the motor nerves, a man has no will whatever. This fact, as is perhaps well known to you, has been found out after a long series of experiments made with the lower animals.

We will take up this question. It is very important to understand this question of Mahat in man, the great principle, the intelligence. This intelligence itself is modified into what we call egoism, and this intelligence is the cause of all the powers in the body. It covers the whole ground, sub-consciousness, consciousness, and super-consciousness.

What are these three states? The sub-conscious state we find in animals, which we call instinct. This is almost infallible, but very limited. Instinct rarely fails. An animal almost instinctively knows a poisonous herb from an edible one, but its instinct is very limited. As soon as something new comes, it is blind. It works like a machine.

Then comes a higher state of knowledge which is fallible and makes mistakes often, but has a larger scope, although it is slow, and this you call reason. It is much larger than instinct, but instinct is surer than reason.

There are more chances of mistakes in reasoning than in instinct. There is a still higher state of the mind, the super-conscious, which belongs only to Yogis, to men who have cultivated it. This is infallible and much more unlimited in its scope than reason. This is the highest state. So we must remember, this Mahat is the real cause of all that is here, that which manifests itself in various ways, covers the whole ground of sub-conscious, conscious, and super-conscious, the three states in which knowledge exists.

Now comes a delicate question which is being always asked. If a perfect God created the universe, why is there imperfection in it? What we call the universe is what we see, and that is only this little plane of consciousness and reason; beyond that we do not see at all. Now the very question is an impossible one. If I take only a small portion out of a mass of something and look at it, it seems to be inharmonious. Naturally. The universe is inharmonious because we make it so.

How? What is reason? What is knowledge? Knowledge is finding the association about things. You go into the street and see a man and say, I know this is a man; because you remember the impressions on your mind, the marks on the Chitta. You have seen many men, and each one has made an impression on your mind; and as you see this man, you refer this to your store and see many similar pictures there; and when you see them, you are satisfied, and you put this new one with the rest. When a new impression comes and it has associations in your mind, you are satisfied; and this state of association is called knowledge.

Knowledge is, therefore, pigeon-holing one experience with the already existing fund of experience, and this is one of the great proofs of the fact that you cannot have any knowledge until you have already a fund in existence. If you are without experience, as some European philosophers think, and that your mind is a *tabula rasa* to begin with, you cannot get any knowledge, because the very fact of knowledge is the recognition of the new by means of associations already existing in the mind.

There must be a store at hand to which to refer a new impression. Suppose a child is born into this world without such a fund, it would be impossible for him ever to get any knowledge. Therefore, the child must have been previously in a state in which he had a fund, and so knowledge is eternally increasing. Slow me a way of getting round this argument.

It is a mathematical fact. Some Western schools of philosophy also hold that there cannot be any knowledge without a fund of past knowledge. They have framed the idea that the child is born with knowledge. These Western philosophers say that the impressions with which the child comes into the world are not due to the child's past, but to the experiences of his forefathers: it is only hereditary transmission. Soon they will find out that this idea is all wrong; some German philosophers are now giving hard blows to these heredity ideas. Heredity is very good, but incomplete, it only explains the physical side. How do you explain the environments influencing us?

Many causes produce one effect. Environment is one of the modifying effects. We make our own environment: as our past is, so we find the present environment. A drunken man naturally gravitates to the lowest slums of the city. You understand what is meant by knowledge.

Knowledge is pigeon-holing a new impression with old ones, recognising a new impression. What is meant by recognition? Finding associations with similar impressions that one already has. Nothing further is meant by knowledge. If that is the case, if knowledge means finding the associations, then it must be that to know anything we have to set the whole series of its similars. Is it not so?

Suppose you take a pebble; to find the association, you have to see the whole series of pebbles similes to it. But with our perception of the universe as a whole we cannot do that, because in the pigeon-hole of our mind there is only one single record of the perception, we have no other perception of the same nature or class, we cannot compare it with any other.

We cannot refer it to its associations. This bit of the universe, cut off by our consciousness, is a startling new thing, because we have not been able to find its associations.

Therefore, we are struggling with it, and thinking it horrible, wicked, and bad; we may sometimes think it is good, but we always think it is imperfect. It is only when we find its associations that the universe can be known. We shall recognise it when we go beyond the universe and consciousness, and then the universe will stand explained.

Until we can do that, all the knocking of our heads against a wall will never explain the universe, because knowledge is the finding of similars, and this conscious plane only gives us one single perception of it. So with our idea of God. All that we see of God is only a part just as we see only one portion of the universe, and all the rest is beyond human cognition. "I, the universal; so great am I that even this universe is but a part of Me." That is why we see God as imperfect, and do not understand Him. The only way to understand Him and the universe is to go beyond reason, beyond consciousness.

"When thou goest beyond the heard and the hearing, the thought and the thinking, then alone wilt thou come to Truth." "Go thou beyond the scriptures, because they teach only up to nature, up to the three qualities." When we go beyond them, we find the harmony, and not before.

The microcosm and the macrocosm are built on exactly the same plan, and in the microcosm we know only one part, the middle part. We know neither the sub-conscious, nor the super-conscious.

We know the conscious only. If a man stands up and says, "I am a sinner", he makes an untrue statement because he does not know himself. He is the most ignorant of men; of himself he knows only one part, because his knowledge covers only a part of the ground he is on. So with this universe, it is possible to know only a part of it with the reason, not the whole of it; for the sub-conscious, the conscious and the super-conscious, the individual Mahat and the universal Mahat, and all the subsequent modifications, constitute the universe. What makes nature (Prakriti) change? We see so far that everything, all Prakriti, is Jada, insentient. It is all compound and insentient.

Wherever there is law, it is proof that the region of its play is insentient. Mind, intelligence, will, and everything else is insentient. But they are all reflecting the sentiency, the "Chit" of some being who is beyond all this, whom the Sankhya philosophers call "Purusha".

The Purusha is the unwitting cause of all the changes in the universe. That is to say, this Purusha, taking Him in the universal sense, is the God of the universe. It is said that the will of the Lord created the universe. It is very good as a common expression, but we see it cannot be true. How could it be will? Will is the third or fourth manifestation in nature. Many things exist before it, *and what created them*? Will is a compound, and everything that is a compound is a product of nature. Will, therefore, could not create nature. So, to say that the will of the Lord created the universe is meaningless.

Our will only covers a little portion of self-consciousness and moves our brain. It is not will that is working your body or that is working the universe. This body is being moved by a power of which will is only a manifestation in one part. Likewise in the universe there is will, but that is only one part of the universe. The whole of the universe is not guided by will; that is why we cannot explain it by the will theory.

Suppose I take it for granted that it is will moving the body, then, when I find I cannot work it at will, I begin to fret and fume. It is my fault, because I had no right to take the will theory for granted. In the same way, if I take the universe and think it is will that moves it and find things which do not coincide, it is my fault. So the Purusha is not will; neither can it be intelligence, because intelligence itself is a compound.

There cannot be any intelligence without some sort of matter corresponding to the brain. Wherever there is intelligence, there must be something akin to that matter which we call brain which becomes lumped together into a particular form and serves the purpose of the brain. Wherever there is intelligence, there must be that matter in some form or other. But intelligence itself is a compound.

What then is this Purusha? It is neither intelligence nor will, but it is the cause of all these. It is its presence that sets them all going and combining. It does not mix with nature; it is not intelligence, or Mahat; but the Self, the pure, is Purusha. "I am the witness, and through my witnessing, nature is producing; all that is sentient and all that is insentient."

What is this sentiency in nature? We find intelligence is this sentiency which is called Chit. The basis of sentiency is in the Purusha, it is the nature of Purusha. It is that which cannot be explained but which is the cause of all that we call knowledge. Purusha is not consciousness, because consciousness is a compound; buts whatever is light and good in consciousness belongs to Purusha.

Purusha is not conscious, but whatever is light in intelligence belongs to Purusha. Sentiency is in the Purusha, but the Purusha is not intelligent, not knowing. The Chit in the Purusha plus Prakriti is what we see around us.

Whatever is pleasure and happiness and light in the universe belongs to Purusha; but it is a compound, because it is Purusha plus Prakriti. "Wherever there is any happiness, wherever there is any bliss, there is a spark of that immortality which is God." "Purusha is the; great attraction of the universe; though untouched by and unconnected with the universe, yet it attracts the whole; universe."

You see a man going after gold, because behind it is a spark of the Purusha though mixed up with a good deal of dirt. When a man loves his children or a woman her husband, what is the attracting power? A spark of Purusha behind them. It is there, only mixed up with "dirt". Nothing else can attract. "In this world of insentiency the Purusha alone is sentient."

This is the Purusha of the Sankhya. As such, it necessarily follows that the Purusha must be omnipresent. That which is not omnipresent must be limited. All limitations are caused; that which is caused must have a beginning and end. If the Purusha is limited, it will die, will not be free, will not be final, but must have some cause.

Therefore it is omnipresent. According to Kapila, there are many Purushas; not one, but an infinite number of them. You and I have each of us one, and so has everyone else; an infinite number of circles, each one infinite, running through this universe. The Purusha is neither mind nor matter, the reflex from it is all that we know. We are sure if it is omnipresent it has neither death nor birth. Nature is casting her shadow upon it, the shadow of birth and death, but it is by its nature pure. So far we have found the philosophy of the Sankhya wonderful.

Next we shall take up the proofs against it. So far the analysis is perfect, the psychology incontrovertible. We find by the division of the senses into organs and instruments that they are not simple, but compound; by dividing egoism into sense and matter, we find that this is also material and that Mahat is also a state of matter, and finally we find the Purusha.

So far there is no objection. But if we ask the Sankhya the question, "Who created nature?" — the Sankhya says that the Purusha and the Prakriti are uncreate and omnipresent, and that of this Purusha there is an infinite number. We shall have to controvert these propositions, and find a better solution, and by so doing we shall come to Advaitism. Our first objection is, how can there be these *two* infinites?

Then our argument will be that the Sankhya is not a perfect generalization, and that we have not found in it a perfect solution. And then we shall see how the Vedantists grope out of all these difficulties and reach a perfect solution, and yet all the glory really belongs to the Sankhya. It is very easy to give a finishing touch to a building when it is constructed.

THE PHILOSOPHY OF ISHVARA

Who is Ishvara? Janmadyasya yatah — "From whom is the birth, continuation, and dissolution of the universe," — He is Ishvara — "the Eternal, the Pure, the Ever-Free, the Almighty, the All-Knowing, the All-Merciful, the Teacher of all teachers"; and above all, Sa Ishvarah anirvachaniya-premasvarupah — "He the Lord is, of His own nature, inexpressible Love."

These certainly are the definitions of a Personal God. Are there then two Gods — the "Not this, not this," the Sat-chit-ananda, the Existence-Knowledge-Bliss of the philosopher, and this God of Love of the Bhakta? No, it is the same Sat-chit-ananda who is also the God of Love, the impersonal and personal in one.

It has always to be understood that the Personal God worshipped by the Bhakta is not separate or different from the Brahman. All is Brahman, the One without a second; only the Brahman, as unity or absolute, is too much of an abstraction to be loved and worshipped; so the Bhakta chooses the relative aspect of Brahman, that is, Ishvara, the Supreme Ruler. To use a simile: Brahman is as the clay or substance out of which an infinite variety of articles are fashioned.

As clay, they are all one; but form or manifestation differentiates them. Before every one of them was made, they all existed potentially in the clay, and, of course, they are identical substantially; but when formed, and so long as the form remains, they are separate and different; the clay-mouse can never become a clay-elephant, because, as manifestations, form alone makes them what they are, though as unformed clay they are all one. Ishvara is the highest manifestation of the Absolute Reality, or in other words, the highest possible reading of the Absolute by the human mind. Creation is eternal, and so also is Ishvara.

In the fourth Pada of the fourth chapter of his *Sutras*, after stating the almost infinite power and knowledge which will come to the liberated soul after the attainment of Moksha,

Vyasa makes the remark, in an aphorism, that none, however, will get the power of creating, ruling, and dissolving the universe, because that belongs to God alone.

In explaining the Sutra it is easy for the dualistic commentators to show how it is ever impossible for a subordinate soul, Jiva, to have the infinite power and total independence of God. The thorough dualistic commentator Madhvacharya deals with this passage in his usual summary method by quoting a verse from the *Varaha Purana*.

In explaining this aphorism the commentator Ramanuja says, "This doubt being raised, whether among the powers of the liberated souls is included that unique power of the Supreme One, that is, of creation etc. of the universe and even the Lordship of all, or whether, without that, the glory of the liberated consists only in the direct perception of the Supreme One, we get as an argument the following: It is reasonable that the liberated get the Lordship of the universe, because the scriptures say, 'He attains to extreme sameness with the Supreme One and all his desires are realised.'

Now extreme sameness and realisation of all desires cannot be attained without the unique power of the Supreme Lord, namely, that of governing the universe.

Therefore, to attain the realisation of all desires and the extreme sameness with the Supreme, we must all admit that the liberated get the power of ruling the whole universe. To this we reply, that the liberated get all the powers except that of ruling the universe. Ruling the universe is guiding the form and the life and the desires of all the sentient and the non-sentient beings.

The liberated ones from whom all that veils His true nature has been removed, only enjoy the unobstructed perception of the Brahman, but do not possess the power of ruling the universe.

This is proved from the scriptural text, "From whom all these things are born, by which all that are born live, unto whom they, departing, return — ask about it. That is Brahman.' If this quality of ruling the universe be a quality common even to the liberated then this text would not apply as a definition of Brahman defining Him through His rulership of the universe. The uncommon attributes alone define a thing; therefore in texts like — 'My beloved boy, alone, in the beginning there existed the One without a second. That saw and felt, "I will give birth to the many."

That projected heat.' — 'Brahman indeed alone existed in the beginning. That One evolved. That projected a blessed form, the Kshatra. All these gods are Kshatras: Varuna, Soma, Rudra, Parjanya, Yama, Mrityu, Ishana.' — 'Atman indeed existed alone in the beginning; nothing else vibrated; He thought of projecting the world; He projected the world after.' — 'Alone Narayana existed; neither Brahma, nor Ishana, nor the Dyava-Prithivi, nor the stars, nor water, nor fire, nor Soma, nor the sun. He did not take pleasure alone.

He after His meditation had one daughter, the ten organs, etc.' — and in others as, 'Who living in the earth is separate from the earth, who living in the Atman, etc.' — the Shrutis speak of the Supreme One as the subject of the work of ruling the universe.... Nor in these descriptions of the ruling of the universe is there any position for the liberated soul, by which such a soul may have the ruling of the universe ascribed to it."

In explaining the next Sutra, Ramanuja says, "If you say it is not so, because there are direct texts in the Vedas in evidence to the contrary, these texts refer to the glory of the liberated in the spheres of the subordinate deities." This also is an easy solution of the difficulty. Although the system of Ramanuja admits the unity of the total, within that totality of existence there are, according to him, eternal differences. Therefore, for all practical purposes, this system also being dualistic, it was easy for Ramanuja to keep the distinction between the personal soul and the Personal God very clear.

We shall now try to understand what the great representative of the Advaita School has to say on the point. We shall see how the Advaita system maintains all the hopes and aspirations of the dualist intact, and at the same time propounds its own solution of the problem in consonance with the high destiny of divine humanity. Those who aspire to retain their individual mind even after liberation and to remain distinct will have ample opportunity of realising their aspirations and enjoying the blessing of the qualified Brahman.

These are they who have been spoken of in the *Bhagavata Purana* thus: "O king, such are the, glorious qualities of the Lord that the sages whose only pleasure is in the Self, and from whom all fetters have fallen off, even they love the Omnipresent with the love that is for love's sake." These are they who are spoken of by the Sankhyas as getting merged in nature in this cycle, so that, after attaining perfection, they may come out in the next as lords of world-systems. But none of these ever becomes equal to God (Ishvara).

Those who attain to that state where there is neither creation, nor created, nor creator, where there is neither knower, nor knowable, nor knowledge, where there is neither *I*, nor *thou*, nor *he*, where there is neither subject, nor object, nor relation, "there, who is seen by whom?" — such persons have gone beyond everything to "where words cannot go nor mind", gone to that which the Shrutis declare as "Not this, not this"; but for those who cannot, or will not reach this state, there will inevitably remain the triune vision of the one undifferentiated Brahman as nature, soul, and the interpenetrating sustainer of both — Ishvara. So, when Prahlada forgot himself, he found neither the universe nor its cause; all was to him one Infinite, undifferentiated by name and form; but as soon as he remembered that he was Prahlada, there was the universe before him and with it the Lord of the universe — "the Repository of an infinite number of blessed qualities".

So it was with the blessed Gopis. So long as they had lost sense of their own personal identity and individuality, they were all Krishnas, and when they began again to think of Him as the One to be worshipped, then they were Gopis again, and immediately

(*Bhagavata*) — "Unto them appeared Krishna with a smile on His lotus face, clad in yellow robes and having garlands on, the embodied conqueror (in beauty) of the god of love."

Now to go back to our Acharya Shankara: "Those", he says, "who by worshipping the qualified Brahman attain conjunction with the Supreme Ruler, preserving their own mind — is their glory limited or unlimited? This doubt arising, we get as an argument: Their glory should be unlimited because of the scriptural texts, 'They attain their own kingdom', 'To him all the gods offer worship', 'Their desires are fulfilled in all the worlds'. As an answer to this, Vyasa writes, 'Without the power of ruling the universe.' Barring the power of creation etc. of the universe, the other powers such as Anima etc. are acquired by the liberated. As to ruling the universe, that belongs to the eternally perfect Ishvara. Why? Because He is the subject of all the scriptural texts as regards creation etc., and the liberated souls are not mentioned therein in any connection whatsoever. The Supreme Lord indeed is alone engaged in ruling the universe. The texts as to creation etc. all point to Him. Besides, there is given the adjective 'ever-perfect'. Also the scriptures say that the powers Anima etc. of the others are from the search after and the worship of God. Therefore they have no place in the ruling of the universe. Again, on account of their possessing their own minds, it is possible that their wills may differ, and that, whilst one desires creation, another may desire destruction. The only way of avoiding this conflict is to make all wills subordinate to some one will. Therefore the conclusion is that the wills of the liberated are dependent on the will of the Supreme Ruler." Bhakti, then, can be directed towards Brahman, only in His personal aspect. — "The way is more difficult for those whose mind is attached to the Absolute!" Bhakti has to float on smoothly with the current of our nature. True it is that we cannot have; any idea of the

Brahman which is not anthropomorphic, but is it not equally true of everything we know?

The greatest psychologist the world has ever known, Bhagavan Kapila, demonstrated ages ago that human consciousness is one of the elements in the make-up of all the objects of our perception and conception, internal as well as external. Beginning with our bodies and going up to Ishvara, we may see that every object of our perception is this consciousness plus something else, whatever that may be; and this unavoidable mixture is what we ordinarily think of as reality. Indeed it is, and ever will be, all of the reality that is possible for the human mind to know. Therefore to say that Ishvara is unreal, because He is anthropomorphic, is sheer nonsense. It sounds very much like the occidentals squabble on idealism and realism, which fearful-looking quarrel has for its foundation a mere play on the word "real". The idea of Ishvara covers all the ground ever denoted and connoted by the word real, and Ishvara is as real as anything else in the universe; and after all, the word real means nothing more than what has now been pointed out. Such is our philosophical conception of Ishvara.

SWAMI VIVEKANANDA'S PHILOSOPHY OF NEO- VEDANTA

Vedanta philosophy was one of the mainly significant ancient philosophies of India which whispered that God alone was real and the visible world was unreal and the absorption of individual soul in the one supreme soul was the goal of every human being. That was described liberation and it could be achieved with the help of true knowledge. Raja Ram Mohan Roy was a supporter of non-dualists monism. He expounded the concept of fatherhood of God and the brotherhood of man. But Vivekananda followed the Vedanta preached through his teacher which was rooted in the traditional Indian wisdom of Bhakti custom, He did not consider in the path of renunciation and asked people to perform their duties in the spirit of self-lessness. There were three significant principles of Neo-Vedanta philosophy of Vivekananda. They were as follows:

Vedanta Whispered in the Oneness flanked by God and Man and the Solidarity of Universe

It did not stand for a life of renunciation but stood for self-less action in the services of humanity. Hence, service of man should be measured as service of Cod. It propagated the principle of universal tolerance and whispered that dissimilar religious faiths were dissimilar paths to reach the goal of liberation. Therefore ; for Swami Vivekananda, Neo-Vedanta philosophy stood 'for service, sacrifice and freedom. He did not want the Neo-Vedantists to remain inactive but to work for the awakening of the masses. He wanted young Indians to dedicate themselves in the cause of resurgence of India.

7

The Hindu View of Life

(*Brooklyn Times*, December 31, 1894)

The Brooklyn Ethical Association, at the Pouch Gallery last night, tendered a reception to Swami Vivekananda. . . . Previous to the reception the distinguished visitor delivered a remarkably interesting lecture on "The Religions of India". Among other things he said:

"The Hindoo's view of life is that we are here to learn; the whole happiness of life is to learn; the human soul is here to love learning and get experience. I am able to read my Bible better by your Bible, and you will learn to read your Bible the better by my Bible. If there is but one religion to be true, all the rest must be true. The same truth has manifested itself in different forms, and the forms are according to the different circumstances of the physical or mental nature of the different nations.

"If matter and its transformation answer for all that we have, there is no necessity for supposing the existence of a soul. But it can [not] be proven that thought has been evolved out of matter. We can not deny that bodies inherit certain tendencies, but those tendencies only mean the physical configuration through which a peculiar mind alone can act in a peculiar way. These peculiar tendencies in that soul have been caused by past actions. A soul with a certain tendency will take birth in a body which is the fittest instrument for the display of that tendency, by the laws of affinity. And this is in perfect accord with science, for science wants to explain everything by habit, and habit is got through repetitions. So these repetitions are also necessary to explain the natural habits of a new-born soul. They were not got in this present life; therefore, they must have come down from past lives. "All religions are so many stages. Each one of them represents the stage through which the human soul passes to realize God. Therefore, not one of them should be neglected. None of the stages are dangerous or bad. They are good. Just as a child becomes a young man, and a young man becomes an old man, so they are travelling from truth to truth; they become dangerous only when they become rigid, and will not move further — when he ceases to grow. If the child refuses to become an old man, then he is diseased, but if they steadily grow, each step will lead them onward until they reach the whole truth. Therefore, we believe in both a personal and impersonal God, and at the same time we believe in all the religions that were, all the religions that are, and all the religions that will be in the world. We also believe we ought not only tolerate these religions, but to accept them.

"In the material physical world, expansion is life, and contraction is death. Whatever ceases to expand ceases to live. Translating this in the moral world we have: If one would expand, he must love, and when he ceases to love he dies. It is your nature; you must, because that is the only law of life. Therefore, we must love God for love's sake, so we must do our duty for duty's sake; we must work for work's sake without looking for any reward — know that you are purer and more perfect, know that this is the real temple of God."

(*Brooklyn Daily Eagle*, December 31, 1894)

After referring to the views of the Mohammedans, the Buddhists and other religious schools of India, the speaker said that the Hindoos received their religion through the revelations of the Vedas, who teach that creation is without beginning or end. They teach that man is a spirit living in a body. The body will die, but the man will not. The spirit will go on living. The soul was not created from nothing for creation means a combination and that means a certain future dissolution. If then the soul was created it must die. Therefore, it was not created. He might be asked how it is that we do not remember anything of our past lives. This could be easily explained. Consciousness is the name only of the surface of the mental ocean, and within its depths are stored up all our experiences. The desire was to find out something that was stable. The mind, the body, all nature, in fact, is changing. This question of finding something that was infinite had long been discussed. One school of which the modern Buddhists are the representatives, teach that everything that could not be solved by the five senses was nonexistent. That every object is dependent upon all others, that it is a delusion that man is an independent entity. The idealists, on the other hand, claim that each individual is an independent body. The true solution of this problem is that nature is a mixture of dependence and independence, of reality and idealism. There is a dependence which is proved by the fact that the movements of our bodies are controlled by our minds, and our minds are controlled by the spirit within us, which Christians call the soul.

Death is but a change. Those who have passed beyond and are occupying high positions there are but the same as those who remain here, and those who are occupying lower positions there are the same as others here. Every human being is a perfect being.

If we sit down in the dark and lament that it is so dark it will profit us nothing, but if we procure matches and strike a light, the darkness goes out immediately. So, if we sit down and lament that our bodies are imperfect, that our souls are imperfect, we are not profited. When we call in the light of reason, then this darkness of doubt will disappear. The object of life is to learn. Christians can learn from the Hindus, and the Hindus from Christians. He could read his Bible better after reading ours. "Tell your children," he said, "that religion is a positive something, and not a negative something.

It is not the teachings of men, but a growth, a development of something higher within our nature that seeks outlet. Every child born into the world is born with a certain accumulated experience. The idea of independence which possesses us shows there is something in us besides mind and body. The body and mind are dependent. The soul that animates us is an independent factor that creates this wish for freedom. If we are not free how can we hope to make the world good or perfect? We hold that we are makers of ourselves, that what we have we make ourselves. We have made it and we can unmake it. We believe in God, the Father of us all, the Creator and Preserver of His children, omnipresent and omnipotent. We believe in a personal God, as you do, but we go further. We believe that we are He. We believe in all the religions that have gone before, in all that now exist and in all that are to come. The Hindu bows down to the all religion [sic] for in this world the idea is addition, not subtraction. We would make up a bouquet of all beautiful colours for God, the Creator, who is a personal God. We must love Cod for love's sake, we must do our duty to Him for duty's sake, and must work for Him for work's sake and must worship Him for worship's sake.

"Books are good but they are only maps. Reading a book by direction of a man I read that so many inches of rain fell during the year. Then he told me to take the book and squeeze it between my hands. I did so and not a drop of water came from it. It was the idea only that the book conveyed. So we can get good from books, from the temple, from the church, from anything, so long as it leads us onward and upward. Sacrifices, genuflections, rumblings and mutterings are not religion. They are all good if they help us to come to a perception of the perfection which we shall realize when we come face to face with Christ. These are words or instructions to us by which we may profit. Columbus, when he discovered this continent, went back and told his countrymen that he had found the new world. They would not believe him, or some would not, and he told them to go and search for themselves. So with us, we read these truths and come in and find the truths for ourselves and then we have a belief which no one can take from us."

After the lecture an opportunity was given those present to question the speaker on any point on which they wished to have his views. Many of them availed themselves of this offer.

8

The Science of Yoga

The teachers of the science of Yoga, therefore, declare that religion is not only based upon the experience of ancient times, but that no man can be religious until he has the same perceptions himself. Yoga is the science which teaches us how to get these perceptions. It is not much use to talk about religion until one has felt it. Why is there so much disturbance, so much fighting and quarrelling in the name of God? There has been more bloodshed in the name of God than for any other cause, because people never went to the fountain-head; they were content only to give a mental assent to the customs of their forefathers, and wanted others to do the same. What right has a man to say he has a soul if he does not feel it, or that there is a God if he does not see Him?

If there is a God we must see Him, if there is a soul we must perceive it; otherwise it is better not to believe. It is better to be an outspoken atheist than a hypocrite. The modern idea, on the one hand, with the "learned" is that religion and metaphysics and all search after a Supreme Being are futile; on the other hand, with the semi-educated, the idea seems to be that these things really have no basis; their only value consists in the fact that they furnish strong motive powers for doing good to the world. If men believe in a God, they may become good, and moral, and so make good citizens. We cannot blame them for holding such ideas, seeing that all the teaching these men get is simply to believe in an eternal rigmarole of words, without any substance behind them. They are asked to live upon words; can they do it? If they could, I should not have the least regard for human nature. Man wants truth, wants to experience truth for himself; when he has grasped it, realised it, felt it within his heart of hearts, then alone, declare the Vedas, would all doubts vanish, all darkness be scattered, and all crookedness be made straight. "Ye children of immortality, even those who live in the highest sphere, the way is found; there is a way out of all this darkness, and that is by perceiving Him who is beyond all darkness; there is no other way."

The science of Raja-Yoga proposes to put before humanity a practical and scientifically worked out method of reaching this truth. In the first place, every science must have its own method of investigation. If you want to become an astronomer and sit down and cry "Astronomy! Astronomy!" it will never come to you. The same with chemistry. A certain method must be followed. You must go to a laboratory, take different substances, mix them up, compound them, experiment with them, and out of that will come a knowledge of chemistry. If you want to be an astronomer, you must go to an observatory, take a telescope, study the stars and planets, and then you will become an astronomer. Each science must have its own methods. I could preach you thousands of sermons, but they would not make you religious, until you practiced the method. These are the truths of the sages of all countries, of all ages, of men pure and unselfish, who had no motive but to do good to the world. They all declare that they have found some truth higher than what the senses can bring to us, and they invite verification. They ask us to take up the method and practice honestly, and then, if we do not find this higher truth, we will have the right to say there is no truth in the claim, but before we have done that, we are not rational in denying the truth of their assertions. So we must work faithfully using the prescribed methods, and light will come.

In acquiring knowledge we make use of generalisations, and generalisation is based upon observation. We first observe facts, then generalise, and then draw conclusions or principles. The knowledge of the mind, of the internal nature of man, of thought, can never be had until we have first the power of observing the facts that are going on within. It is comparatively easy to observe facts in the external world, for many instruments have been invented for the purpose, but in the internal world we have no instrument to help us. Yet we know we must observe in order to have a real science. Without a proper analysis, any science will be hopeless — mere theorising. And that is why all the psychologists have been quarrelling among themselves since the beginning of time, except those few who found out the means of observation.

The science of Raja-Yoga, in the first place, proposes to give us such a means of observing the internal states. The instrument is the mind itself. The power of attention, when properly guided, and directed towards the internal world, will analyse the mind, and illumine facts for us. The powers of the mind are like rays of light dissipated; when they are concentrated, they illumine. This is our only means of knowledge. Everyone is using it, both in the external and the internal world; but, for the psychologist, the same minute observation has to be directed to the internal world, which the scientific man directs to the external; and this requires a great deal of practice. From our childhood upwards we have been taught only to pay attention to things external, but never to things internal; hence most of us have nearly lost the faculty of observing the internal mechanism. To turn the mind as it were, inside, stop it from going outside, and then to concentrate all its powers, and throw them upon the mind itself, in order that it may know its own nature, analyse itself, is very hard work. Yet that is the only way to anything which will be a scientific approach to the subject.

What is the use of such knowledge? In the first place, knowledge itself is the highest reward of knowledge, and secondly, there is also utility in it. It will take away all our misery. When by analysing his own mind, man comes face to face, as it were, with something which is never destroyed, something which is, by its own nature, eternally pure and perfect, he will no more be miserable, no more unhappy. All misery comes from fear, from unsatisfied desire. Man will find that he never dies, and then he will have no more fear of death. When he knows that he is perfect, he will have no more vain desires, and both these causes being absent, there will be no more misery — there will be perfect bliss, even while in this body.

There is only one method by which to attain this knowledge, that which is called concentration. The chemist in his laboratory concentrates all the energies of his mind into one focus, and throws them upon the materials he is analysing, and so finds out their secrets. The astronomer concentrates all the energies of his mind and projects them through his telescope upon the skies; and the stars, the sun, and the moon, give up their secrets to him. The more I can concentrate my thoughts on the matter on which I am talking to you, the more light I can throw upon you. You are listening to me, and the more you concentrate your thoughts, the more clearly you will grasp what I have to say. How has all the knowledge in the world been gained but by the concentration of the powers of the mind? The world is ready to give up its secrets if we only know how to knock, how to give it the necessary blow. The strength and force of the blow come through concentration. There is no limit to the power of the human mind. The more concentrated it is, the more power is brought to bear on one point; that is the secret.

It is easy to concentrate the mind on external things, the mind naturally goes outwards; but not so in the case of religion, or psychology, or metaphysics, where the subject and the object, are one. The object is internal, the mind itself is the object, and it is necessary to study the mind itself — mind studying mind. We know that there is the power of the mind called reflection. I am talking to you. At the same time I am standing aside, as it were, a second person, and knowing and hearing what I am talking. You work and think at the same time, while a portion of your mind stands by and sees what you are thinking. The powers of the mind should be concentrated and turned back upon itself, and as the darkest places reveal their secrets before the penetrating rays of the sun, so will this concentrated mind penetrate its own innermost secrets. Thus will we come to the basis of belief, the real genuine religion. We will perceive for ourselves whether we have souls, whether life is of five minutes or of eternity, whether there is a God in the universe or more. It will all be revealed to us. This is what Raja-Yoga proposes to teach. The goal of all its teaching is how to concentrate the minds, then, how to discover the innermost recesses of our own minds, then, how to generalise their contents and form our own conclusions from them. It, therefore, never asks the question what our religion is, whether we are Deists or Atheists, whether Christians, Jews, or Buddhists. We are human beings; that is sufficient. Every human being has the right and the power to seek for religion. Every human being has the right to ask the reason, why, and to have his question answered by himself, if he only takes the trouble.

So far, then, we see that in the study of this Raja-Yoga no faith or belief is necessary. Believe nothing until you find it out for yourself; that is what it teaches us. Truth requires no prop to make it stand. Do you mean to say that the facts of our awakened state require any dreams or imaginings to prove them? Certainly not. This study of Raja-Yoga takes a long time and constant practice. A part of this practice is physical, but in the main it is mental. As we proceed we shall find how intimately the mind is connected with the body. If we believe that the mind is simply a finer part of the body, and that mind acts upon the body, then it stands to reason that the body must react upon the mind. If the body is sick, the mind becomes sick also. If the body is healthy, the mind remains healthy and strong. When one is angry, the mind becomes disturbed. Similarly when the mind is disturbed, the body also becomes disturbed. With the majority of mankind the mind is greatly under the control of the body, their mind being very little developed. The vast mass of humanity is very little removed from the animals. Not only so, but in many instances, the power of control in them is little higher than that of the lower animals. We have very little command of our minds. Therefore to bring that command about, to get that control over body and mind, we must take certain physical helps. When the body is sufficiently controlled, we can attempt the manipulation of the mind. By manipulating the mind, we shall be able to bring it under our control, make it work as we like, and compel it to concentrate its powers as we desire.

According to the Raja-Yogi, the external world is but the gross form of the internal, or subtle. The finer is always the cause, the grosser the effect. So the external world is the effect, the internal the cause. In the same way external forces are simply the grosser parts, of which the internal forces are the finer. The man who has discovered and learned how to manipulate the internal forces will get the whole of nature under his control. The Yogi proposes to himself no less a task than to master the whole universe, to control the whole of nature. He wants to arrive at the point where what we call "nature's laws" will have no influence over him, where he will be able to get beyond them all. He will be master of the whole of nature, internal and external. The progress and civilisation of the human race simply mean controlling this nature.

Different races take to different processes of controlling nature. Just as in the same society some individuals want to control the external nature, and others the internal, so, among races, some want to control the external nature, and others the internal. Some say that by controlling internal nature we control everything. Others that by controlling external nature we control everything. Carried to the extreme both are right, because in nature there is no such division as internal or external. These are fictitious limitations that never existed. The externalists and the internalists are destined to meet at the same point, when both reach the extreme of their knowledge. Just as a physicist, when he pushes his knowledge to its limits, finds it melting away into metaphysics, so a metaphysician will find that what he calls mind and matter are but apparent distinctions, the reality being One.

The end and aim of all science is to find the unity, the One out of which the manifold is being manufactured, that One existing as many. Raja-Yoga proposes to start from the internal world, to study internal nature, and through that, control the whole — both internal and external. It is a very old attempt. India has been its special stronghold, but it was also attempted by other nations. In Western countries it was regarded as mysticism and people who wanted to practice it were either burned or killed as witches and sorcerers. In India, for various reasons, it fell into the hands of persons who destroyed ninety per cent of the knowledge, and tried to make a great secret of the remainder. In modern times many so-called teachers have arisen in the West worse than those of India, because the latter knew something, while these modern exponents know nothing.

Anything that is secret and mysterious in these systems of Yoga should be at once rejected. The best guide in life is strength. In religion, as in all other matters, discard everything that weakens you, have nothing to do with it. Mystery-mongering weakens the human brain. It has well-nigh destroyed Yoga — one of the grandest of sciences. From the time it was discovered, more than four thousand years ago, Yoga was perfectly delineated, formulated, and preached in India. It is a striking fact that the more modern the commentator the greater the mistakes he makes, while the more ancient the writer the more rational he is. Most of the modern writers talk of all sorts of mystery. Thus Yoga fell into the hands of a few persons who made it a secret, instead of letting the full blaze of daylight and reason fall upon it. They did so that they might have the powers to themselves. In the first place, there is no mystery in what I teach. What little I know I will tell you. So far as I can reason it out I will do so, but as to what I do not know I will simply tell you what the books say. It is wrong to believe blindly. You must exercise your own reason and judgment; you must practice, and see whether these things happen or not. Just as you would take up any other science, exactly in the same manner you should take up this science for study. There is neither mystery nor danger in it. So far as it is true, it ought to be preached in the public streets, in broad daylight. Any attempt to mystify these things is productive of great danger.

Before proceeding further, I will tell you a little of the Sankhya philosophy, upon which the whole of Raja-Yoga is based. According to the Sankhya philosophy, the genesis of perception is as follows: the affections of external objects are carried by the outer instruments to their respective brain centres or organs, the organs carry the affections to the mind, the mind to the determinative faculty, from this the Purusha (the soul) receives them, when perception results. Next he gives the order back, as it were, to the motor centres to do the needful. With the exception of the Purusha all of these are material, but the mind is much finer matter than the external instruments. That material of which the mind is composed goes also to form the subtle matter called the Tanmatras. These become gross and make the external matter. That is the psychology of the Sankhya. So that between the intellect and the grosser matter outside there is only a difference in degree. The Purusha is the only thing which is immaterial. The mind is an instrument, as it were, in the hands of the soul, through which the soul catches external objects. The mind is constantly changing and vacillating, and can, when perfected, either attach itself to several organs, to one, or to none. For instance, if I hear the clock with great attention, I will not, perhaps, see anything although my eyes may be open, showing that the mind was not attached to the seeing organ, while it was to the hearing organ. But the perfected mind can be attached to all the organs simultaneously. It has the reflexive power of looking back into its own depths. This reflexive power is what the Yogi wants to attain; by concentrating the powers of the mind, and turning them inward, he seeks to know what is happening inside. There is in this no question of mere belief; it is the analysis arrived at by certain philosophers. Modern physiologists tell us that the eyes are not the organ of vision, but that the organ is in one of the nerve centres of the brain, and so with all the senses; they also tell us that these centres are formed of the same material as the brain itself. The Sankhyas also tell us the same thing The former is a statement on the physical side, and the latter on the psychological side; yet both are the same. Our field of research lies beyond this. The Yogi proposes to attain that fine state of perception in which he can perceive all the different mental states. There must be mental perception of all of them. One can perceive how the sensation is travelling, how the mind is receiving it, how it is going to the determinative faculty, and how this gives it to the Purusha. As each science requires certain preparations and has its own method, which must be followed before it could be understood, even so in Raja-Yoga.

Certain regulations as to food are necessary; we must use that food which brings us the purest mind. If you go into a menagerie, you will find this demonstrated at once. You see the elephants, huge animals, but calm and gentle; and if you go towards the cages of the lions and tigers, you find them restless, showing how much difference has been made by food. All the forces that are working in this body have been produced out of food; we see that every day. If you begin to fast, first your body will get weak, the physical forces will suffer; then after a few days, the mental forces will suffer also. First, memory will fail. Then comes a point, when you are not able to think, much less to pursue any course of reasoning. We have, therefore, to take care what sort of food we eat at the beginning, and when we have got strength enough, when our practice is well advanced, we need not be so careful in this respect. While the plant is growing it must be hedged round, lest it be injured; but when it becomes a tree, the hedges are taken away. It is strong enough to withstand all assaults

A Yogi must avoid the two extremes of luxury and austerity. He must not fast, nor torture his flesh. He who does so, says the Gita, cannot be a Yogi: He who fasts, he who keeps awake, he who sleeps much, he who works too much, he who does no work, none of these can be a Yogi (Gita, VI, 16).

THE ESSENCE OF RAJA YOGA

The fire of Yoga burns the cage of sin that is around a man. Knowledge becomes purified and Nirvana is directly obtained. From Yoga comes knowledge; knowledge again helps the Yogi. He who combines in himself both Yoga and knowledge, with him the Lord is pleased. Those that practice Mahayoga, either once a day, or twice a day, or thrice, or always, know them to be gods. Yoga is divided into two parts. One is called Abhava, and the other, Mahayoga. Where one's self is meditated upon as zero, and bereft of quality, that is called Abhava. That in which one sees the self as full of bliss and bereft of all impurities, and one with God, is called Mahayoga. The Yogi, by each one, realises his Self. The other Yogas that we read and hear of, do not deserve to be ranked with the excellent Mahayoga in which the Yogi finds himself and the whole universe as God. This is the highest of all Yogas. Yama, Niyama, Asana, Pranayama, Pratyahara, Dharana, Dhyana, and Samadhi are the steps in Raja-Yoga, of which non-injury, truthfulness, non-covetousness, chastity, not receiving anything from another are called Yama.

This purifies the mind, the Chitta. Never producing pain by thought, word, and deed, in any living being, is what is called Ahimsa, non-injury. There is no virtue higher than non-injury. There is no happiness higher than what a man obtains by this attitude of non-offensiveness, to all creation. By truth we attain fruits of work.

Through truth everything is attained. In truth everything is established. Relating facts as they are — this is truth. Not taking others' goods by stealth or by force, is called Asteya, non-covetousness. Chastity in thought, word, and deed, always, and in all conditions, is what is called Brahmacharya. Not receiving any present from anybody, even when one is suffering terribly, is what is called Aparigraha. The idea is, when a man receives a gift from another, his heart becomes impure, he becomes low, he loses his independence, he becomes bound and attached. The following are helps to success in Yoga and are called Niyama or regular habits and observances; Tapas, austerity; Svadhyaya, study; Santosha, contentment; Shaucha, purity; Ishvara-pranidhana, worshipping God.

Fasting, or in other ways controlling the body, is called physical Tapas. Repeating the Vedas and other Mantras, by which the Sattva material in the body is purified, is called study, Svadhyaya. There are three sorts of repetitions of these Mantras. One is called the verbal, another semi-verbal, and the third mental.

The verbal or audible is the lowest, and the inaudible is the highest of all. The repetition which is loud is the verbal; the next one is where only the lips move, but no sound is heard. The inaudible repetition of the Mantra, accompanied with the thinking of its meaning, is called the "mental repetition," and is the highest.

The sages have said that there are two sorts of purification, external and internal. The purification of the body by water, earth, or other materials is the external purification, as bathing etc. Purification of the mind by truth, and by all the other virtues, is what is called internal purification. Both are necessary. It is not sufficient that a man should be internally pure and externally dirty. When both are not attainable the internal purity is the better, but no one will be a Yogi until he has both. Worship of God is by praise, by thought, by devotion.

We have spoken about Yama and Niyama. The next is Asana (posture). The only thing to understand about it is leaving the body free, holding the chest, shoulders, and head straight. Then comes Pranayama. Prana means the vital forces in one's own body, Ayama means controlling them. There are three sorts of Pranayama, the very simple, the middle, and the very high. Pranayama is divided into three parts: filling, restraining, and emptying. When you begin with twelve seconds it is the lowest Pranayama; when you begin with twenty-four seconds it is the middle Pranayama; that Pranayama is the best which begins with thirty-six seconds.

In the lowest kind of Pranayama there is perspiration, in the medium kind, quivering of the body, and in the highest Pranayama levitation of the body and influx of great bliss. There is a Mantra called the Gayatri. It is a very holy verse of the Vedas. "We meditate on the glory of that Being who has produced this universe; may He enlighten our minds."

Om is joined to it at the beginning and the end. In one Pranayama repeat three Gayatris. In all books they speak of Pranayama being divided into Rechaka (rejecting or exhaling), Puraka (inhaling), and Kurnbhaka (restraining, stationary). The Indriyas, the organs of the senses, are acting outwards and coming in contact with external objects. Bringing them under the control of the will is what is called Pratyahara or gathering towards oneself.

Fixing the mind on the lotus of the heart, or on the centre of the head, is what is called Dharana. Limited to one spot, making that spot the base, a particular kind of mental waves rises; these are not swallowed up by other kinds of waves, but by degrees become prominent, while all the others recede and finally disappear. Next the multiplicity of these waves gives place to unity and one wave only is left in the mind. This is Dhyana, meditation. When no basis is necessary, when the whole of the mind has become one wave, one-formedness, it is called Samadhi. Bereft of all help from places and centres, only the meaning of the thought is present. If the mind can be fixed on the centre for twelve seconds it will be a Dharana, twelve such Dharanas will be a Dhyana, and twelve such

Dhyanas will be a Samadhi. Where there is fire, or in water or on ground which is strewn with dry leaves, where there are many ant-hills, where there are wild animals, or danger, where four streets meet, where there is too much noise, where there are many wicked persons, Yoga must not be practiced.

This applies more particularly to India. Do not practice when the body feels very lazy or ill, or when the mind is very miserable and sorrowful. Go to a place which is well hidden, and where people do not come to disturb you. Do not choose dirty places. Rather choose beautiful scenery, or a room in your own house which is beautiful. When you practice, first salute all the ancient Yogis, and your own Guru, and God, and then begin.

Dhyana is spoken of, and a few examples are given of what to meditate upon. Sit straight, and look at the tip of your nose. Later on we shall come to know how that concentrates the mind, how by controlling the two optic nerves one advances a long way towards the control of the arc of reaction, and so to the control of the will. Here are a few specimens of meditation. Imagine a lotus upon the top of the head, several inches up, with virtue as its centre, and knowledge as its stalk. The eight petals of the lotus are the eight powers of the Yogi.

Inside, the stamens and pistils are renunciation. If the Yogi refuses the external powers he will come to salvation. So the eight petals of the lotus are the eight powers, but the internal stamens and pistils are extreme renunciation, the renunciation of all these powers. Inside of that lotus think of the Golden One, the Almighty, the Intangible, He whose name is Om, the Inexpressible, surrounded with effulgent light. Meditate on that.

Another meditation is given. Think of a space in your heart, and in the midst of that space think that a flame is burning. Think of that flame as your own soul and inside the flame is another effulgent light, and that is the Soul of your soul, God. Meditate upon that in the heart. Chastity, non-injury, forgiving even the greatest enemy, truth, faith in the

Lord, these are all different Vrittis. Be not afraid if you are not perfect in all of these; work, they will come. He who has given up all attachment, all fear, and all anger, he whose whole soul has gone unto the Lord, he who has taken refuge in the Lord, whose heart has become purified, with whatsoever desire he comes to the Lord, He will grant that to him. Therefore worship Him through knowledge, love, or renunciation.

"He who hates none, who is the friend of all, who is merciful to all, who has nothing of his own, who is free from egoism, who is even-minded in pain and pleasure, who is forbearing, who is always satisfied, who works always in Yoga, whose self has become controlled, whose will is firm, whose mind and intellect are given up unto Me, such a one is My beloved Bhakta. From whom comes no disturbance, who cannot be disturbed by others, who is free from joy, anger, fear, and anxiety, such a one is My beloved. He who does not depend on anything, who is pure and active, who does not care whether good comes or evil, and never becomes miserable, who has given up all efforts for himself; who is the same in praise or in blame, with a silent, thoughtful mind, blessed with what little comes in his way, homeless, for the whole world is his home, and who is steady in his ideas, such a one is My beloved Bhakta." Such alone become Yogis. There was a great god-sage called Narada.

Just as there are sages among mankind, great Yogis, so there are great Yogis among the gods. Narada was a good Yogi, and very great. He travelled everywhere. One day he was passing through a forest, and saw a man who had been meditating until the white ants had built a huge mound round his body — so long had he been sitting in that position. He said to Narada, "Where are you going?" Narada replied, "I am going to heaven." "Then ask God when He will be merciful to me; when I shall attain freedom." Further on Narada saw another man. He was jumping about, singing, dancing, and said, "Oh, Narada, where are you going?" His voice and his gestures were wild. Narada said, "I am going to heaven."

"Then, ask when I shall be free." Narada went on. In the course of time he came again by the same road, and there was the man who had been meditating with the ant-hill round him. He said, "Oh, Narada, did you ask the Lord about me?" "Oh, yes." "What did He say?" "The Lord told me that you would attain freedom in four more births." Then the man began to weep and wail, and said, "I have meditated until an ant-hill has grown around me, and I have four more births yet!" Narada went to the other man. "Did you ask my question?" "Oh, yes. Do you see this tamarind tree? I have to tell you that as many leaves as there are on that tree, so many times, you shall be born, and then you shall attain freedom." The man began to dance for joy, and said, "I shall have freedom after such a short time!" A voice came, "My child, you will have freedom this minute." That was the reward for his perseverance. He was ready to work through all those births, nothing discouraged him. But the first man felt that even four more births were too long. Only perseverance, like that of the man who was willing to wait aeons brings about the highest result.

DHARANA ON RAJA YOGA

The next step is called Pratyahara. What is this? You know how perceptions come. First of all there are the external instruments, then the internal organs acting in the body through the brain centres, and there is the mind. When these come together and attach themselves to some external object, then we perceive it. At the same time it is a very difficult thing to concentrate the mind and attach it to one organ only; the mind is a slave.

We hear "Be good," and "Be good," and "Be good," taught all over the world. There is hardly a child, born in any country in the world, who has not been told, "Do not steal," "Do not tell a lie," but nobody tells the child how he can help doing them. Talking will not help him. Why should he not become a thief? We do not teach him how not to steal; we simply tell him, "Do not steal." Only when we teach him to control his mind do we really help him. All actions, internal and external, occur when the mind joins itself to certain centres, called the organs. Willingly or unwillingly it is drawn to join itself to the centres, and that is why people do foolish deeds and feel miserable, which, if the mind were under control, they would not do. What would be the result of controlling the mind? It then would not join itself to the centres of perception, and, naturally, feeling and willing would be under control. It is clear so far. Is it possible? It is perfectly possible. You see it in modern times; the faith-healers teach people to deny misery and pain and evil. Their philosophy is rather roundabout, but it is a part of Yoga upon which they have somehow stumbled. Where they succeed in making a person throw off suffering by denying it, they really use a part of Pratyahara, as they make the mind of the person strong enough to ignore the senses. The hypnotists in a similar manner, by their suggestion, excite in the patient a sort of morbid Pratyahara for the time being. The so-called hypnotic suggestion can only act upon a weak mind. And until the operator, by means of fixed gaze or otherwise, has succeeded in putting the mind of the subject in a sort of passive, morbid condition, his suggestions never work.

Now the control of the centres which is established in a hypnotic patient or the patient of faith-healing, by the operator, for a time, is reprehensible, because it leads to ultimate ruin. It is not really controlling the brain centres by the power of one's own will, but is, as it were, stunning the patient's mind for a time by sudden blows which another's will delivers to it. It is not checking by means of reins and muscular strength the mad career of a fiery team, but rather by asking another to deliver heavy blows on the heads of the horses, to stun them for a time into gentleness. At each one of these processes the man operated upon loses a part of his mental energies, till at last, the mind, instead of gaining the power of perfect control, becomes a shapeless, powerless mass, and the only goal of the patient is the lunatic asylum.

Every attempt at control which is not voluntary, not with the controller's own mind, is not only disastrous, but it defeats the end. The goal of each soul is freedom, mastery — freedom from the slavery of matter and thought, mastery of external and internal nature. Instead of leading towards that, every will-current from another, in whatever form it comes, either as direct control of organs, or as forcing to control them while under a morbid condition, only rivets one link more to the already existing heavy chain of bondage of past thoughts, past superstitions. Therefore, beware how you allow yourselves to be acted upon by others. Beware how you unknowingly bring another to ruin. True, some succeed in doing good to many for a time, by giving a new trend to their propensities, but at the same time, they bring ruin to millions by the unconscious suggestions they throw around, rousing in men and women that morbid, passive, hypnotic condition which makes them almost soulless at last. Whosoever, therefore, asks any one to believe blindly, or drags people behind him by the controlling power of his superior will, does an injury to humanity, though he may not intend it. Therefore use your own minds, control body and mind yourselves, remember that until you are a diseased person, no extraneous will can work upon you; avoid everyone, however great and good he may be, who asks you to believe blindly. All over the world there have been dancing and jumping and howling sects, who spread like infection when they begin to sing and dance and preach; they also are a sort of hypnotists. They exercise a singular control for the time being over sensitive persons, alas! often, in the long run, to degenerate whole races. Ay, it is healthier for the individual or the race to remain wicked than be made apparently good by such morbid extraneous control. One's heart sinks to think of the amount of injury done to humanity by such irresponsible yet well-meaning religious fanatics. They little know that the minds which attain to sudden spiritual upheaval under their suggestions, with music and prayers, are simply making themselves passive, morbid, and powerless, and opening themselves to any other suggestion, be it ever so evil. Little do these ignorant, deluded persons dream that whilst they are congratulating themselves upon their miraculous power to transform human hearts, which power they think was poured upon them by some Being above the clouds, they are sowing the seeds of future decay, of crime, of lunacy, and of death. Therefore, beware of everything that takes away your freedom. Know that it is dangerous, and avoid it by all the means in your power.

He who has succeeded in attaching or detaching his mind to or from the centres at will has succeeded in Pratyahara, which means, "gathering towards," checking the outgoing powers of the mind, freeing it from the thraldom of the senses. When we can do this, we shall really possess character; then alone we shall have taken a long step towards freedom; before that we are mere machines. How hard it is to control the mind! Well has it been compared to the maddened monkey. There was a monkey, restless by his own nature, as all monkeys are. As if that were not enough some one made him drink freely of wine, so that he became still more restless. Then a scorpion stung him. When a man is stung by a scorpion, he jumps about for a whole day; so the poor monkey found his condition worse than ever. To complete his misery a demon entered into him. What language can describe the uncontrollable restlessness of that monkey? The human mind is like that monkey, incessantly active by its own nature; then it becomes drunk with the wine of desire, thus increasing its turbulence. After desire takes possession comes the sting of the scorpion of jealousy at the success of others, and last of all the demon of pride enters the mind, making it think itself of all importance. How hard to control such a mind!

The first lesson, then, is to sit for some time and let the mind run on. The mind is bubbling up all the time. It is like that monkey jumping about. Let the monkey jump as much as he can; you simply wait and watch. Knowledge is power, says the proverb, and that is true. Until you know what the mind is doing you cannot control it. Give it the rein; many hideous thoughts may come into it; you will be astonished that it was possible for you to think such thoughts. But you will find that each day the mind's vagaries are becoming less and less violent, that each day it is becoming calmer. In the first few months you will find that the mind will have a great many thoughts, later you will find that they have somewhat decreased, and in a few more months they will be fewer and fewer, until at last the mind will be under perfect control; but we must patiently practice every day. As soon as the steam is turned on, the engine must run; as soon as things are before us we must perceive; so a man, to prove that he is not a machine, must demonstrate that he is under the control of nothing. This controlling of the mind, and not allowing it to join itself to the centres, is Pratyahara. How is this practised? It is a tremendous work, not to be done in a day. Only after a patient, continuous struggle for years can we succeed. After you have practised Pratyahara for a time, take the next step, the Dharana, holding the mind to certain points.

What is meant by holding the mind to certain points? Forcing the mind to feel certain parts of the body to the exclusion of others. For instance, try to feel only the hand, to the exclusion of other parts of the body. When the Chitta, or mind-stuff, is confined and limited to a certain place it is Dharana. This Dharana is of various sorts, and along with it, it is better to have a little play of the imagination. For instance, the mind should be made to think of one point in the heart. That is very difficult; an easier way is to imagine a lotus there. That lotus is full of light, effulgent light. Put the mind there. Or think of the lotus in the brain as full of light, or of the different centres in the Sushumna mentioned before.

The Yogi must always practice. He should try to live alone; the companionship of different sorts of people distracts the mind; he should not speak much, because to speak distracts the mind; not work much, because too much work distracts the mind; the mind cannot be controlled after a whole day's hard work. One observing the above rules becomes a Yogi. Such is the power of Yoga that even the least of it will bring a great amount of benefit. It will not hurt anyone, but will benefit everyone. First of all, it will tone down nervous excitement, bring calmness, enable us to see things more clearly. The temperament will be better, and the health will be better. Sound health will be one of the first signs, and a beautiful voice. Defects in the voice will be changed. This will be among the first of the many effects that will come. Those who practise hard will get many other signs. Sometimes there will be sounds, as a peal of bells heard at a distance, commingling, and falling on the ear as one continuous sound. Sometimes things will be seen, little specks of light floating and becoming bigger and bigger; and when these things come, know that you are progressing fast. Those who want to be Yogis, and practice hard, must take care of their diet at first.

But for those who want only a little practice for everyday business sort of life, let them not eat too much; otherwise they may eat whatever they please. For those who want to make rapid progress, and to practice hard, a strict diet is absolutely necessary. They will find it advantageous to live only on milk and cereals for some months. As the organisation becomes finer and finer, it will be found in the beginning that the least irregularity throws one out of balance. One bit of food more or less will disturb the whole system, until one gets perfect control, and then one will be able to eat whatever one likes.

When one begins to concentrate, the dropping of a pin will seem like a thunderbolt going through the brain. As the organs get finer, the perceptions get finer. These are the stages through which we have to pass, and all those who persevere will succeed. Give up all argumentation and other distractions. Is there anything in dry intellectual jargon? It only throws the mind off its balance and disturbs it. Things of subtler planes have to be realised. Will talking do that? So give up all vain talk. Read only those books which have been written by persons who have had realisation.

Be like the pearl oyster. There is a pretty Indian fable to the effect that if it rains when the star Svati is in the ascendant, and a drop of rain falls into an oyster, that drop becomes a pearl. The oysters know this, so they come to the surface when that star shines, and wait to catch the precious raindrop.

When a drop falls into them, quickly the oysters close their shells and dive down to the bottom of the sea, there to patiently develop the drop into the pearl. We should be like that. First hear, then understand, and then, leaving all distractions, shut your minds to outside influences, and devote yourselves to developing the truth within you.

There is the danger of frittering away your energies by taking up an idea only for its novelty, and then giving it up for another that is newer. Take one thing up and do it, and see the end of it, and before you have seen the end, do not give it up. He who can become mad with an idea, he alone sees light. Those that only take a nibble here and a nibble there will never attain anything. They may titillate their nerves for a moment, but there it will end. They will be slaves in the hands of nature, and will never get beyond the senses. Those who really want to be Yogis must give up, once for all, this nibbling at things.

Take up one idea. Make that one idea your life — think of it, dream of it, live on that idea. Let the brain, muscles, nerves, every part of your body, be full of that idea, and just leave every other idea alone. This is the way to success, and this is the way great spiritual giants are produced. Others are mere talking machines. If we really want to be blessed, and make others blessed, we must go deeper. The first step is not to disturb the mind, not to associate with persons whose ideas are disturbing. All of you know that certain persons, certain places, certain foods, repel you. Avoid them; and those who want to go to the highest, must avoid all company, good or bad. Practise hard; whether you live or die does not matter. You have to plunge in and work, without thinking of the result. If you are brave enough, in six months you will be a perfect Yogi. But those who take up just a bit of it and a little of everything else make no progress.

It is of no use simply to take a course of lessons. To those who are full of Tamas, ignorant and dull — those whose minds never get fixed on any idea, who only crave for something to amuse them — religion and philosophy are simply objects of entertainment. These are the unpersevering. They hear a talk, think it very nice, and then go home and forget all about it. To succeed, you must have tremendous perseverance, tremendous will. "I will drink the ocean," says the persevering soul, "at my will mountains will crumble up." Have that sort of energy, that sort of will, work hard, and you will reach the goal.

STEPS IN RAJA-YOGA

Raja-Yoga is divided into eight steps. The first is Yama — non-killing, truthfulness, non-stealing, continence, and non-receiving of any gifts. Next is Niyama — cleanliness, contentment, austerity, study, and self-surrender to God. Then comes Asana, or posture; Pranayama, or control of Prana; Pratyahara, or restraint of the senses from their objects; Dharana, or fixing the mind on a spot; Dhyana, or meditation; and Samadhi, or superconsciousness. The Yama and Niyama, as we see, are moral trainings; without these as the basis no practice of Yoga will succeed. As these two become established, the Yogi will begin to realise the fruits of his practice; without these it will never bear fruit. A Yogi must not think of injuring anyone, by thought, word, or deed. Mercy shall not be for men alone, but shall go beyond, and embrace the whole world.

The next step is Asana, posture. A series of exercises, physical and mental, is to be gone through every day, until certain higher states are reached. Therefore it is quite necessary that we should find a posture in which we can remain long. That posture which is the easiest for one should be the one chosen. For thinking, a certain posture may be very easy for one man, while to another it may be very difficult. We will find later on that during the study of these psychological matters a good deal of activity goes on in the body. Nerve currents will have to be displaced and given a new channel. New sorts of vibrations will begin, the whole constitution will be remodelled as it were. But the main part of the activity will lie along the spinal column, so that the one thing necessary for the posture is to hold the spinal column free, sitting erect, holding the three parts — the chest, neck, and head — in a straight line. Let the whole weight of the body be supported by the ribs, and then you have an easy natural postures with the spine straight. You will easily see that you cannot think very high thoughts with the chest in. This portion of the Yoga is a little similar to the Hatha-Yoga which deals entirely with the physical body, its aim being to make the physical body very strong. We have nothing to do with it here, because its practices are very difficult, and cannot be learned in a day, and, after all, do not lead to much spiritual growth. Many of these practices you will find in Delsarte and other teachers, such as placing the body in different postures, but the object in these is physical, not psychological. There is not one muscle in the body over which a man cannot establish a perfect control. The heart can be made to stop or go on at his bidding, and each part of the organism can be similarly controlled.

The result of this branch of Yoga is to make men live long; health is the chief idea, the one goal of the Hatha-Yogi. He is determined not to fall sick, and he never does. He lives long; a hundred years is nothing to him; he is quite young and fresh when he is 150, without one hair turned grey. But that is all. A banyan tree lives sometimes 5000 years, but it is a banyan tree and nothing more. So, if a man lives long, he is only a healthy animal. One or two ordinary lessons of the Hatha-Yogis are very useful. For instance, some of you will find it a good thing for headaches to drink cold water through the nose as soon as you get up in the morning; the whole day your brain will be nice and cool, and you will never catch cold. It is very easy to do; put your nose into the water, draw it up through the nostrils and make a pump action in the throat.

After one has learned to have a firm erect seat, one has to perform, according to certain schools, a practice called the purifying of the nerves. This part has been rejected by some as not belonging to Raja-Yoga, but as so great an authority as the commentator Shankaracharya advises it, I think fit that it should be mentioned, and I will quote his own directions from his commentary on the Shvetashvatara Upanishad: "The mind whose dross has been cleared away by Pranayama, becomes fixed in Brahman; therefore Pranayama is declared. First the nerves are to be purified, then comes the power to practice Pranayama. Stopping the right nostril with the thumb, through the left nostril fill in air, according to capacity; then, without any interval, throw the air out through the right nostril, closing the left one. Again inhaling through the right nostril eject through the left, according to capacity; practicing this three or five times at four hours of the day, before dawn, during midday, in the evening, and at midnight, in fifteen days or a month purity of the nerves is attained; then begins Pranayama."

Practice is absolutely necessary. You may sit down and listen to me by the hour every day, but if you do not practice, you will not get one step further. It all depends on practice. We never understand these things until we experience them. We will have to see and feel them for ourselves. Simply listening to explanations and theories will not do. There are several obstructions to practice. The first obstruction is an unhealthy body: if the body is not in a fit state, the practice will be obstructed. Therefore we have to keep the body in good health; we have to take care of what we eat and drink, and what we do. Always use a mental effort, what is usually called "Christian Science," to keep the body strong. That is all — nothing further of the body. We must not forget that health is only a means to an end. If health were the end, we would be like animals; animals rarely become unhealthy.

The second obstruction is doubt; we always feel doubtful about things we do not see. Man cannot live upon words, however he may try. So, doubt comes to us as to whether there is any truth in these things or not; even the best of us will doubt sometimes: With practice, within a few days, a little glimpse will come, enough to give one encouragement and hope. As a certain commentator on Yoga philosophy says, "When one proof is obtained, however little that may be, it will give us faith in the whole teaching of Yoga." For instance, after the first few months of practice, you will begin to find you can read another's thoughts; they will come to you in picture form. Perhaps you will hear something happening at a long distance, when you concentrate your mind with a wish to hear. These glimpses will come, by little bits at first, but enough to give you faith, and strength, and hope. For instance, if you concentrate your thoughts on the tip of your nose, in a few days you will begin to smell most beautiful fragrance, which will be enough to show you that there are certain mental perceptions that can be made obvious without the contact of physical objects. But we must always remember that these are only the means; the aim, the end, the goal, of all this training is liberation of the soul. Absolute control of nature, and nothing short of it, must be the goal. We must be the masters, and not the slaves of nature; neither body nor mind must be our master, nor must we forget that the body is mine, and not I the body's.

A god and a demon went to learn about the Self from a great sage. They studied with him for a long time. At last the sage told them, "You yourselves are the Being you are seeking." Both of them thought that their bodies were the Self. They went back to their people quite satisfied and said, "We have learned everything that was to be learned; eat, drink, and be merry; we are the Self; there is nothing beyond us." The nature of the demon was ignorant, clouded; so he never inquired any further, but was perfectly contented with the idea that he was God, that by the Self was meant the body. The god had a purer nature. He at first committed the mistake of thinking: I, this body, am Brahman: so keep it strong and in health, and well dressed, and give it all sorts of enjoyments. But, in a few days, he found out that could not be the meaning of the sage, their master; there must be something higher. So he came back and said, "Sir, did you teach me that this body was the Self? If so, I see all bodies die; the Self cannot die." The sage said, "Find it out; thou art That." Then the god thought that the vital forces which work the body were what the sage meant. But after a time, he found that if he ate, these vital forces remained strong, but, if he starved, they became weak. The god then went back to the sage and said, "Sir, do you mean that the vital forces are the Self ?" The sage said, "Find out for yourself; thou art That." The god returned home once more, thinking that it was the mind, perhaps, that was the Self. But in a short while he saw that thoughts were so various, now good, again bad; the mind was too changeable to be the Self. He went back to the sage and said, "Sir, I do not think that the mind is the Self; did you mean that?" "No," replied the sage, "thou art That; find out for yourself." The god went home, and at last found that he was the Self, beyond all thought, one without birth or death, whom the sword cannot pierce or the fire burn, whom the air cannot dry or the water melt, the beginningless and endless, the immovable, the intangible, the omniscient, the omnipotent Being; that It was neither the body nor the mind, but beyond them all. So he was satisfied; but the poor demon did not get the truth, owing to his fondness for the body.

This world has a good many of these demoniac natures, but there are some gods too. If one proposes to teach any science to increase the power of sense-enjoyment, one finds multitudes ready for it. If one undertakes to show the supreme goal, one finds few to listen to him. Very few have the power to grasp the higher, fewer still the patience to attain to it. But there are a few also who know that even if the body can be made to live for a thousand years, the result in the end will be the same. When the forces that hold it together go away, the body must fall. No man was ever born who could stop his body one moment from changing. Body is the name of a series of changes. "As in a river the masses of water are changing before you every moment, and new masses are coming, yet taking similar form, so is it with this body." Yet the body must be kept strong and healthy. It is the best instrument we have.

This human body is the greatest body in the universe, and a human being the greatest being. Man is higher than all animals, than all angels; none is greater than man. Even the Devas (gods) will have to come down again and attain to salvation through a human body. Man alone attains to perfection, not even the Devas. According to the Jews and Mohammedans, God created man after creating the angels and everything else, and after creating man He asked the angels to come and salute him, and all did so except Iblis; so God cursed him and he became Satan. Behind this allegory is the great truth that this human birth is the greatest birth we can have. The lower creation, the animal, is dull, and manufactured mostly out of Tamas. Animals cannot have any high thoughts; nor can the angels, or Devas, attain to direct freedom without human birth. In human society, in the same way, too much wealth or too much poverty is a great impediment to the higher development of the soul. It is from the middle classes that the great ones of the world come. Here the forces are very equally adjusted and balanced.

Returning to our subject, we come next to Pranayarna, controlling the breathing. What has that to do with concentrating the powers of the mind? Breath is like the fly-wheel of this machine, the body. In a big engine you find the fly-wheel first moving, and that motion is conveyed to finer and finer machinery until the most delicate and finest mechanism in the machine is in motion. The breath is that fly-wheel, supplying and regulating the motive power to everything in this body.

There was once a minister to a great king. He fell into disgrace. The king, as a punishment, ordered him to be shut up in the top of a very high tower. This was done, and the minister was left there to perish. He had a faithful wife, however, who came to the tower at night and called to her husband at the top to know what she could do to help him. He told her to return to the tower the following night and bring with her a long rope, some stout twine, pack thread, silken thread, a beetle, and a little honey. Wondering much, the good wife obeyed her husband, and brought him the desired articles. The husband directed her to attach the silken thread firmly to the beetle, then to smear its horns with a drop of honey, and to set it free on the wall of the tower, with its head pointing upwards. She obeyed all these instructions, and the beetle started on its long journey. Smelling the honey ahead it slowly crept onwards, in the hope of reaching the honey, until at last it reached the top of the tower, when the minister grasped the beetle, and got possession of the silken thread. He told his wife to tie the other end to the pack thread, and after he had drawn up the pack thread, he repeated the process with the stout twine, and lastly with the rope. Then the rest was easy. The minister descended from the tower by means of the rope, and made his escape. In this body of ours the breath motion is the "silken thread"; by laying hold of and learning to control it we grasp the pack thread of the nerve currents, and from these the stout twine of our thoughts, and lastly the rope of Prana, controlling which we reach freedom.

We do not know anything about our own bodies; we cannot know. At best we can take a dead body, and cut it in pieces, and there are some who can take a live animal and cut it in pieces in order to see what is inside the body. Still, that has nothing to do with our own bodies. We know very little about them. Why do we not? Because our attention is not discriminating enough to catch the very fine movements that are going on within. We can know of them only when the mind becomes more subtle and enters, as it were, deeper into the body. To get the subtle perception we have to begin with the grosser perceptions. We have to get hold of that which is setting the whole engine in motion. That is the Prana, the most obvious manifestation of which is the breath. Then, along with the breath, we shall slowly enter the body, which will enable us to find out about the subtle forces, the nerve currents that are moving all over the body. As soon as we perceive and learn to feel them, we shall begin to get control over them, and over the body. The mind is also set in motion: by these different nerve currents, so at last we shall reach the state of perfect control over the body and the mind, making both our servants. Knowledge is power. We have to get this power. So we must begin at the beginning, with Pranayama, restraining the Prana. This Pranayama is a long subject, and will take several lessons to illustrate it thoroughly. We shall take it part by part.

We shall gradually see the reasons for each exercise and what forces in the body are set in motion. All these things will come to us, but it requires constant practice, and the proof will come by practice. No amount of reasoning which I can give you will be proof to you, until you have demonstrated it for yourselves. As soon as you begin to feel these currents in motion all over you, doubts will vanish, but it requires hard practice every day. You must practice at least twice every day, and the best times are towards the morning and the evening. When night passes into day, and day into night, a state of relative calmness ensues. The early morning and the early evening are the two periods of calmness. Your body will have a like tendency to become calm at those times. We should take advantage of that natural condition and begin then to practice. Make it a rule not to eat until you have practiced; if you do this, the sheer force of hunger will break your laziness. In India they teach children never to eat until they have practiced or worshipped, and it becomes natural to them after a time; a boy will not feel hungry until he has bathed and practiced.

Those of you who can afford it will do better to have a room for this practice alone. Do not sleep in that room, it must be kept holy. You must not enter the room until you have bathed, and are perfectly clean in body and mind. Place flowers in that room always; they are the best surroundings for a Yogi;

also pictures that are pleasing. Burn incense morning and evening. Have no quarrelling, nor anger, nor unholy thought in that room. Only allow those persons to enter it who are of the same thought as you. Then gradually there will be an atmosphere of holiness in the room, so that when you are miserable, sorrowful, doubtful, or your mind is disturbed, the very fact of entering that room will make you calm. This was the idea of the temple and the church, and in some temples and churches you will find it even now, but in the majority of them the very idea has been lost. The idea is that by keeping holy vibrations there the place becomes and remains illumined. Those who cannot afford to have a room set apart can practice anywhere they like. Sit in a straight posture, and the first thing to do is to send a current of holy thought to all creation. Mentally repeat, "Let all beings be happy; let all beings be peaceful; let all beings be blissful." So do to the east, south, north and west. The more you do that the better you will feel yourself. You will find at last that the easiest way to make ourselves healthy is to see that others are healthy, and the easiest way to make ourselves happy is to see that others are happy. After doing that, those who believe in God should pray — not for money, not for health, nor for heaven; pray for knowledge and light; every other prayer is selfish. Then the next thing to do is to think of your own body, and see that it is strong and healthy; it is the best instrument you have. Think of it as being as strong as adamant, and that with the help of this body you will cross the ocean of life. Freedom is never to be reached by the weak. Throw away all weakness. Tell your body that it is strong, tell your mind that it is strong, and have unbounded faith and hope in yourself.

9

Hindu Philosophic Thought

The first group of religious ideas that we see coming up — I mean recognised religious ideas, and not the very low ideas, which do not deserve the name of religion — all include the idea of inspiration and revealed books and so forth. The first group of religious ideas starts with the idea of God. Here is the universe, and this universe is created by a certain Being. Everything that is in this universe has been created by Him. Along with that, at a later stage, comes the idea of soul — that there is this body, and something inside this body which is not the body. This is the most primitive idea of religion that we know. We can find a few followers of that in India, but it was given up very early.

The Indian religions take a peculiar start. It is only by strict analysis, and much calculation and conjecture, that we can ever think that that stage existed in Indian religions. The tangible state in which we find them is the next step, not the first one. At the earliest step the idea of creation is very peculiar, and it is that the whole universe is created out of zero, at the will of God; that all this universe did not exist, and out of this nothingness all this has come. In the next stage we find this conclusion is questioned. How can existence be produced out of nonexistence? At the first step in the Vedanta this question is asked. If this universe is existent it must have come out of something, because it was very easy to see that nothing comes out of nothing, anywhere. All work that is done by human hands requires materials. If a house is built, the material was existing before; if a boat is made the material existed before; if any implements are made, the materials were existing before. So the effect is produced. Naturally, therefore, the first idea that this world was created out of nothing was rejected, and some material out of which this world was created was wanted. The whole history of religion, in fact, is this search after that material.

Out of what has all this been produced? Apart from the question of the efficient cause, or God, apart from the question that God created the universe, the great question of all questions is: Out of what did He create it? All the philosophies are turning, as it were, on this question. One solution is that nature, God, and soul are eternal existences, as if three lines are running parallel eternally, of which nature and soul comprise what they call the dependent, and God the independent Reality. Every soul, like every particle of matter, is perfectly dependent on the will of God. Before going to the other steps we will take up the idea of soul, and then find that with all the Vedantic philosophers, there is one tremendous departure from all Western philosophy. All of them have a common psychology. Whatever their philosophy may have been, their psychology is the same in India, the old Sankhya psychology. According to this, perception occurs by the transmission of the vibrations which first come to the external sense-organs, from the external to the internal organs, from the internal organs to the mind, from the mind to the Buddhi, from the Buddhi or intellect, to something which is a unit, which they call the Atman. Coming to modern physiology, we know that it has found centres for all the different sensations. First it finds the lower centres, and then a higher grade of centres, and these two centres exactly correspond with the internal organs and the mind, but not one centre has been found which controls all the other centres. So physiology cannot tell what unifies all these centres. Where do the centres get united? The centres in the brain are all different. and there is not one centre which controls all the other centres; therefore, so far as it goes, the Indian psychology stands unchallenged upon this point. We must have this unification, something upon which the sensations will be reflected, to form a complete whole. Until there is that something, I cannot have any idea of you, or a picture, or anything else. If we had not that unifying something, we would only see, then after a while breathe, then hear, and so on, and while I heard a man talking I would not see him at all, because all the centres are different.

This body is made of particles which we call matter, and it is dull and insentient. So is what the Vedantists call the fine body. The fine body, according to them, is a material but transparent body, made of very fine particles, so fine that no microscope can see them. What is the use of that? It is the receptacle of the fine forces. Just as this gross body is the receptacle of the gross forces, so the fine body is the receptacle of the fine forces, which we call thought, in its various modifications. First is the body, which is gross matter, with gross force. Force cannot exist without matter. It must require some matter to exist, so the grosser forces work in the body; and those very forces become finer; the very force which is working in a gross form, works in a fine form, and becomes thought. There is no distinction between them, simply one is the gross and the other the fine manifestation of the same thing. Neither is there any distinction between this fine body and the gross body. The fine body is also material, only very fine matter; and just as this gross body is the instrument that works the gross forces, so the fine body is the instrument that works the fine forces. From where do all these forces come? According to Vedanta philosophy, there are two things in nature, one of which they call Akasha, which is the substance, infinitely fine, and the other they call Prana, which is the force. Whatever you see, or feel, or hear, as air, earth, or anything is material — the product of Akasha. It goes on and becomes finer and finer, or grosser and grosser, changing under the action of Prana. Like Akasha, Prana is omnipresent, and interpenetrating everything. Akasha is like the water, and everything else in the universe is like blocks of ice, made out of that water, and floating in the water, and Prana is the power that changes this Akasha into all these various forms. The gross body is the instrument made out of Akasha, for the manifestation of Prana in gross forms, as muscular motion, or walking, sitting, talking, and so forth. That fine body is also made of Akasha, a very fine form of Akasha, for the manifestation of the same Prana in the finer form of thought. So, first there is this gross body. Beyond that is this fine body, and beyond that is the Jiva, the real man. Just as the nails can be pared off many times and yet are still part of our bodies, not different, so is our gross body related to the fine. It is not that a man has a fine and also a gross body; it is the one body only, the part which endures longer is the fine body, and that which dissolves sooner is the gross. Just as I can cut this nail any number of times, so, millions of times I can shed this gross body, but the fine body will remain. According to the dualists, this Jiva or the real man is very fine, minute.

So far we see that man is a being, who has first a gross body which dissolves very quickly, then a fine body which remains through aeons, and then a Jiva. This Jiva, according to the Vedanta philosophy, is eternal, just as God is eternal. Nature is also eternal, but changefully eternal. The material of nature — Prana and Akasha — is eternal, but it is changing into different forms eternally. But the Jiva is not manufactured either of Akasha or Prana; it is immaterial and, therefore, will remain for ever. It is not the result of any combination of Prana and Akasha, and whatever is not the result of combination, will never be destroyed, because destruction is going back to causes. The gross body is a compound of Akasha and Prana and, therefore, will be decomposed The fine body will also be decomposed, after a long time, but the Jiva is simple, and will never be destroyed. It was never born for the same reason. Nothing simple can be born. The same argument applies. That which is a compound only can be born. The whole of nature comprising millions and millions of souls is under the will of God. God is all-pervading, omniscient, formless, and He is working through nature day and night. The whole of it is under His control. He is the eternal Ruler. So say the dualists. Then the question comes: If God is the ruler of this universe, why did He create such a wicked universe, why must we suffer so much? They say, it is not God's fault. It is our fault that we suffer. Whatever we sow we reap. He did not do anything to punish us. Man is born poor, or blind, or some other way. What is the reason? He had done something before, he was born that way. The Jiva has been existing for all time, was never created. It has been doing all sorts of things all the time. Whatever we do reacts upon us. If we do good, we shall have happiness, and if evil, unhappiness. So the Jiva goes on enjoying and suffering, and doing all sorts of things.

What comes after death? All these Vedanta philosophers admit that this Jiva is by its own nature pure. But ignorance covers its real nature, they say. As by evil deeds it has covered itself with ignorance, so by good deeds it becomes conscious of its own nature again. Just as it is eternal, so its nature is pure. The nature of every being is pure.

When through good deeds all its sins and misdeeds have been washed away, then the Jiva becomes pure again, and when it becomes pure, it goes to what is called Devayana. Its organ of speech enters the mind. You cannot think without words. Wherever there is thought, there must be words. As words enter the mind, so the mind is resolved into the Prana, and the Prana into the Jiva. Then the Jiva gets quickly out of the body, and goes to the solar regions. This universe has sphere after sphere. This earth is the world sphere, in which are moons, suns, and stars. Beyond that here is the solar sphere, and beyond that another which they call the lunar sphere. Beyond that there is the sphere which they call the sphere of lightning, the electric sphere, and when the Jiva goes there, there comes another Jiva, already perfect, to receive it, and takes it to another world, the highest heaven, called the Brahmaloka, where the Jiva lives eternally, no more to be born or to die. It enjoys through eternity, and gets all sorts of powers, except the power of creation. There is only one ruler of the universe, and that is God. No one can become God; the dualists maintain that if you say you are God, it is a blasphemy. All powers except the creative come to the Jiva, and if it likes to have bodies, and work in different parts of the world, it can do so. If it orders all the gods to come before it, if it wants its forefathers to come, they all appear at its command. Such are its powers that it never feels any more pain, and if it wants, it can live in the Brahmaloka through all eternity. This is the highest man, who has attained the love of God, who has become perfectly unselfish, perfectly purified, who has given up all desires, and who does not want to do anything except worship and love God.

There are others that are not so high, who do good works, but want some reward. They say they will give so much to the poor, but want to go to heaven in return. When they die, what becomes of them? The speech enters the mind, the mind enters the Prana, the Prana enters the Jiva, and the Jiva gets out, and goes to the lunar sphere, where it has a very good time for a long period. There it enjoys happiness, so long as the effect of its good deeds endures. When the same is exhausted, it descends, and once again enters life on earth according to its desires. In the lunar sphere the Jiva becomes what we call a god, or what the Christians or Mohammedans call an angel. These gods are the names of certain positions; for instance, Indra, the king of the gods, is the name of a position; thousands of men get to that position. When a virtuous man who has performed the highest of Vedic rites dies, he becomes a king of the gods; by that time the old king has gone down again, and become man. Just as kings change here, so the gods, the Devas, also have to die. In heaven they will all die. The only deathless place is Brahrnaloka, where alone there is no birth and death. So the Jivas go to heaven, and have a overly good time, except now and then when the demons Give them chase. In our mythology it is said there are demons, who sometimes trouble the gods. In all mythologies, you read how these demons and the gods fought, and the demons sometimes conquered the gods, although many times, it seems, the demons did not do so many wicked things as the gods. In all mythologies, for instance, you find the Devas fond of women. So after their reward is finished, they fall down again, come through the clouds, "through the rains, and thus get into some grain or plant and find their way into the human body, when the grain. or plant is eaten by men. The father gives them the material out of which to get a fitting body. When the material suits them no longer, they have to manufacture other bodies. Now there are the very wicked fellows, who do, all sorts of diabolical things; they are born again as animals, and if they are very bad, they are born as very low animals, or become plants, or stones.

In the Deva form they make no Karma at all; only man makes Karma. Karma means work which will produce effect. When a man dies and becomes a Deva, he has only a period of pleasure, and during that time makes no fresh Karma; it is simply a reward for his past good Karma. When the good Karma is worked out, then the remaining Karma begins to take effect, and he comes dozen to earth. He becomes man again, and if he does very good works, and purifies himself, he goes to Brahmaloka and comes back no more. The animal is a state of sojourn for the Jiva evolving from lower forms. In course of time the animal becomes man. It is a significant fact that as the human population is increasing, the animal population is decreasing.

The animal souls are all becoming men. So many species of animals have become men already. Where else have they gone? In the Vedas, there is no mention of hell. But our Puranas, the later books of our scriptures, thought that no religion could be complete, unless hells were attached to it, and so they invented all sorts of hells. In some of these, men are sawed in half, and continually tortured, but do not die. They are continually feeling intense pain, but the books are merciful enough to say it is only for a period. Bad Karma is worked out in that state and then they come back on earth, and get another chance. So this human form is the great chance. It is called the Karma-body, in which we decide our fate. We are running in a huge circle, and this is the point in the circle which determines the future.

So this is considered the most important form that there is. Man is greater than the gods. So far with dualism, pure and simple. Next comes the higher Vedantic philosophy which says, that this cannot be. God is both the material and the efficient cause of this universe. If you say there is a God who is an infinite Being, and a soul which is also infinite, and a nature which is also infinite, you can go on multiplying infinites without limit which is simply absurd; you smash all logic. So God is both the material and the efficient cause of the universe; He projects this universe out of Himself. Then how is it that God has become these walls and this table, that God has become the pig, and the murderer, and all the evil things in the world? We say that God is pure. How can He become all these degenerate things? Our answer is: just as I am a soul and have a body, and in a sense, this body is not different from me, yet I, the real I, in fact, am not the body. For instance, I say, I am a child, a young man, or an old man, but my soul has not changed. It remains the same soul. Similarly, the whole universe, comprising all nature and an infinite number of souls, is, as it were, the infinite body of God. He is interpenetrating the whole of it. He alone is unchangeable, but nature changes, and soul changes. He is unaffected by changes in nature and soul. In what way does nature change? In its forms; it takes fresh forms. But the soul cannot change that way. The soul contracts and expands in knowledge. It contracts by evil deeds. Those deeds which contract the real natural knowledge and purity of the soul are called evil deeds. Those deeds, again, which bring out the natural glory of the soul, are called good deeds. All these souls were pure, but they have become contracted; through the mercy of God, and by doing good deeds, they will expand and recover their natural purity. Everyone has the same chance, and in the long run, must get out. But this universe will not cease, because it is eternal. This is the second theory. The first is called dualism. The second holds that there are God, soul, and nature, and soul and nature form the body of God, and, therefore, these three form one unit. It represents a higher stage of religious development and goes by the name of qualified monism. In dualism, the universe is conceived as a large machine set going by God while in qualified monism, it is conceived as an organism, interpenetrated by the Divine Self.

The last are the non-dualists. They raise the question also, that God must be both the material and the efficient cause of this universe. As such, God has become the whole of this universe and there is no going against it. And when these other people say that God is the soul, and the universe is the body, and the body is changing, but God is changeless, the non-dualists say, all this is nonsense. In that case what is the use of calling God the material cause of this universe? The material cause is the cause become effect; the effect is nothing but the cause in another form. Wherever you see an effect, it is the cause reproduced. If the universe is the effect, and God the cause, it must be the reproduction of God. If you say that the universe is the body of God, and that the body becomes contracted and fine and becomes the cause, and out of that the universe is evolved, the non-dualists say that it is God Himself who has become this universe. Now comes a very fine question. If this God has become this universe, you and all these things are God. Certainly. This book is God, everything is God. My body is God, and my mind is God, and my soul is God. Then why are there so many Jivas? Has God become divided into millions of Jivas? Does that one God turn into millions of Jivas?

Then how did it become so? How can that infinite power and substance, the one Being of the universe, become divided? It is impossible to divide infinity. How can that pure Being become this universe? If He has become the universe, He is changeful, and if He is changeful, He is part of nature, and whatever is nature and changeful is born and dies. If our God is changeful, He must die some day. Take note of that. Again, how much of God has become this universe ? If you say X (the unknown algebraical quantity), then God is God minus X now, and, therefore, not the same God as before this creation, because so much has become this universe.

So the non-dualists say, "This universe does not exist at all; it is all illusion. The whole of this universe, these Devas, gods, angels, and all the other beings born and dying, all this infinite number of souls coming up and going down, are all dreams." There is no Jiva at all. How can there be many? It is the one Infinity. As the one sun, reflected on various pieces of water, appears to be many, and millions of globules of water reflect so many millions of suns, and in each globule will be a perfect image of the sun, yet there is only one sun, so are all these Jivas but reflections in different minds. These different minds are like so many different globules, reflecting this one Being. God is being reflected in all these different Jivas. But a dream cannot be without a reality, and that reality is that one Infinite Existence. You, as body, mind, or soul, are a dream, but what you really are, is Existence, Knowledge, Bliss. You are the God of this universe. You are creating the whole universe and drawing it in. Thus says the Advaitist. So all these births and rebirths, coming and going are the figments of Maya. You are infinite. Where can you go? The sun, the moon, and the whole universe are but drops in your transcendent nature. How can you be born or die? I never was born, never will be born. I never had father or mother, friends or foes, for I am Existence, Knowledge, Bliss Absolute. I am He, I am He. So, what is the goal, according to this philosophy? That those who receive this knowledge are one with the universe. For them, all heavens and even Brahmaloka are destroyed, the whole dream vanishes, and they find themselves the eternal God of the universe. They attain their real individuality, with its infinite knowledge and bliss, and become free. Pleasures in little things cease. We are finding pleasure in this little body, in this little individuality.

How much greater the pleasure when this whole universe is my body! If there is pleasure in one body, how much more when all bodies are mine! Then is freedom attained. And this is called Advaita, the non-dualistic Vedanta philosophy. These are the three steps which Vedanta philosophy has taken, and we cannot go any further, because we cannot go beyond unity. When a science reaches a unity, it cannot by any manner of means go any further. You cannot go beyond this idea of the Absolute.

Advaita Philosophy

All people cannot take up this Advaita philosophy; it is hard. First of all, it is very hard to understand it intellectually. It requires the sharpest of intellects, a bold understanding. Secondly, it does not suit the vast majority of people. So there are these three steps. Begin with the first one. Then by thinking of that and understanding it, the second will open itself. Just as a race advances, so individuals have to advance. The steps which the human race has taken to reach to the highest pinnacles of religious thought, every individual will have to take. Only, while the human race took millions of years to reach from one step to another, individuals may live the whole life of the human race in a much shorter duration. But each one of us will have to go through these steps. Those of you who are non-dualists look back to the period of your lives when you were strong dualists. As soon as you think you are a body and a mind, you will have to take the whole of this dream. If you take one portion, you must take the whole. The man who says, here is this world, and there is no (Personal) God, is a fool; because if there is a world, there will have to be a cause, and that is what is called God. You cannot have an effect without knowing that there is a cause. God will only vanish when this world vanishes; then you will become God (Absolute), and this world will be no longer for you. So long as the dream that you are a body exists, you are bound to see yourself as being born and dying; but as soon as that dream vanishes, so will the dream vanish that you are being born and dying, and so will the other dream that there is a universe vanish. That very thing which we now see as the universe will appear to us as God (Absolute), and that very God who has so long been external will appear to be internal, as our own Self.

THE COMMON BASES OF HINDUISM

On his arrival at Lahore the Swamiji was accorded a grand reception by the leaders, both of the Arya Samaj and of the Sanatana Dharma Sabha. During his brief stay in Lahore, Swamiji delivered three lectures. The first of these was on "The Common Bases of Hinduism", the second on "Bhakti", and the third one was the famous lecture on "The Vedanta". On the first occasion he spoke as follows: This is the land which is held to be the holiest even in holy Aryavarta; this is the Brahmavarta of which our great Manu speaks. This is the land from whence arose that mighty aspiration after the Spirit, ay, which in times to come, as history shows, is to deluge the world. This is the land where, like its mighty rivers, spiritual aspirations have arisen and joined their strength, till they travelled over the length and breadth of the world and declared themselves with a voice of thunder. This is the land which had first to bear the brunt of all inroads and invasions into India; this heroic land had first to bare its bosom to every onslaught of the outer barbarians into Aryavarta. This is the land which, after all its sufferings, has not yet entirely lost its glory and its strength. Here it was that in later times the gentle Nanak preached his marvellous love for the world. Here it was that his broad heart was opened and his arms outstretched to embrace the whole world, not only of Hindus, but of Mohammedans too. Here it was that one of the last and one of the most glorious heroes of our race, Guru Govinda Singh, after shedding his blood and that of his dearest and nearest for the cause of religion, even when deserted by those for whom this blood was shed, retired into the South to die like a wounded lion struck to the heart, without a word against his country, without a single word of murmur.

Here, in this ancient land of ours, children of the land of five rivers, I stand before you, not as a teacher, for I know very little to teach, but as one who has come from the east to exchange words of greeting with the brothers of the west, to compare notes. Here am I, not to find out differences that exist among us, but to find where we agree. Here am I trying to understand on what ground we may always remain brothers, upon what foundations the voice that has spoken from eternity may become stronger and stronger as it grows. Here am I trying to propose to you something of constructive work and not destructive. For criticism the days are past, and we are waiting for constructive work. The world needs, at times, criticisms even fierce ones; but that is only for a time, and the work for eternity is progress and construction, and not criticism and destruction. For the last hundred years or so, there has been a flood of criticism all over this land of ours, where the full play of Western science has been let loose upon all the dark spots, and as a result the corners and the holes have become much more prominent than anything else. Naturally enough there arose mighty intellects all over the land, great and glorious, with the love of truth and justice in their hearts, with the love of their country, and above all, an intense love for their religion and their God; and because these mighty souls felt so deeply, because they loved so deeply, they criticised everything they thought was wrong. Glory unto these mighty spirits of the past! They have done so much good; but the voice of the present day is coming to us, telling, "Enough!" There has been enough of criticism, there has been enough of fault-finding, the time has come for the rebuilding, the reconstructing; the time has come for us to gather all our scattered forces, to concentrate them into one focus, and through that, to lead the nation on its onward march, which for centuries almost has been stopped. The house has been cleansed; let it be inhabited anew. The road has been cleared. March children of the Aryans!

Gentlemen, this is the motive that brings me before you, and at the start I may declare to you that I belong to no party and no sect. They are all great and glorious to me, I love them all, and all my life I have been attempting to find what is good and true in them. Therefore, it is my proposal tonight to bring before you points where we are agreed, to find out, if we can, a ground of agreement; and if through the grace of the Lord such a state of things be possible, let us take it up, and from theory carry it out into practice. We are Hindus. I do not use the word Hindu in any bad sense at all, nor do I agree with those that think there is any bad meaning in it. In old times, it simply meant people who lived on the other side of the Indus; today a good many among those who hate us may have put a bad interpretation upon it, but names are nothing.

Upon us depends whether the name Hindu will stand for everything that is glorious, everything that is spiritual, or whether it will remain a name of opprobrium, one designating the downtrodden, the worthless, the heathen. If at present the word Hindu means anything bad, never mind; by our action let us be ready to show that this is the highest word that any language can invent. It has been one of the principles of my life not to be ashamed of my own ancestors. I am one of the proudest men ever born, but let me tell you frankly, it is not for myself, but on account of my ancestry. The more I have studied the past, the more I have looked back, more and more has this pride come to me, and it has given me the strength and courage of conviction, raised me up from the dust of the earth, and set me working out that great plan laid out by those great ancestors of ours. Children of those ancient Aryans, through the grace of the Lord may you have the same pride, may that faith in your ancestors come into your blood, may it become a part and parcel of your lives, may it work towards the salvation of the world!

Before trying to find out the precise point where we are all agreed, the common ground of our national life, one thing we must remember. Just as there is an individuality in every man, so there is a national individuality. As one man differs from another in certain particulars, in certain characteristics of his own, so one race differs from another in certain peculiar characteristics; and just as it is the mission of every man to fulfil a certain purpose in the economy of nature, just as there is a particular line set out for him by his own past Karma, so it is with nations — each nation has a destiny to fulfil, each nation has a message to deliver, each nation has a mission to accomplish. Therefore, from the very start, we must have to understand the mission of our own race, the destiny it has to fulfil, the place it has to occupy in the march of nations, the note which it has to contribute to the harmony of races. In our country, when children, we hear stories how some serpents have jewels in their heads, and whatever one may do with the serpent, so long as the jewel is there, the serpent cannot be killed. We hear stories of giants and ogres who had souls living in certain little birds, and so long as the bird was safe, there was no power on earth to kill these giants; you might hack them to pieces, or do what you liked to them, the giants could not die. So with nations, there is a certain point where the life of a nation centres, where lies the nationality of the nation, and until that is touched, the nation cannot die. In the light of this we can understand the most marvellous phenomenon that the history of the world has ever known. Wave after wave of Barbarian conquest has rolled over this devoted land of ours. "Allah Ho Akbar!" has rent the skies for hundreds of years, and no Hindu knew what moment would be his last. This is the most suffering and the most subjugated of all the historic lands of the world. Yet we still stand practically the same race, ready to face difficulties again and again if necessary; and not only so, of late there have been signs that we are not only strong, but ready to go out, for the sign of life is expansion.

We find today that our ideas and thoughts are no more cooped up within the bounds of India, but whether we will it or not, they are marching outside, filtering into the literature of nations, taking their place among nations, and in some, even getting a commanding dictatorial position. Behind this we find the explanation that the great contribution to the sum total of the world's progress from India is the greatest, the noblest, the sublimest theme that can occupy the mind of man — it is philosophy and spirituality.

Our ancestors tried many other things; they, like other nations, first went to bring out the secrets of external nature as we all know, and with their gigantic brains that marvellous race could have done miracles in that line of which the world could have been proud for ever. But they gave it up for something higher; something better rings out from the pages of the Vedas: "That science is the greatest which makes us know Him who never changes!"

The science of nature, changeful, evanescent, the world of death, of woe, of misery, may be great, great indeed; but the science of Him who changes not, the Blissful One, where alone is peace, where alone is life eternal, where alone is perfection, where alone all misery ceases — that, according to our ancestors, was the sublimest science of all. After all, sciences that can give us only bread and clothes and power over our fellowmen, sciences that can teach us only how to conquer our fellow-beings, to rule over them, which teach the strong to domineer over the weak — those they could have discovered if they willed.

But praise be unto the Lord, they caught at once the other side, which was grander, infinitely higher, infinitely more blissful, till it has become the national characteristic, till it has come down to us, inherited from father to son for thousands of years, till it has become a part and parcel of us, till it tingles in every drop of blood that runs through our veins, till it has become our second nature, till the name of religion and Hindu have become one.

This is the national characteristic, and this cannot be touched. Barbarians with sword and fire, barbarians bringing barbarous religions, not one of them could touch the core, not one could touch the "jewel", not one had the power to kill the "bird" which the soul of the race inhabited. This, therefore, is the vitality of I the race, and so long as that remains, there is no power under the sun that can kill the race.

All the tortures and miseries of the world will pass over without hurting us, and we shall come out of the flames like Prahlada, so long as we hold on to this grandest of all our inheritances, spirituality. If a Hindu is not spiritual I do not call him a Hindu. In other countries a man may be political first, and then he may have a little religion, but here in India the first and the foremost duty of our lives is to be spiritual first, and then, if there is time, let other things come. Bearing this in mind we shall be in a better position to understand why, for our national welfare, we must first seek out at the present day all the spiritual forces of the race, as was done in days of yore and will be done in all times to come. National union in India must be a gathering up of its scattered spiritual forces. A nation in India must be a union of those whose hearts beat to the same spiritual tune.

There have been sects enough in this country. There are sects enough, and there will be enough in the future, because this has been the peculiarity of our religion that in abstract principles so much latitude has been given that, although afterwards so much detail has been worked out, all these details are the working out of principles, broad as the skies above our heads, eternal as nature herself. Sects, therefore, as a matter of course, must exist here, but what need not exist is sectarian quarrel. Sects must be but sectarianism need not.

The world would not be the better for sectarianism, but the world cannot move on without having sects. One set of men cannot do everything. The almost infinite mass of energy in the world cannot tie managed by a small number of people. Here, at once we see the necessity that forced this division of labour upon us — the division into sects. For the use of spiritual forces let there be sects; but is there any need that we should quarrel when our most ancient books declare that this differentiation is only apparent, that in spite of all these differences there is a thread of harmony, that beautified unity, running through them all? Our most ancient books have declared: — "That which exists is One; sages call Him by various names." Therefore, if there are these sectarian struggles, if there are these fights among the different sects, if there is jealousy and hatred between the different sects in India, the land where all sects have always been honoured, it is a shame on us who dare to call ourselves the descendants of those fathers. There are certain great principles in which, I think, we — whether Vaishnavas, Shaivas, Shaktas, or Ganapatyas, whether belonging to the ancient Vedantists or the modern ones, whether belonging to the old rigid sects or the modern reformed ones — are all one, and whoever calls himself a Hindu, believes in these principles. Of course there is a difference in the interpretation, in the explanation of these principles, and that difference should be there, and it should be allowed, for our standard is not to bind every man down to our position.

It would be a sin to force every man to work out our own interpretation of things, and to live by our own methods. Perhaps all who are here will agree on the first point that we believe the Vedas to be the eternal teachings of the secrets of religion. We all believe that this holy literature is without beginning and without end, coeval with nature, which is without beginning and without end; and that all our religious differences, all our religious struggles must end when we stand in the presence of that holy book; we are all agreed that this is the last court of appeal in all our spiritual differences. We may take different points of view as to what the Vedas are.

There may be one sect which regards one portion as more sacred than another, but that matters little so long as we say that we are all brothers in the Vedas, that out of these venerable, eternal, marvellous books has come everything that we possess today, good, holy, and pure. Well, therefore, if we believe in all this, let this principle first of all be preached broadcast throughout the length and breadth of the land. If this be true, let the Vedas have that prominence which they always deserve, and which we all believe in. First, then, the Vedas. The second point we all believe in is God, the creating, the preserving power of the whole universe, and unto whom it periodically returns to come out at other periods and manifest this wonderful phenomenon, called the universe.

We may differ as to our conception of God. One may believe in a God who is entirely personal, another may believe in a God who is personal and yet not human, and yet another may believe in a God who is entirely impersonal, and all may get their support from the Vedas. Still we are all believers in God; that is to say, that man who does not believe in a most marvellous Infinite Power from which everything has come, in which everything lives, and to which everything must in the end return, cannot be called a Hindu. If that be so, let us try to preach that idea all over the land. Preach whatever conception you have to give, there is no difference, we are not going to fight over it, but preach God; that is all we want. One idea may be better than another, but, mind you, not one of them is bad. One is good, another is better, and again another may be the best, but the word bad does not enter the category of our religion. Therefore, may the Lord bless them all who preach the name of God in whatever form they like! The more He is preached, the better for this race. Let our children be brought up in this idea, let this idea enter the homes of the poorest and the lowest, as well as of the richest and the highest — the idea of the name of God.

The third idea that I will present before you is that, unlike all other races of the world, we do not believe that this world was created only so many thousand years ago, and is going to be destroyed eternally on a certain day. Nor do we believe that the human soul has been created along with this universe just out of nothing. Here is another point I think we are all able to agree upon. We believe in nature being without beginning and without end; only at psychological periods this gross material of the outer universe goes back to its finer state, thus to remain for a certain period, again to be projected outside to manifest all this infinite panorama we call nature. This wavelike motion was going on even before time began, through eternity, and will remain for an infinite period of time.

Next, all Hindus believe that man is not only a gross material body; not only that within this there is the finer body, the mind, but there is something yet greater — for the body changes and so does the mind — something beyond, the Atman — I cannot translate the word to you for any translation will be wrong — that there is something beyond even this fine body, which is the Atman of man, which has neither beginning nor end, which knows not what death is. And then this peculiar idea, different from that of all other races of men, that this Atman inhabits body after body until there is no more interest for it to continue to do so, and it becomes free, not to be born again, I refer to the theory of Samsara and the theory of eternal souls taught by our Shastras. This is another point where we all agree, whatever sect we may belong to. There may be differences as to the relation between the soul and God. According to one sect the soul may be eternally different from God, according to another it may be a spark of that infinite fire, yet again according to others it may be one with that Infinite. It does not matter what our interpretation is, so long as we hold on to the one basic belief that the soul is infinite, that this soul was never created, and therefore will never die, that it had to pass and evolve into various bodies, till it attained perfection in the human one — in that we are all agreed.

And then comes the most differentiating, the grandest, and the most wonderful discovery in the realms of spirituality that has ever been made. Some of you, perhaps, who have been studying Western thought, may have observed already that there is another radical difference severing at one stroke all that is Western from all that is Eastern. It is this that we hold, whether we are Shaktas, Sauras, or Vaishnavas, even whether we are Bauddhas or Jainas, we all hold in India that the soul is by its nature pure and perfect, infinite in power and blessed.

Only, according to the dualist, this natural blissfulness of the soul has become contracted by past bad work, and through the grace of God it is again going to open out and show its perfection; while according to the monist, even this idea of contraction is a partial mistake, it is the veil of Maya that causes us to think the, soul has lost its powers, but the powers are there fully manifest.

Whatever the difference may be, we come to the central core, and there is at once an irreconcilable difference between all that is Western and Eastern. The Eastern is looking inward for all that is great and good. When we worship, we close our eyes and try to find God within. The Western is looking up outside for his God. To the Western their religious books have been inspired, while with us our books have been expired; breath-like they came, the breath of God, out of the hearts of sages they sprang, the Mantra-drashtas.

This is one great point to understand, and, my friends, my brethren, let me tell you, this is the one point we shall have to insist upon in the future. For I am firmly convinced, and I beg you to understand this one fact - no good comes out of the man who day and night thinks he is nobody. If a man, day and night, thinks he is miserable, low, and nothing, nothing he becomes. If you say yea, yea, "I am, I am", so shall you be; and if you say "I am not", think that you are not, and day and night meditate upon the fact that you are nothing, ay, nothing shall you be. That is the great fact which you ought to remember.

We are the children of the Almighty, we are sparks of the infinite, divine fire.

How can we be nothings? We are everything, ready to do everything, we can do everything, and man must do everything. This faith in themselves was in the hearts of our ancestors, this faith in themselves was the motive power that pushed them forward and forward in the march of civilisation; and if there has been degeneration, if there has been defect, mark my words, you will find that degradation to have started on the day our people lost this faith in themselves. Losing faith in one's self means losing faith in God. Do you believe in that infinite, good Providence working in and through you? If you believe that this Omnipresent One, the Antaryamin, is present in every atom, is through and through, Ota-prota, as the Sanskrit word goes, penetrating your body, mind and soul, how can you lose, heart?

I may be a little bubble of water, and you may be a mountain-high wave. Never mind! The infinite ocean is the background of me as well as of you. Mine also is that infinite ocean of life, of power, of spirituality, as well as yours. I am already joined — from my very birth, from the very fact of my life — I am in Yoga with that infinite life and infinite goodness and infinite power, as you are, mountain-high though you may be. Therefore, my brethren, teach this life-saving, great, ennobling, grand doctrine to your children, even from their very birth. You need not teach them Advaitism; teach them Dvaitism, or any "ism" you please, but we have seen that this is the common "ism" all through India; this marvellous doctrine of the soul, the perfection of the soul, is commonly believed in by all sects. As says our great philosopher Kapila, if purity has not been the nature of the soul, it can never attain purity afterwards, for anything that was not perfect by nature, even if it attained to perfection, that perfection would go away again. If impurity is the nature of man, then man will have to remain impure, even though he may be pure for five minutes. The time will come when this purity will wash out, pass away, and the old natural impurity will have its sway once more. Therefore, say all our philosophers, good is our nature, perfection is our nature, not imperfection, not impurity — and we should remember that. Remember the beautiful example of the great sage who, when he was dying, asked his mind to remember all his mighty deeds and all his mighty thoughts. There you do not find that he was teaching his mind to remember all his weaknesses and all his follies. Follies there are, weakness there must be, but remember your real nature always — that is the only way to cure the weakness, that is the only way to cure the follies.

It seems that these few points are common among all the various religious sects in India, and perhaps in future upon this common platform, conservative and liberal religionists, old type and new type, may shake bands. Above all, there is another thing to remember, which I am sorry we forget from time to time, that religion, in India, means realisation and nothing short of that. "Believe in the doctrine, and you are safe", can never be taught to us, for we do not believe in that. You are what you make yourselves. You are, by the grace of God and your own exertions, what you are. Mere believing in certain theories and doctrines will not help you much. The mighty word that came out from the sky of spirituality in India was Anubhuti, realisation, and ours are the only books which declare again and again: "The Lord is to be seen". Bold, brave words indeed, but true to their very core; every sound, every vibration is true. Religion is to be realised, not only heard; it is not in learning some doctrine like a parrot. Neither is it mere intellectual assent — that is nothing; but it must come into us. Ay, and therefore the greatest proof that we have of the existence of a God is not because our reason says so, but because God has been seen by the ancients as well as by the moderns. We believe in the soul not only because there are good reasons to prove its existence, but, above all, because there have been in the past thousands in India, there are still many who have realised, and there will be thousands in the future who will realise and see their own souls. And there is no salvation for man until he sees God, realises his own soul. Therefore, above all, let us understand this, and the more we understand it the less we shall have of sectarianism in India, for it is only that man who has realised God and seen Him, who is religious. In him the knots have been cut asunder, in him alone the doubts have subsided; he alone has become free from the fruits of action who has seen Him who is nearest of the near and farthest of the far. Ay, we often mistake mere prattle for religious truth, mere intellectual perorations for great spiritual realisation, and then comes sectarianism, then comes fight. If we once understand that this realisation is the only religion, we shall look into our own hearts and find how far we are towards realising the truths of religion. Then we shall understand that we ourselves are groping in darkness, and are leading others to grope in the same darkness, then we shall cease from sectarianism, quarrel, arid fight. Ask a man who wants to start a sectarian fight, "Have you seen God? Have you seen the Atman? If you have not, what right have you to preach His name — you walking in darkness trying to lead me into the same darkness — the blind leading the blind, and both falling into the ditch?"

Therefore, take more thought before you go and find fault with others. Let them follow their own path to realisation so long as they struggle to see truth in their own hearts; and when the broad, naked truth will be seen, then they will find that wonderful blissfulness which marvellously enough has been testified to by every seer in India, by every one who has realised the truth. Then words of love alone will come out of that heart, for it has already been touched by Him who is the essence of Love Himself. Then and then alone, all sectarian quarrels will cease, and we shall be in a position to understand, to bring to our hearts, to embrace, to intensely love the very word Hindu and every one who bears that name. Mark me, then and then alone you are a Hindu when the very name sends through you a galvanic shock of strength. Then and then alone you are a Hindu when every man who bears the name, from any country, speaking our language or any other language, becomes at once the nearest and the dearest to you.

Then and then alone you are a Hindu when the distress of anyone bearing that name comes to your heart and makes you feel as if your own son were in distress.

Then and then alone you are a Hindu when you will be ready to bear everything for them, like the great example I have quoted at the beginning of this lecture, of your great Guru Govind Singh. Driven out from this country, fighting against its oppressors, after having shed his own blood for the defence of the Hindu religion, after having seen his children killed on the battlefield — ay, this example of the great Guru, left even by those for whose sake he was shedding his blood and the blood of his own nearest and dearest — he, the wounded lion, retired from the field calmly to die in the South, but not a word of curse escaped his lips against those who had ungratefully forsaken him!

Mark me, every one of you will have to be a Govind Singh, if you want to do good to your country. You may see thousands of defects in your countrymen, but mark their Hindu blood.

They are the first Gods you will have to worship even if they do everything to hurt you, even if everyone of them send out a curse to you, you send out to them words of love. If they drive you out, retire to die in silence like that mighty lion, Govind Singh.

Such a man is worthy of the name of Hindu; such an ideal ought to be before us always. All our hatchets let us bury; send out this grand current of love all round.

Let them talk of India's regeneration as they like. Let me tell you as one who has been working — at least trying to work — all his life, that there is no regeneration for India until you be spiritual. Not only so, but upon it depends the welfare of the whole world. For I must tell you frankly that the very foundations of Western civilisation have been shaken to their base. The mightiest buildings, if built upon the loose sand foundations of materialism, must come to grief one day, must totter to their destruction some day.

The history of the world is our witness. Nation after nation has arisen and based its greatness upon materialism, declaring man was all matter. Ay, in Western language, a man gives up the ghost, but in our language a man gives up his body. The Western man is a body first, and then he has a soul; with us a man is a soul and spirit, and he has a body.

Therein lies a world of difference. All such civilisations, therefore, as have been based upon such sand foundations as material comfort and all that, have disappeared one after another, after short lives, from the face of the world; but the civilisation of India and the other nations that have stood at India's feet to listen and learn, namely, Japan and China, live even to the present day, and there are signs even of revival among them.

Their lives are like that of the Phoenix, a thousand times destroyed, but ready to spring up again more glorious. But a materialistic civilisation once dashed down, never can come up again; that building once thrown down is broken into pieces once for all. Therefore have patience and wait, the future is in store for us.

Do not be in a hurry, do not go out to imitate anybody else. This is another great lesson we have to remember; imitation is not civilisation. I may deck myself out in a Raja's dress, but will that make me a Raja? An ass in a lion's skin never makes a lion.

Imitation, cowardly imitation, never makes for progress. It is verily the sign of awful degradation in a man. Ay, when a man has begun to hate himself, then the last blow has come. When a man has begun to be ashamed of his ancestors, the end has come. Here am I, one of the least of the Hindu race, yet proud of my race, proud of my ancestors. I am proud to call myself a Hindu, I am proud that I am one of your unworthy servants. I am proud that I am a countryman of yours, you the descendants of the sages, you the descendants of the most glorious Rishis the world ever saw.

Therefore have faith in yourselves, be proud of your ancestors, instead of being ashamed of them. And do not imitate, do not imitate! Whenever you are under the thumb of others, you lose your own independence. If you are working, even in spiritual things, at the dictation of others, slowly you lose all faculty, even of thought. Bring out through your own exertions what you have, but do not imitate, yet take what is good from others.

We have to learn from others. You put the seed in the ground, and give it plenty of earth, and air, and water to feed upon; when the seed grows into the plant and into a gigantic tree, does it become the earth, does it become the air, or does it become the water? It becomes the mighty plant, the mighty tree, after its own nature, having absorbed everything that was given to it. Let that be your position. We have indeed many things to learn from others, yea, that man who refuses to learn is already dead. Declares our Manu:

> *"Take the jewel of a woman for your wife, though she be of inferior descent. Learn supreme knowledge with service even from the man of low birth; and even from the Chandala, learn by serving him the way to salvation."*
> *Learn everything that is good from others, but bring it in, and in your own way absorb it; do not become others. Do not be dragged away out of this Indian life; do not for a moment think that it would be better for India if all the Indians dressed, ate, and behaved like another race. You know the difficulty of giving up a habit of a few years. The Lord knows how many thousands of years are in your blood; this national specialised life has been flowing in one way, the Lord knows for how many thousands of years; and do you mean to say that that mighty stream, which has nearly reached its ocean, can go back to the snows of its Himalayas again? That*

> *is impossible! The struggle to do so would only break it. Therefore, make way for the life-current of the nation. Take away the blocks that bar the way to the progress of this mighty river, cleanse its path, dear the channel, and out it will rush by its own natural impulse, and the nation will go on careering and progressing.*

These are the lines which I beg to suggest to you for spiritual work in India. There are many other great problems which, for want of time, I cannot bring before you this night. For instance, there is the wonderful question of caste. I have been studying this question, its pros and cons, all my life; I have studied it in nearly every province in India. I have mixed with people of all castes in nearly every part of the country, and I am too bewildered in my own mind to grasp even the very significance of it. The more I try to study it, the more I get bewildered. Still at last I find that a little glimmer of light is before me, I begin to feel its significance just now. Then there is the other great problem about eating and drinking. That is a great problem indeed. It is not so useless a thing as we generally think. I have come to the conclusion that the insistence which we make now about eating and drinking is most curious and is just going against what the Shastras required, that is to say, we come to grief by neglecting the proper purity of the food we eat and drink; we have lost the true spirit of it.

There are several other questions which I want to bring before you and show how these problems can be solved, how to work out the ideas; but unfortunately the meeting could not come to order until very late, and I do not wish to detain you any longer now. I will, therefore, keep my ideas about caste and other things for a future occasion.

Now, one word more and I will finish about these spiritual ideas. Religion for a long time has come to be static in India. What we want is to make it dynamic. I want it to be brought into the life of everybody. Religion, as it always has been in the past, must enter the palaces of kings as well as the homes of the poorest peasants in the land. Religion, the common inheritance, the universal birthright of the race, must be brought free to the door of everybody. Religion in India must be made as free and as easy of access as is God's air. And this is the kind of work we have to bring about in India, but not by getting up little sects and fighting on points of difference. Let us preach where we all agree and leave the differences to remedy themselves. As I have said to the Indian people again and again, if there is the darkness of centuries in a room and we go into the room and begin to cry, "Oh, it is dark, it is dark!", will the darkness go?

Bring in the light and the darkness will vanish at once. This is the secret of reforming men. Suggest to them higher things; believe in man first. Why start with the belief that man is degraded and degenerated? I have never failed in my faith in man in any case, even taking him at his worst. Wherever I had faith in man, though at first the prospect was not always bright, yet it triumphed in the long run. Have faith in man, whether he appears to you to be a very learned one or a most ignorant one.

Have faith in man, whether he appears to be an angel or the very devil himself. Have faith in man first, and then having faith in him, believe that if there are defects in him, if he makes mistakes, if he embraces the crudest and the vilest doctrines, believe that it is not from his real nature that they come, but from the want of higher ideals. If a man goes towards what is false, it is because he cannot get what is true. Therefore the only method of correcting what is false is by supplying him with what is true.

Do this, and let him compare. You give him the truth, and there your work is done. Let him compare it in his own mind with what he has already in him; and, mark my words, if you have really given him the truth, the false must vanish, light must dispel darkness, and truth will bring the good out. This is the way if you want to reform the country spiritually; this is the way, and not fighting, not even telling people that what they are doing is bad. Put the good before them, see how eagerly they take it, see how the divine that never dies, that is always living in the human, comes up awakened and stretches out its hand for all that is good, and all that is glorious.

May He who is the Creator, the Preserver, and the Protector of our race, the God of our forefathers, whether called by the name of Vishnu, or Shiva, or Shakti, or Ganapati, whether He is worshipped as Saguna or as Nirguna, whether He is worshipped as personal or as impersonal, may He whom our forefathers knew and addressed by the words, — "That which exists is One; sages call Him by various names" — may He enter into us with His mighty love; may He shower His blessings on us, may He make us understand each other, may He make us work for each other with real love, with intense love for truth, and may not the least desire for our own personal fame, our own personal prestige, our own personal advantage, enter into this great work of me spiritual regeneration of India!

10

Sacrifice as a Spiritual Discipline

In the July 2003 editorial, 'We, God and the Universe', we saw that the macrocosm (God) and the microcosm (we) are under dynamic equilibrium at different levels: the gross, the subtle and the causal. The divinity behind the individual's body and mind is called Atman, and that behind the universe and the cosmic mind, Brahman. And ultimately, Atman and Brahman are identical according to the famous Upanishadic equation '*Ayam atma brahma,* This Atman is Brahman.'(1) Realization of this identity is the goal of life, goal of religion.

With this background we shall examine an important verse in the *Bhagavadgita*: 'The world is bound by work because work is not performed as a sacrifice. Therefore, O son of Kunti, work for the sake of sacrifice, devoid of attachment to it.'

Yajna: Different Interpretations

By sacrifice, Sri Shankaracharya and Sri Shridhara Svamin mean 'God', citing '*Yajno vai vishnuh,* Yajna is Vishnu.' Sri Ramanuja interprets sacrifice as the Vedic yajna. Sant Jnaneshvar advocates looking upon one's duty itself as an obligatory sacrifice. Yajna as a fire ritual, or offering of oblations to gods through fire, has almost fallen into disuse now. Therefore, looking upon *sacrifice* as Vishnu and performing actions for the Lord, and considering one's duty itself as a sacrifice seem to be more relevant interpretations meriting deeper analysis. A third important point emerges from the Gita verse cited: Sri Krishna asks Arjuna to work for the sake of sacrifice (yajna), *devoid of attachment to work*. That underlines the fact that detachment (from work and its outcome) is the main factor in work performed in a spirit of sacrifice.

Work for the Lord

According to the first interpretation, working for the sake of yajna implies working for God, not out of selfish interests. Such work frees us from the good and bad effects of work. Sri Krishna shows how such a work is done: 'Whatever you do, whatever you eat, whatever you offer as oblation in a sacrifice, whatever gifts or service you give, whatever austerities you perform - O son of Kunti, do that all as an offering unto me.'(4) With a slight modification this can serve as an 'offering' verse: 'Whatever I do … O God, I offer that all unto you.' A person who works for the Lord remembers that God is the Prime Mover of all activities. It is God who directs our thoughts and actions from within as the *antaryamin* (Inner Controller). Such an aspirant offers the fruits of his actions to that Prime Mover: 'I take refuge in that primal Purusha, from whom have streamed forth the eternal activity (of projection, sustenance and dissolution).' Repeatedly offering his actions to the indwelling supreme Spirit, he undergoes self-renewal and learns to look upon himself more and more as a spark of divinity, part of the luminous ultimate Reality. The hold on him of his body-mind complex thus gradually wears thin.

For such an aspirant, even the simple act of prostration before images of God becomes a significant spiritual practice. With each prostration he offers his body, mind and buddhi - the slightly awakened Self - to the supreme Spirit pervading the holy Image. He feels spiritually renewed with such a simple but qualitatively uplifting act and gradually develops detachment from his body and mind. His focus gradually shifts to the Deity that dwells within him, as his real 'I'. Such an aspirant does not look upon his little awakening as some non-dual realization. His little awakening does not preclude his prostration before images of God or His incarnations. He knows the difference between him and God (or an incarnation): In him the awakening or realization is so feeble that he needs to struggle to keep his mind above the pull of the body and the senses. An incarnation of God - as in the case of Sri Ramakrishna - has his mind riveted to the Infinite all the time, and with great difficulty brings his mind *down* to the normal plane, to show humanity the path to God. The spiritual aspirant's prostration before images of God is a symbolic sacrifice of his partially awakened Self (and body-mind) in the supreme Spirit behind the image or in the divine fire of realization of the incarnation.

It may be parenthetically remembered that Sri Ramakrishna never found any incongruity in prostrating before the image of Bhavatarini in the Dakshineswar temple, even after scaling heights of non-dual experiences and beyond.

Working for God also includes selfless participation in a movement furthering the mission of an incarnation of God; for according to Sri Ramakrishna, 'There is no doubt that God exists in all things; but the manifestations of his Power are different in different beings. The greatest manifestation of His Power is through an Incarnation. Again in some Incarnations there is a complete manifestation of God's Power. It is the Shakti, the Power of God, that is born as an Incarnation.'

Performing One's Duties as Sacrifice

The wheels of social life can revolve smoothly only if individuals discharge their responsibilities, conscious of their impact on the good of society as a whole. None can remain in a mental island and isolate himself from the welfare of others. Discharging to perfection one's duties without prompting from others - other people or rules of the state - is another way of performing work as a sacrifice. The interrelatedness of the activities of the members of society and the resultant social harmony are brought out clearly in the following words of a former Vice President of the Ramakrishna Order:

Production and distribution of consumable commodities is done through an exchange of services by capitalists, technocrats, labour, the distributor and the consumer. All these factors functioning within the good of the whole social order in view and contributing their respective services and receiving their due rewards without any party trying to take undue advantage of the others - may be called yajna in the social sense. All this is based on work and a person who seeks all the benefits of society but keeps quiet and fails to contribute his share for social good can be described as an exploiter and a thief as the Gita does. The difference in this interpretation is that, in place of the divine agencies, only the social environment is taken for mutual exchange of services and rewards. This explanation sublimates the ritualistic yajna.

God Himself Works

An important verse from the third chapter of the Gita lends another dimension to work done in a spirit of sacrifice. Sri Krishna says: 'O Partha, I have no duty to speak of. There is nothing in the three worlds that I have not gained; nor is there anything that I have to gain. Still I continue to work.'

God takes a human form with a special mission: to uplift humanity from animal nature to human nature to divine nature. Avatara means 'one who has descended'. Here the descent is from a state of pure undivided Consciousness, Brahman, to a human form, with associated pain and misery - not a mean sacrifice on God's part. God assumes a human form whenever there is decline in dharma, righteousness, and prevalence of adharma, unrighteousness. Sri Krishna further clarifies the concept of incarnation: 'Though I am birthless, of changeless nature and the Lord of all beings, yet having my Prakriti (maya) under my control I come into being by my own maya.

A mother went for shopping along with her four-year-old daughter. They saw someone across the street, walking along with some policemen. 'Who is he?' asked the child. 'He is a thief being taken to the police station,' replied the mother. A couple of days later, the child asked her again, pointing out someone accompanied by policemen, 'Who is that thief, mom?' The mother hurriedly shut the child's mouth and said, 'No, my dear, he is not a thief. He is the Governor of our state; the police are offering him protection.'

There was police escort in both the cases. But the governor had the police under his control, while the thief was under police control. This example is cited to prove an important Vedantic point: Brahman appears as an incarnation of God, or functions as Ishvara, with maya under Its control. The individual souls - all of us - on the other hand, are under maya's control.

Whatever an incarnation of God does is for the welfare of humanity, uplift of dharma being his primary concern. He is subject to sufferings in the world; he undergoes struggles like an ordinary spiritual aspirant, practises spiritual disciplines and shows that it is possible to live a God-centred life amid the world and its lures and problems. Students of the lives of Sri Ramakrishna and Sri Sarada Devi, his spiritual consort, can appreciate the point.

Sri Krishna is an important character in that monumental epic, the *Mahabharata*. Even some apparently controversial actions of his have this one aim: uplift of dharma. He lived what he preached in the Gita: calmness amid intense activity and absolute freedom from selfishness and attachment. Citing his own case, Sri Krishna encourages Arjuna - and through him, us - to work without attachment, without anxiety for the outcome.

God's Work: Another Viewpoint

A second way of looking at God's work is to analyse his functions as Ishvara, Personal God. We need to recap on some points we discussed in the July 2003 editorial. In the God-Soul-Universe triangle all the three vertices of the triangle stand or fall together. As long as our individuality is real to us, God and the universe continue to be real. According to Swami Vivekananda, Personal God is the highest reading of the Absolute [Brahman] by the human mind.

We also saw in the said editorial that Ishvara (Personal God) is the macrocosmic counterpart of the microcosmic causal body, which the individual soul dons during deep sleep. Just as we have a gross body and a subtle mind, even so Ishvara has a gross body (the entire universe) and a subtle mind (the cosmic Mind, of which all individual minds are, as it were, parts). Incidentally, according to qualified non-dualism, besides the universe, we, individual souls, also constitute Ishvara's body. And Ishvara is the Soul of our souls.

This background is to help us appreciate that the ceaseless flow of ideas in the cosmic Mind constitute Ishvara's mental activities, and the unceasing, but rhythmic, movements of galaxies, stars, planets and solar systems are His physical activities. Ishvara Himself is unattached to these activities. He has no likes or dislikes towards anyone, nor does He take note of anyone's merits or demerits. (5.15) He is a silent witness to the happenings in His creation. (He responds to His devotees' prayers; He can bring about inexplicable trans-formation in their lives and can alter the course of their destiny - all this is true, but we are not discussing them here.) Ishvara is ever conscious of His divinity and a perfect embodiment of the 'inaction amid action and action amid inaction' described in the *Gita*. (4.18)

In order to be free from maya and realize his potential divinity, man needs to emulate his macrocosmic counterpart in his thoughts and activities: not giving way to lethargy, trying to practise calmness amid activity and expecting nothing in return. In other words, he needs to hold his body, mind and spirit as a sacrifice to the supreme Spirit, and offers in It the fruits of his actions.

Sacrifice and Detachment

Attachment to work results from selfishness, an offshoot of the feelings of 'I' and 'mine'. As a corollary, detachment from work and its results implies giving up selfishness. Swamiji equates unselfishness with God Himself(12) and traces the root of misery to selfishness:

This 'I and mine' causes the whole misery. With the sense of possession comes selfishness, and selfishness brings on misery. Every act of selfishness or thought of selfishness makes us attached to something, and immediately we are made slaves. Each wave in the Chitta [mind-stuff] that says 'I and mine' immediately puts a chain round us and makes us slaves; and the more we say 'I and mine', the more slavery grows, the more misery increases. Therefore Karma-Yoga tells us to enjoy the beauty of all the pictures in the world, but not to identify ourselves with any of them. Never say 'mine'. Whenever we say a thing is 'mine', misery will immediately come. Do not even say 'my child' in your mind. Possess the child, but do not say 'mine'. If you do, then will come the misery. Do not say 'my house', do not say 'my body'. The whole difficulty is there. The body is neither yours, nor mine, nor anybody's. These bodies are coming and going by the laws of nature, but we are free, standing as witness. This body is no more free than a picture or a wall. Why should we be attached so much to a body? If somebody paints a picture, he does it and passes on. Do not project that tentacle of selfishness, 'I must possess it'. As soon as that is projected, misery will begin.

So Karma-Yoga says, first destroy the tendency to project this tentacle of selfishness, and when you have the power of checking it, hold it in and do not allow the mind to get into the ways of selfishness. (1.100-1)

An unselfish attitude coupled with an attitude of worship and adoration towards the recipient of service can help us in the process of attunement with the macrocosm, in simulating the actions of God. In the words of Swa-miji, 'When you are doing any work, do not think of anything beyond. Do it as worship, as the highest worship, and devote your whole life to it for the time being.' (1.71) 'And this is the gist of all worship - to be pure and to do good to others.' (3.141)

In sum, sacrifice involves renunciation of selfishness and cultivation of detachment from the fruits of actions. This will pave the way for the ultimate sacrifice: renunciation of attachment to the body-mind complex, offering one's self as an oblation into the imperishable supreme Self - the supreme sacrifice that lends meaning to human life.

11

Last Days of His Life

Swami Vivekananda disembarked in Bombay and immediately entrained for Calcutta, arriving at the Belur Math late in the evening of December 9, 1900. The Swami had not informed anybody of his return. The gate of the monastery was locked for the night. He heard the dinner bell, and in his eagerness to join the monks at their meal, scaled the gate. There was great rejoicing over his homecoming.

At the Math Swami Vivekananda was told about the passing away of his beloved disciple Mr. Sevier at Mayavati in the Himalayas. This was the sad news of which he had had a presentiment in Egypt. He was greatly distressed, and on December 11 wrote to Miss MacLeod: 'Thus two great Englishmen (The other was Mr. Goodwin.) gave up their lives for us - us, the Hindus.

This is martyrdom, if anything is.' Again he wrote to her on December 26: 'He was cremated on the bank of the river that flows by his ashrama, a la Hindu, covered with garlands, the brahmins carrying the body and the boys chanting the Vedas. The cause has already two martyrs. It makes me love dear England and its heroic breed. The Mother is watering the plant of future India with the best blood of England. Glory unto Her!'

The Swami stayed at the Math for eighteen days and left for Mayavati to see Mrs. Sevier. The distance from the railroad station to the monastery at Mayavati was sixty-five miles. The Swami did not give the inmates sufficient time to arrange for his comfortable transportation.

He left the railroad station in a hurry in the company of Shivananda and Sadananda. The winter of that year was particularly severe in the Himalayas; there was a heavy snowfall on the way, and in his present state of health he could hardly walk. He reached the monastery, however, on January 3, 1901.

The meeting with Mrs. Sevier stirred his emotions. He was delighted, however, to see the magnificent view of the eternal snow and also the progress of the work. Because of the heavy winter, he was forced to stay indoors most of the time. It was a glorious occasion for the members of the ashrama.

The Swami's conversation was inspiring. He spoke of the devotion of his Western disciples to his cause, and in this connexion particularly mentioned the name of Mr. Sevier. He also emphasized the necessity of loyalty to the work undertaken, loyalty to the leader, and loyalty to the organization. But the leader, the Swami said, must command respect and obedience by his character. While at Mayavati, in spite of a suffocating attack of asthma, he was busy with his huge correspondence and wrote three articles for the magazine Prabuddha Bharata. The least physical effort exhausted him. One day he exclaimed, 'My body is done for!'

The Advaita Ashrama at Mayavati had been founded, as may be remembered, with a view to enabling its members to develop their spiritual life through the practice of the non-dualistic discipline. All forms of ritual and worship were strictly excluded. But some of the members, accustomed to rituals, had set apart a room as the shrine, where a picture of Sri Ramakrishna was installed and worshipped daily. One morning the Swami chanced to enter this room while the worship was going on. He said nothing at that time, but in the evening severely reprimanded the inmates for violating the rules of the monastery. As he did not want to hurt their feelings too much, he did not ask them to discontinue the worship, but it was stopped by the members themselves. One of them, however, whose heart was set on dualistic worship, asked the advice of the Holy Mother. She wrote: 'Sri Ramakrishna was all Advaita and preached Advaita. Why should you not follow Advaita? All his disciples are Advaitins.'

After his return to the Belur Math, the Swami said in the course of a conversation: 'I thought of having one centre at least from which the external worship of Sri Ramakrishna would be excluded. But I found that the Old Man had already established himself even there. Well! Well!'

The above incident should not indicate any lack of respect in Swami Vivekananda for Sri Ramakrishna or dualistic worship. During the last few years of his life he showed a passionate love for the Master. Following his return to the Belur Math he arranged, as will be seen presently, the birthday festival of Sri Ramakrishna and the worship of the Divine Mother, according to traditional rituals.

The Swami's real nature was that of a lover of God, though he appeared outwardly as a philosopher. But in all his teachings, both in India and abroad, he had emphasized the non-dualistic philosophy. For Ultimate Reality, in the Hindu spiritual tradition, is non-dual. Dualism is a stage on the way to non-dualism. Through non-dualism alone, in the opinion of the Swami, can the different dualistic concepts of the Personal God be harmonized. Without the foundation of the non-dualistic Absolute, dualism breeds fanaticism, exclusiveness, and dangerous emotionalism. He saw both in India and abroad a caricature of dualism in the worship conducted in the temples, churches, and other places of worship.

In India the Swami found that non-dualism had degenerated into mere dry intellectual speculation. And so he wanted to restore non-dualism to its pristine purity. With that end in view he had established the Advaita Ashrama at Mayavati, overlooking the gorgeous eternal snow of the Himalayas, where the mind naturally soars to the contemplation of the Infinite, and there he had banned all vestiges of dualistic worship. In the future, the Swami believed, all religions would receive a new orientation from the non-dualistic doctrine and spread goodwill among men.

On his way to Mayavati Swami Vivekananda had heard the melancholy news of the passing away of the Raja of Khetri, his faithful disciple, who had borne the financial burden of his first trip to America. The Raja had undertaken the repairing of a high tower of the Emperor Akbar's tomb near Agra, and one day, while inspecting the work, had missed his footing, fallen several feet, and died. 'Thus', wrote the Swami to Mary Hale, 'we sometimes come to grief on account of our zeal for antiquity. Take care, Mary, don't be too zealous about your piece of Indian antiquity.' (Referring to himself.) 'So you see', the Swami wrote to Mary again, 'things are gloomy with me just now and my own health is wretched. Yet I am sure to bob up soon and am waiting for the next turn.' The Swami left Mayavati on January 18, and travelled four days on slippery slopes, partly through snow, before reaching the railroad station. He arrived at the Belur Math on January 24.

Swami Vivekananda had been in his monastery for seven weeks when pressing invitations for a lecture trip began to pour in from East Bengal. His mother, furthermore, had expressed an earnest desire to visit the holy places situated in that part of India. On January 26 he wrote to Mrs. Ole Bull: 'I am going to take my mother on pilgrimage....This is the one great wish of a Hindu widow. I have brought only misery to my people all my life. I am trying to fulfil this one wish of hers.'

On March 18, in the company of a large party of his sannyasin disciples, the Swami left for Dacca, the chief city of East Bengal, and arrived the next day. He was in poor health, suffering from both asthma and diabetes. During an asthmatic attack, when the pain was acute, he said half dreamily: 'What does it matter! I have given them enough for fifteen hundred years.' But he had hardly any rest. People besieged him day and night for instruction. In Dacca he delivered two public lectures and also visited the house of Nag Mahashay, where he was entertained by the saint's wife.

Next he proceeded to Chandranath, a holy place near Chittagong, and to sacred Kamakhya in Assam. While in Assam he spent several days at Shillong in order to recover his health, and there met Sir Henry Cotton, the chief Government official and a friend of the Indians in their national aspiration. The two exchanged many ideas, and at Sir Henry's request the Government physician looked after the Swami's health.

Vivekananda returned to the Belur Monastery in the second week of May. Concerning the impressions of his trip, he said that a certain part of Assam was endowed with incomparable natural beauty. The people of East Bengal were more sturdy, active, and resolute than those of West Bengal. But in religious views they were rather conservative and even fanatical.

He had found that some of the gullible people believed in pseudo-Incarnations, several of whom were living at that time in Dacca itself. The Swami had exhorted the people to cultivate manliness and the faculty of reasoning.

To a sentimental young man of Dacca he had said: 'My boy, take my advice; develop your muscles and brain by eating good food and by healthy exercise, and then you will be able to think for yourself. Without nourishing food your brain seems to have weakened a little.' On another occasion, in a public meeting, he had declared, referring to youth who had very little physical stamina, 'You will be nearer to Heaven through football than through the study of the Gita.'

The brother disciples and his own disciples were much concerned about the Swami's health, which was going from bad to worse. The damp climate of Bengal did not suit him at all; it aggravated his asthma, and further, he was very, very tired. He was earnestly requested to lead a quiet life, and to satisfy his friends the Swami lived in the monastery for about seven months in comparative retirement. They tried to entertain him with light talk. But he could not be dissuaded from giving instruction to his disciples whenever the occasion arose.

He loved his room on the second storey, in the southeast corner of the monastery building, to which he joyfully returned from his trips to the West or other parts of India. This large room with four windows and three doors served as both study and bedroom. In the corner to the right of the entrance door stood a mirror about five feet high, and near this, a rack with his ochre clothes. In the middle of the room was an iron bedstead with a spring mattress, which had been given to him by one of his Western disciples. But he seldom used it; for he preferred to sleep on a small couch placed by its side. A writing-table with letters, manuscripts, pen, ink, paper, and blotting-pad, a call-bell, some flowers in a metal vase, a photograph of the Master, a deer-skin which he used at the time of meditation, and a small table with a tea-set completed the furnishings.

Here he wrote, gave instruction to his disciples and brother monks, received friends, communed with God in meditation, and sometimes ate his meals. And it was in this room that he ultimately entered into the final ecstasy from which he never returned to ordinary consciousness. The room has been preserved as it was while the Swami was in his physical body, everything in it being kept as on the last day of his life, the calendar on the wall reading July 4, 1902.

On December 19, 1900, he wrote to an American disciple: 'Verily I am a bird of passage. Gay and busy Paris, grim old Constantinople, sparkling little Athens, and pyramidal Cairo are left behind, and here I am writing in my room on the Ganga, in the Math. It is so quiet and still! The broad river is dancing in the bright sunshine, only now and then an occasional cargo boat breaking the silence with the splashing of the waves. It is the cold season here, but the middle of the day is warm and bright every day. It is like the winter of southern California.

Everything is green and gold, and the grass is like velvet, yet the air is cold and crisp and delightful.'

After the Swami's return from East Bengal he lived a relaxed life in the monastery, surrounded by his pet animals: the dog Bagha, the she-goat Hansi, an antelope, a stork, several cows and sheep and ducks and geese, and a kid called Matru who was adorned with a collar of little bells, and with whom the Swami ran and played like a child. The animals adored him, Matru, the little kid, who had been - so he pretended - a relation of his in a previous existence, slept in his room. When it died he grieved like a child and said to a disciple: 'How strange! Whomsoever I love dies early.' Before milking Hansi for his tea, he always asked her permission. Bagha who took part in the Hindu ceremonies, went to bathe in the Ganga with the devotees on sacred occasions, as for instance when the gongs and conchs announced the end of an eclipse. He was, in a sense, the leader of the group of animals at the Math. After his death he was given a burial in the grounds of the monastery.

Referring to his pet animals he wrote to an American disciple on September 7, 1901: 'The rains have come down in right earnest, and it is a deluge - pouring, pouring, pouring, night and day. The river is rising, flooding the banks; the ponds and tanks have overflowed. I have just now returned from lending a hand in cutting a deep drain to take off the water from the Math grounds. The rainwater stands at places some feet deep. My huge stork is full of glee and so are the ducks and geese. My tame antelope fled from the Math and gave us some days of anxiety in finding him out. One of my ducks unfortunately died yesterday. She had been gasping for breath more than a week. One of my waggish old monks says, "Sir, it is no use living in the Kaliyuga, when ducks catch cold from damp and rain, and frogs sneeze!" One of the geese had her plumes falling off. Knowing no other method of treatment, I left her some minutes in a tub of water mixed with mild carbolic, so that it might either kill or heal - and she is all right now.'

Thus Swami Vivekananda tried to lead a carefree life at the monastery, sometimes going about the grounds clad in his loin-cloth, sometimes supervising the cooking arrangements and himself preparing some delicacies for the inmates, and sometimes joining his disciples and brother monks in the singing of devotional music. At other times he imparted spiritual instruction to the visitors, or engaged in deep thought whenever his inner spirit was stirred up, occupied himself with serious study in his room, or explained to the members of the Math the intricate passages of the scriptures and unfolded to them his scheme of future work.

Though his body was wearing away day by day, his mind was luminous. At times his eyes assumed a far-away look, showing how tired he was of the world. One day he said, 'For one thing we may be grateful: this life is not eternal.'

The illness did not show any sign of abatement, but that did not dampen his spirit to work. When urged to rest, he said to a disciple: 'My son, there is no rest for me. That which Sri Ramakrishna called "Kali" took possession of my body and soul three or four days before his passing away. That makes me work and work and never lets me keep still or look to my personal comfort.' Then he told the disciple how the Master, before his passing away, had transmitted his spiritual power to him.

During the later part of 1901 the Swami observed all the religious festivals at the Math. The Divine Mother was worshipped in strict orthodox fashion during the Durga-puja, Lakshmi-puja and Kali-puja. On the occasion of the Durga-puja the poor were given a sumptuous feast. Thus the Swami demonstrated the efficacy of religious rituals in the development of the spiritual life. In February 1902 the birth anniversary of Sri Ramakrishna was celebrated at the Belur Math, and over thirty thousand devotees gathered for the occasion. But the Swami was feverish. He was confined to his room by the swelling of his legs. From the windows he watched the dancing and the music of the devotees.

To the disciple who was attending him the Swami said: 'He who has realized the Atman becomes a storehouse of great power. From him as the centre a spiritual force emanates, working within a certain radius; people who come within this circle become inspired with his ideas and are overwhelmed by them.

Thus without much religious striving they derive benefit from the spiritual experience of an illumined person. This is called grace.' 'Blessed are those,' the Swami continued, 'who have seen Sri Ramakrishna. All of you, too, will get his vision. When you have come here, you are very near to him. Nobody has been able to understand him who came on earth as Sri Ramakrishna. Even his own nearest devotees have no real clue to it. Only some have a little inkling of it. All will understand in time.'

It is said that the spot immediately beneath a lamp is dark. And so it was that the orthodox people of the neighbouring villages hardly understood the ideas and ideals of the Belur Math. The monks there did not in all respects lead the life of orthodox sannyasins. Devotees from abroad frequented the monastery. In matters of food and dress the inmates were liberal. Thus they became the butt of criticism. The villagers invented scandals about them and the passengers on the boats passing along the Ganga would point out the monastery with an accusing finger.

When the Swami heard all this he said: 'That is good. It is a law of nature. That is the way with all founders of religion. Without persecution superior ideas cannot penetrate into the heart of society.'

But the criticism of the neighbours in time gave place to pride in having in their midst so many saintly souls.

Many distinguished Indians used to visit the Swami at this time. With some of them he discussed the idea of founding a Vedic Institution for the promotion of the ancient Aryan culture and the knowledge of Sanskrit. This was one of the

Swami's favourite thoughts, on which he dwelt even on the last day of his life on earth.

Towards the end of 1901 two learned Buddhists from Japan came to the Belur Math to induce the Swami to attend a Congress of Religions that was being contemplated in Japan at that time. One of them was the famous artist and art critic Okakura, and the other Oda, the head priest of a Buddhist temple. The Swami became particularly fond of Okakura and said, 'We are two brothers who meet again, having come from the ends of the earth.' Though pressed by the visitors, he could not accept the invitation to go to Japan, partly because of his failing health and partly because he was sceptical that the Japanese would appreciate the monastic ideal of the Non-dualistic Vedanta. In a letter to a Western lady written in June 1902, the Swami made the following interesting observation about the connexion between the monastic ideal and fidelity in married life:

In my opinion, a race must first cultivate a great respect for motherhood, through the sanctification and inviolability of marriage, before it can attain to the ideal of perfect chastity. The Roman Catholics and the Hindus, holding marriage sacred and inviolate, have produced great chaste men and women of immense power. To the Arab, marriage is a contract or a forceful possession, to be dissolved at will, and we do not find there the development of the idea of the virgin of the brahmacharin. Modern Buddhism - having fallen among races who had not yet come up to the evolution of marriage - has made a travesty of monasticism. So until there is developed in Japan a great and sacred ideal about marriage (apart from mutual attraction and love), I do not see how there can be great monks and nuns. As you have come to see that the glory of life is chastity, so my eyes also have been opened to the necessity of this great sanctification for the vast majority, in order that a few lifelong chaste powers may be produced.

The Swami used to say that absolute loyalty and devotion between husbands and wives for three successive generations find their expression in the birth of an ideal monk. Okakura earnestly requested the Swami to accompany him on a visit to Bodh-Gaya, where Buddha had attained illumination. Taking advantage of several weeks' respite from his ailment, the Swami accepted the invitation. He also desired to see Varanasi. The trip lasted through January and February 1902, and was a fitting end to all his wanderings. He arrived at Bodh-Gaya on the morning of his last birthday and was received with genuine courtesy and hospitality by the orthodox Hindu monk in charge of the temple.

This and the similar respect and affection shown by the priests in Varanasi proved the extent of his influence over men's hearts. It may be remembered that Bodh-Gaya had been the first of the holy places he had visited during Sri Ramakrishna's lifetime. And some years later, when he was still an unknown monk, he had said farewell to Varanasi with the words: 'Till that day when I fall on society like a thunderbolt I shall visit this place no more.'

In Varanasi the Swami was offered a sum of money by a Maharaja to establish a monastery there. He accepted the offer and, on his return to Calcutta, sent Swami Shivananda to organize the work. Even before Swami Vivekananda's visit to Varanasi, several young men, under the Swami's inspiration, had started a small organization for the purpose of providing destitute pilgrims with food, shelter, and medical aid. Delighted with their unselfish spirit, the Swami said to them: 'You have the true spirit, my boys, and you will always have my love and blessings! Go on bravely; never mind your poverty. Money will come. A great thing will grow out of it, surpassing your fondest hopes.' The Swami wrote the appeal which was published with the first report of the 'Ramakrishna Home of Service,' as the institution came to be called. In later years it became the premier institution of its kind started by the Ramakrishna Mission.

The Swami returned from Varanasi. But hardly had he arrived at Belur when his illness showed signs of aggravation in the damp air of Bengal. During the last year and a half of his life he was, off and on, under the strict supervision of his physicians. Diabetes took the form of dropsy.

His feet swelled and certain parts of his body became hypersensitive. He could hardly close his eyes in sleep. A native physician made him follow a very strict regime: he had to avoid water and salt. For twenty-one days he did not allow a drop of water to pass through his throat. To a disciple he said: 'The body is only a tool of the mind. What the mind dictates the body will have to obey. Now I do not even think of water. I do not miss it at all.... I see I can do anything.'

Though his body was subjected to a devitalizing illness, his mind retained its usual vigour. During this period he was seen reading the newly published Encyclopaedia Britannica. One of his householder disciples remarked that it was difficult to master these twenty-five volumes in one life.

But the Swami had already finished ten volumes and was busy reading the eleventh. He told the disciple to ask him any question from the ten volumes he had read, and to the latter's utter amazement the Swami not only displayed his knowledge of many technical subjects but even quoted the language of the book here and there. He explained to the disciple that there was nothing miraculous about it. A man who observed strict chastity in thought and action, he declared, could develop the retentive power of the mind and reproduce exactly what he had heard or read but once, even years before.

The regeneration of India was the ever recurring theme of the Swami's thought. Two of the projects dear to his heart were the establishment of a Vedic College and a convent for women. The latter was to be started on the bank of the Ganga under the direction of the Holy Mother and was to be completely separated from the Belur Monastery. The teachers trained in the convent were to take charge of the education of Indian women along national lines.

But the Swami's heart always went out in sympathy for the poor and neglected masses. During the later part of 1901 a number of Santhal labourers were engaged in levelling the grounds about the monastery. They were poor and outside the pale of society. The Swami felt an especial joy in talking to them, and listened to the accounts of their misery with great compassion. One day he arranged a feast for them and served them with delicacies that they had never before tasted. Then, when the meal was finished, the Swami said to them: 'You are Narayanas. Today I have entertained the Lord Himself by feeding you.'

He said to a disciple: 'I actually saw God in them. How guileless they are!' Afterwards he said, addressing the inmates of the Belur Math: 'See how simple-hearted these poor, illiterate people are! Will you be able to relieve their miseries to some extent at least? Otherwise of what use is our wearing the ochre robe of the sannyasin? To be able to sacrifice everything for the good of others is real monasticism. Sometimes I think within myself: "What is the good of building monasteries and so forth? Why not sell them and distribute the money among the poor, indigent Narayanas? What homes should we care for, we who have made the tree our shelter? Alas! How can we have the heart to put a morsel into our mouths, when our countrymen have not enough wherewith to feed or clothe themselves?...Mother, shall there be no redress for them?" One of the purposes of my going out to preach religion to the West, as you know, was to see if I could find any means of providing for the people of my country. Seeing their poverty and distress, I think sometimes: "Let us throw away all the paraphernalia of worship - blowing the conch and ringing the bell and waving the lights before the image....Let us throw away all pride of learning and study of the scriptures and all spiritual disciplines for the attainment of personal liberation. Let us go from village to village, devoting ourselves to the service of the poor.

Let us, through the force of our character and spirituality and our austere living, convince the rich about their duties to the masses, and get money and the means wherewith to serve the poor and the distressed....Alas! Nobody in our country thinks for the low, the poor, the miserable! Those who are the backbone of the nation, whose labour produces food, those whose one day's absence from work raises a cry of general distress in the city - where is the man in our country who sympathizes with them, who shares in their joys and sorrows? Look how, for want of sympathy on the part of the Hindus, thousands of pariahs are becoming Christians in the Madras Presidency!

Don't think that it is merely the pinch of hunger that drives them to embrace Christianity. It is simply because they do not get your sympathy. You are continually telling them: "Don't touch me." "Don't touch this or that!" Is here any fellow-feeling or sense of dharma left in the country? There is only "Don't-touchism" now! Kick out all such degrading usages! How I wish to abolish the barriers of "Don't-touchism" and go out and bring together one and all, crying: "Come, all ye that are poor and destitute, fallen and downtrodden! We are one in the name of Ramakrishna!" Unless they are elevated, the Great Mother India will never awake! What are we good for if we cannot provide facilities for their food and clothing? Alas, they are ignorant of the ways of the world and hence fail to eke out a living though labouring hard day and night for it. Gather all your forces together to remove the veil from their eyes. What I see clear as daylight is that the same Brahman, the same Sakti, is in them as in me! Only there is a difference in the degree of manifestation - that is all. Have you ever seen a country in the whole history of the world rise unless there was a uniform circulation of the national blood all over the body? Know for certain that not much can be done with that body one limb of which is paralysed, even though the other limbs are healthy.'

One of the lay disciples pointed out the difficulty of establishing unity and harmony among the diverse sects in India. Vivekananda replied with irritation:

'Don't come here any more if you think any task too difficult. Through the grace of the Lord, everything becomes easy of achievement. Your duty is to serve the poor and the distressed without distinction of caste and creed.

What business have you to consider the fruits of your action? Your duty is to go on working, and everything will set itself right in time, and work by itself.

My method of work is to construct, and not to destroy that which is already existing....You are all intelligent boys and profess to be my disciples - tell me what you have done. Couldn't you give away one life for the sake of others? Let the reading of Vedanta and the practice of meditation and the like be left for the next life! Let this body go in the service of others - and then I shall know you have not come to me in vain!'

A little later he said:

'After so much tapasya, austerity, I have known that the highest truth is this: "He is present in all beings. These are all the manifested forms of Him. There is no other God to seek for! He alone is worshipping God, who serves all beings."'

In this exhortation is found Vivekananda's message in all its vividness. These words are addressed to India and the Western world alike.

The west, too, has its pariahs. He who exploits another man, near or distant, offends God and will pay for it sooner or later. All men are sons of the same God, all bear within them the same God. He who wishes to serve must serve man - and in the first instance, man in the humblest, poorest, most degraded form. Only by breaking down the barriers between man and man can one usher in the kingdom of heaven on earth.

There were moments when Vivekananda felt gloomy. His body was wasting away, and only a few young men came forward to help him in his work. He wanted more of them who, fired with indomitable faith in God and in themselves, would renounce everything for the welfare of others. He used to say that with a dozen such people he could divert into a new channel the whole thought-current of the country. Disregarding his physical suffering, he constantly inspired his disciples to cultivate this new faith.

Thus we see him, one day, seated on a canvas cot under the mango tree in the courtyard of the monastery. Sannyasins and brahmacharins about him were busy doing their daily duties.

One was sweeping the courtyard with a big broom. Swami Premananda, after his bath, was climbing the steps to the shrine. Suddenly Swami Vivekananda's eyes became radiant. Shaking with emotion, he said to a disciple:

'Where will you go to seek Brahman? He is immanent in all beings. Here, here is the visible Brahman! Shame on those who, neglecting the visible Brahman, set their minds on other things! Here is the visible Brahman before you as tangible as a fruit in one's hand! Can't you see? Here - here - is Brahman!'

These words struck those around him with a kind of electric shock. For a quarter of an hour they remained glued to the spot, as if petrified. The broom in the hand of the sweeper stopped. Premananda fell into a trance. Everyone experienced an indescribable peace. At last the Swami said to Premananda, 'Now go to worship.'

The brother disciples tried to restrain the Swami's activities, especially instruction to visitors and seekers. But he was unyielding. 'Look here!' he said to them one day. 'What good is this body?

Let it go in helping others. Did not the Master preach until the very end? And shall I not do the same? I do not care a straw if the body goes. You cannot imagine how happy I am when I find earnest seekers after truth to talk to. In the work of waking up Atman in my fellow men I shall gladly die again and again!' Till the very end the Swami remained the great leader of the monastery, guiding with a firm hand the details of its daily life, in spite of his own suffering. He insisted upon thorough cleanliness and examined the beds to see that they were aired and properly taken care of. He drew up a weekly time-table and saw that it was scrupulously observed. The classes on the Vedas and the Puranas were held daily, he himself conducting them when his health permitted. He discouraged too much ritualism in the chapel.

He warned the monks against exaggerated sentimentalism and narrow sectarianism.

But the leader kept a stern watch on the practice of daily meditation on the part of the inmates of the monastery. The bell sounded at fixed hours for meals, study, discussion, and meditation.

About three months before his death he made it a rule that at four o'clock in the morning a hand-bell should be rung from room to room to awaken the monks. Within half an hour all should be gathered in the chapel to meditate. But he was always before them.

He got up at three and went to the chapel, where he sat facing the north, meditating motionless for more than two hours. No one was allowed to leave his seat before the Swami set the example.

As he got up, he chanted softly, 'Siva! Siva!' Bowing to the image of Sri Ramakrishna, he would go downstairs and pace the courtyard, singing a song about the Divine Mother or Siva. Naturally his presence in the chapel created an intense spiritual atmosphere. Swami Brahmananda said: 'Ah! One at once becomes absorbed if one sits for meditation in company with Naren! I do not feel this when I sit alone.'

Once, after an absence of several days on account of illness, he entered the chapel and found only two monks there. He became annoyed; in order to discipline the absentees he forbade them to eat their meals at the monastery. They had to go out and beg their food. He did not spare anyone, even a beloved brother disciple for whom he cherished the highest respect and who happened to be absent from the chapel that morning. Another day, he found a brother disciple, Swami Shivananda, in bed at the hour of meditation.

He said to the latter 'Brother! I know you do not need meditation. You have already realized the highest goal through the grace of Sri Ramakrishna. But you should daily meditate with the youngsters in order to set an example to them.'

From that day on, Shivananda, whether ill or well, always communed with God during the early hours of the morning. In his old age, when it became physically impossible for him to go to the chapel, he used to sit on his bed for meditation.

But the Swami, preoccupied as he was with the training of his Indian disciples, never forgot his Western ones. Their welfare, too, was always in his thought and prayer.

To Miss MacLeod he wrote on June 14, 1901:

Well, Joe, keep health and spirits up....Gloire et honneur await you - and mukti. The natural ambition of woman is, through marriage, to climb up leaning upon a man; but those days are gone. You shall be great without the help of any man, just as you are, plain, dear Joe - our Joe, everlasting Joe....

We have seen enough of this life not to care for any of its bubbles, have we not, Joe? For months I have been practising to drive away all sentiments; therefore I stop here, and good-bye just now.

It was ordained by Mother that we should work together; it has been already for the good of many; it shall be for the good of many more. So let it be. It is useless planning useless high flights; Mother will find her own way...rest assured.

To Mary Hale, on August 27, 1901 he wrote with his usual wit:

I would that my health were what you expected - at least to be able to write you a long letter. It is getting worse, in fact, every day - and so many complications and botherations without that, I have ceased to notice it at all. I wish you all joy in your lovely Suisse chalet - splendid health, good appetite, and a light study of Swiss or other antiquities just to liven things up a bit.

I am so glad that you are breathing the free air of the mountains, but sorry that Sam is not in the best of health. Well, there is no anxiety about it; he has naturally such a fine physique.

'Woman's moods and man's luck - the gods themselves do not know, not to speak of men.'

My instincts may be very feminine - but what I am exercised with just this moment is that you get a little bit of manliness about you. Oh!

Mary, your brain, health, beauty, everything, is going to waste just for the lack of that one essential - assertion of individuality. Your haughtiness, spirit, etc. are all nonsense - only mockery. You are at best a boarding-school girl - no backbone! no backbone!

Alas! this lifelong leading-string business ! This is very harsh, very brutal - but I can't help it. I love you, Mary - sincerely, genuinely. I can't cheat you with namby-pamby sugar candies. Nor do they ever come to me.

Then again, I am a dying man; I have no time to fool in. Wake up, girl! I expect now from you letters of the right slashing order. Give it right straight - I need a good deal of rousing....

I am in a sense a retired man. I don't keep much note of what is going on about the Movement. Then the Movement is getting bigger and it is impossible for one man to know all about it minutely. I now do nothing except try to eat and sleep and nurse my body the rest of the time.

Good-bye, dear Mary. Hope we shall meet again somewhere in this life - but meeting or no meeting, I remain ever your loving brother, Vivekananda.

To his beloved disciple Nivedita he wrote on February 12, 1902: 'May all powers come unto you!

May Mother Herself be your hands and mind! It is immense power - irresistible - that I pray for you, and, if possible, along with it infinite peace....

'If there was any truth in Sri Ramakrishna, may He take you into His leading, even as He did me, nay, a thousand times more!'

And again, to Miss MacLeod: 'I can't, even in imagination, pay the immense debt of gratitude I owe you. Wherever you are you never forget my welfare; and there, you are the only one that bears all my burdens, all my brutal outbursts....' The sun, enveloped in a golden radiance, was fast descending to the horizon.

The last two months of the Swami's life on earth had been full of events foreshadowing the approaching end. Yet few had thought the end so near. Soon after his return from Varanasi the Swami greatly desired to see his sannyasin disciples and he wrote to them to come to the Belur Math, even if only for a short time.

'Many of his disciples from distant parts of the world,' writes Sister Nivedita, 'gathered round the Swami. Ill as he looked, there was none probably who suspected how near the end had come. Yet visits were paid and farewells exchanged that it had needed voyages half round the world to make.'

More and more the Swami was seen to free himself from all responsibilities, leaving the work to other hands. 'How often,' he said, 'does a man ruin his disciples by remaining always with them !

When men are once trained, it is essential that their leader leave them, for without his absence they cannot develop themselves.' 'Plants,' he had said some time before, 'always remain small under a big tree.' Yet the near and dear ones thought that he would certainly live three or four years more.

He refused to express any opinion on the question of the day. 'I can no more enter into outside affairs,' he said; 'I am already on the way.'

On another occasion he said: 'You may be right; but I cannot enter any more into these matters. I am going down into death.' News of the world met with but a far-away rejoinder from him. On May 15, 1902, he wrote to Miss MacLeod, perhaps for the last time: 'I am somewhat better, but of course far from what I expected.

A great idea of quiet has come upon me. I am going to retire for good - no more work for me. If possible, I will revert to my old days of begging. All blessings attend you, Joe; you have been a good angel to me.'

But it was difficult for him to give up what had been dearer to him than his life: the work. On the last Sunday before the end he said to one of his disciples: 'You know the work is always my weak point. When I think that might come to an end, I am all undone.' He could easily withdraw from weakness and attachment, but the work still retained its power to move him.

Sri Ramakrishna and the Divine Mother preoccupied his mind. He acted as if he were the child of the Mother or the boy playing at the feet of Sri Ramakrishna at Dakshineswar. He said, 'A great tapasya and meditation has come upon me, and I am making ready for death.'

His disciples and spiritual brothers were worried to see his contemplative mood.

They remembered the words of Sri Ramakrishna that Naren, after his mission was completed, would merge for ever into samadhi, and that he would refuse to live in his physical body if he realized who he was.

A brother monk asked him one day, quite casually, 'Do you know yet who you are?' The unexpected reply, 'Yes, I now know!' awed into silence everyone present. No further question was asked. All remembered the story of the great nirvikalpa samadhi of Naren's youth, and how, when it was over, Sri Ramakrishna had said: 'Now the Mother has shown you everything.

But this realization, like the jewel locked in a box, will be hidden away from you and kept in my custody. I will keep the key with me. Only after you have fulfilled your mission on this earth will the box be unlocked, and you will know everything as you have known now.'

They also remembered that in the cave of Amarnath, in the summer of 1898, he had received the grace of Siva - not to die till he himself should will to do so. He was looking death in the face unafraid as it drew near.

Everything about the Swami in these days was deliberate and significant, yet none could apprehend its true import. People were deceived by his outer cheerfulness. From the beginning of June he appeared to be regaining his health.

One day, about a week before the end, he bade a disciple bring him the Bengali almanac. He was seen several times on subsequent days studying the book intently, as if he was undecided about something he wanted to know.

After the passing away, the brother monks and disciples realized that he had been debating about the day when he should throw away the mortal body. Ramakrishna, too, had consulted the almanac before his death.

Three days before the mahasamadhi, Vivekananda pointed out to Swami Premananda a particular spot on the monastery grounds where he wished his body to be cremated.

On Wednesday the Swami fasted, following the orthodox rule: it was the eleventh day of the moon.

Sister Nivedita came to the monastery to ask him some questions about her school; but he was not interested and referred her to some other Swamis. He insisted, however, on serving Nivedita the morning meal. To quote the Sister's words:

Each dish, as it was offered - boiled seeds of the jack-fruit, boiled potatoes, plain rice, and ice-cold milk - formed the subject of playful chat; and finally, to end the meal, he himself poured the water over her hands, and dried them with a towel.

'It is I who should do these things for you, Swamiji! Not you for me!' was the protest naturally offered. But his answer was startling in its solemnity - 'Jesus washed the feet of his disciples!'

Something checked the answer, 'But that was the last time!' as it rose to the lips, and the words remained unuttered. This was well. For here also, the time had come.

There was nothing sad or grave about the Swami during these days. Efforts were made not to tire him. Conversations were kept as light as possible, touching only upon the pet animals that surrounded him, his garden experiments, books, and absent friends.

But all the while one was conscious of a luminous presence of which the Swami's bodily form seemed only a shadow or symbol. The members of the monastery had never felt so strongly as now, before him, that they stood in the presence of an infinite light; yet none was prepared to see the end so soon, least of all on that Friday, July the Fourth, on which he appeared so much stronger and healthier than he had been for years.

On the supreme day, Friday, he rose very early. Going to the chapel, alone, he shut the windows and bolted the doors, contrary to his habit, and meditated for three hours. Descending the stairs of the shrine, he sang a beautiful song about Kali:

Is Kali, my Mother, really black?

The Naked One, though black She seems,

Lights the Lotus of the heart.

Men call Her black, but yet my mind

Will not believe that She is so:

Now She is white, now red, now blue;

Now She appears as yellow, too.

I hardly know who Mother is,

Though I have pondered all my life:

Now Purusha, now Prakriti,

And now the Void, She seems to be.

To meditate on all these things

Confounds poor Kamalakanta's wits.

Then he said, almost in a whisper: 'If there were another Vivekananda, then he would have understood what this Vivekananda has done! And yet - how many Vivekanandas shall be born in time!'

He expressed the desire to worship Mother Kali at the Math the following day, and asked two of his disciples to procure all the necessary articles for the ceremony. Next he asked the disciple Suddhananda to read a passage from the Yajurveda with the commentary of a well-known expositor.

The Swami said that he did not agree with the commentator and exhorted the disciple to give a new interpretation of the Vedic texts.

He partook of the noon meal with great relish, in company with the members of the Math, though usually, at that time, he ate alone in his room because of his illness. Immediately afterwards, full of life and humour, he gave lessons to the brahmacharins for three hours on Sanskrit grammar. In the afternoon he took a walk for about two miles with Swami Premananda and discussed his plan to start a Vedic College in the monastery.

'What will be the good of studying the Vedas?' Premananda asked.

'It will kill superstition,' Swami Vivekananda said.

On his return the Swami inquired very tenderly concerning every member of the monastery. Then he conversed for a long time with his companions on the rise and fall of nations. 'India is immortal,' he said, 'if she persists in her search for God. But if she goes in for politics and social conflict, she will die.'

At seven o'clock in the evening the bell rang for worship in the chapel.

The Swami went to his room and told the disciple who attended him that none was to come to him until called for. He spent an hour in meditation and telling his beads, then called the disciple and asked him to open all the windows and fan his head.

He lay down quietly on his bed and the attendant thought that he was either sleeping or meditating.

At the end of an hour his hands trembled a little and he breathed once very deeply.

There was a silence for a minute or two, and again he breathed in the same manner. His eyes became fixed in the centre of his eyebrows, his face assumed a divine expression, and eternal silence fell.

'There was,' said a brother disciple of the Swami, 'a little blood in his nostrils, about his mouth, and in his eyes.' According to the Yoga scriptures, the life-breath of an illumined yogi passes out through the opening on the top of the head, causing the blood to flow in the nostrils and the mouth.

The great ecstasy took place at ten minutes past nine. Swami Vivekananda passed away at the age of thirty-nine years, five months, and twenty-four days, thus fulfilling his own prophecy: 'I shall not live to be forty years old.'

The brother disciples thought that he might have fallen into samadhi, and chanted the Master's name to bring back his consciousness. But he remained on his back motionless.

Physicians were sent for and the body was thoroughly examined. In the doctor's opinion life was only suspended; artificial respiration was tried. At midnight, however, Swami

Vivekananda was pronounced dead, the cause, according to medical science, having been apoplexy or sudden failure of the heart. But the monks were convinced that their leader had voluntarily cast off his body in samadhi, as predicted by Sri Ramakrishna.

In the morning people poured in from all quarters. Nivedita sat by the body and fanned it till it was brought down at 2 p.m. to the porch leading to the courtyard. It was covered with ochre robes and decorated with flowers. Incense was burnt and a religious service was performed with lights, conch-shells, and bells.

The brother monks and disciples took their final leave and the procession started, moving slowly through the courtyard and across the lawn, till it reached the vilva tree near the spot where the Swami himself had desired his body to be cremated.

The funeral pyre was built and the body was consigned to the flames kindled with sandalwood. Across the Ganga, on the other bank, Ramakrishna had been cremated sixteen years before.

Nivedita began to weep like a child, rolling on the ground. Suddenly the wind blew into her lap a piece of the ochre robe from the pyre, and she received it as a blessing.

It was dusk when the flames subsided. The sacred relics were gathered and the pyre was washed with the water of the Ganga. The place is now marked by a temple, the table of the altar standing on the very spot where the Swami's body rested in the flames.

Gloom and desolation fell upon the monastery. The monks prayed in the depths of their hearts: 'O Lord! Thy will be done!' But deep beneath their grief all felt that this was not the end. The words of the leader, uttered long before his death, rang in their ears:

'It may be that I shall find it good to get outside my body - to cast it off like a worn-out garment. But I shall not cease to work. I shall inspire men everywhere, until the world shall know that it is one with God.'

And: 'May I be born again and again, and suffer thousands of miseries, so that I may worship the only God that exists, the only God I believe in, the sum total of all souls.'

For centuries to come people everywhere will be inspired by Swami Vivekananda's message: O man! first realize that you are one with Brahman - aham Brahmasmi - and then realize that the whole universe is verily the same Brahman - sarvam khalvidam Brahma.

Bibliography

Benjamin, Joseph: *Scheduled Castes in Indian Politics and Society*, Ess Ess Publications, New Delhi, 1989.

Biswas, C.C. : *Bengal's Response to Gandhi*, Kolkata, Minerva Associates, 2004.

Bose, S. C., *The Indian Struggle, 1920-1942*, Bombay, Asia Publishing House, 1964.

Calvocoressi, Peter, and Guy Wint: *The Total War: the Story of World War II*, New York, Pantheon Books, 1972.

Carlisle Robertson: *Rammohan Ray, The Essential Writings of Raja*, Delhi, 1999.

Chatterjee, Partha: *Caste and Subaltern Consciousness*, Oxford University Press, Delhi, 1994.

Edwardes, Michael: *The Last Years of British India*, Cleveland, World Pub. Co., 1964.

George, Davis : *Dynamics of Power : The Gandhian Perspective*, New Delhi, Frank Bros. & Co., 2000.

Glen, M. and Johnson, S. B.: *Social Mobility Among Untouchables*, Vikas, New Delhi, 1979.

Gupta, S.P. Das : *Rabindranath Tagore : Thought Relics: New Expanded Version*, Kolkata, Sadesh, 2007.

Hauser, Walter: *Peasant Organisation in India: A Case Study of the Bihar Kisan Sabha, 1929-1942*. Chicago University, 1961.

Joshi, V.C.: *Vivekananda and the Process of Modernization in India*, Delhi, 1975.

Karve, Irawati: *Hindu Society: An Interpretation*, Sangam Press, Poona, 1961.

Kopf, David: *The Brahmo Samaj and the Shaping of the Modern Indian Mind*. Princeton, 1979.

Kumar, Ravindra : *Gandhian Thoughts : An Overview*, New Delhi, Gyan, 2006.

Madhavananda, Swami : *Shankaracharya: Vivekachudamani*, Calcutta: Advaita Ashrama, 1970,

Majumdar, R. C.: *Jibanera Smritideepe*, Calcutta, General Printers and Publishers, 1978.

Mishra, Anil Dutta : *Challenges of 21 Century : Gandhian Alternatives*, New Delhi, Mittal Pub., 2003.

Murthi, R.K. : *Discovery of Nehru*, Indian Pub., Delhi, 1993.

Nair, A. M.: *An Indian Freedom Fighter in Japan*, Bombay, Orient Longman, 1983.

Narula, Sanjay : *Indian Politics*, New Delhi, Murari Lal and Sons, 2007.

Niharranjan Ray: *Rammohun Roy: A Bi-Centenary Tribute*, New Delhi, 1974.

Noorani, A.G. : *Indian Political Trials : 1775-1947*, New Delhi, Oxford University Press, 2005.

O'Malley, L. S. S.: *Indian Caste Customs*, Vikas Publishing House, Delhi, 1974.

Partha, C.: *Caste and Subaltern Consciousness*, Oxford University Press, Delhi, 1994.

Patel, Asha : *Gandhian Vision of Rural Development : Its Relevance in Present Time*, New Delhi, Decent Books, 2005.

Ray, Dalia : *The Parsees of Calcutta*, Sujan, Kolkata, 2005.

Sanghavi, Nagindas : *The Agony of Arrival : Gandhi : The South Africa Years*, New Delhi, Rupa & Co., 2006.

Sanyal, Bandana : *Achalayatan : The Petrified Place, Rabindranath Tagore*, New Delhi, Rupa, 2006.

Sharma, S.R. : *Gandhi : Ahimsa and Non Violence in Practice*, Delhi, Cosmo, 2001.

Silverberg, James: *Social Mobility in the Caste System in India*, Mouton Publishers, The Hague, 1968.

Singhal, Rahul : *The Eternal Saga of Love : Devdas*, Pentagon Paperbacks, Delhi, 2002.

Sophia Dobson: *The Life and Letters of Vivekananda*, Calcutta, 1962.

Toye, Hugh: *The Springing Tiger: A Study of a Revolutionary*, London, Cassell, 1959.

Vidyarthi, L. P. and Mishra, N.: *Harijan Today: Sociological, Economic, Political, Religious and Cultural Analysis*, Classical Publications, New Delhi, 1977.

Yogesh, A.: *The Changing Frontiers of Caste*, National Publishing House, Delhi, 1968.

Index

A

Advaita Philosophy, 206.
Another Viewpoint, 230.

B

Belur Math, 20, 234, 236, 237, 241, 242, 243, 246, 253.
Bhagavad Gita, 13, 131.

C

Caste System, 68, 71.
Chicago Parliament, 49.
Chicago World Parliament, 65.
Common Bases of Hinduism, 207.

D

Democracy, 29, 30, 71.
Dharana on Raja Yoga, 180.

E

Essence of Raja Yoga, 175.

F

Freedom, 29, 30, 36, 56, 69, 73, 83, 111, 112, 160, 164, 179, 180, 182, 183, 192, 193, 195, 206, 230.

H

Hindu Believes, 53.
Hindu Philosophic Thought, 196.
Hindu Religion, 56, 63, 74, 82, 135, 220.
Hindu View of Life, 161.

M

Monastic Brotherhood, 18.

P

Paper on Hinduism, 97.
Parliament of Religions, 20, 37, 43, 45, 46, 48, 49, 65, 66, 77.
Pratyahara, 175, 177, 180, 181, 183, 184, 187.

R

Raja Yoga, 77, 175, 180.
Reform Movements, 13.

S

Sankhya Philosophy, 143, 146, 173, 180.
Science of Yoga, 166.
Social Change, 71, 72, 73.
Social Reformers, 19.

Spiritual Discipline, 226.
Sri Ramakrishna Teacher, 133.
Steps in Raja-Yoga, 175, 187.

T

Teachings of Vivekananda, 16.

U

Upanishads, 13, 14, 96, 114.

V

Vedic Religious, 85.
Visit to America, 34.

W

Works of Swami Vivekananda, 69, 75, 76, 77, 78, 80.
World Parliament, 65.
Worldwide Spiritual Regeneration, 28.

❑❑❑